REFUGEE PROTECTION IN CANADA
For Iranian Christian Convert Claimants

CHARLES MWEWA

ACP
AFRICA IN CANADA
PRESS

2023

First published in 2020.

Republished by:

AFRICA IN CANADA PRESS
Ottawa, Ontario
Canada
www.acpress.ca
www.charlesmwewa.com

ISBN: 978-1-988251-20-2

DEDICATION

For

Tashany-Idyllia

CONTENTS

ABBREVIATIONS

AI	Amnesty International
AIIS	Amnesty International's International Secretariat
AMAR	Statistical Centre of Iran
ANM	Advancing Native Missions
BBC	British Broadcasting Corporation
BCC	Blind Carbon Copy
BOC	Basis of Claim
CBN	Christian Broadcasting Network
CBSA	Canada Border Services Agency
CIC	Citizenship and Immigration Canada
CNO	Computer Network Operations
COI	Country of Origin Information
CPC	Country of Particular Concern
CPJ	Committee to Protect Journalists
CR	Convention Refugee
CRDD	Convention Refugee Determination Division
CSW	Christian Solidarity Worldwide
DFAT	Department of Foreign Affairs and Trade
DIS	Danish Immigration Service
DPI	Deep Packet Inspection
DRC	Danish Refugee Council
DW	Deutsche Welle
FATA	Iranian Cyber Police
FIDH	International Federation for Human Rights
GARs	Government-Assisted Refugees
H&C	Humanitarian and Compassionate
HRA	Human Rights Activists in Iran
HRC	Human Rights Council
HRWF	Human Rights Without Frontiers
IAD	Immigration Appeal Division
IAGCI	Independent Advisory Group on Country Information

ICAC	Integrated Claim Analysis Centre
ICHRI	International Campaign for Human Rights in Iran
ICI	Iranian Christians International
ID	Immigration Division
IFHP	Interim Federal Health Program
IHRDC	Iran Human Rights Documentation Centre
IPC	Islamic Penal Code
IRB	Immigration and Refugee Board of Canada
IRCC	Immigration Refugees and Citizenship Canada
IRFA	International Religious Freedom Act
IRGC	Islamic Revolutionary Guards Corps
IRPA	Immigration and Refugee Protection Act
ISPs	Internet Service Providers
LANDINFO	Danish Refugee Council
LoC	US Library of Congress
MOI	Iran's Ministry of Intelligence
MRG	Minority Rights Group International
NDP	National Documentation Package
NGO	Non-Governmental Organization
NIN	National Information Network
NPR	National Public Radio
OHIP	Ontario Health Insurance Plan
PIF	Personal Information Form
POE	Point of Entry
RAD	Refugee Appeal Division
RDS	Refugee Determination System
RPCD	Refugee Protection Claimant's Document
RPD	Refugee Protection Division
RSF	Reporters Sans Frontières
UN	United Nations
UNHCR	United Nations High Commissioner for Refugees
USCIRF	United States Commission on International

LIST OF CASES

Abawaji, Abdulwahid Haji Hassen v. M.C.I. (F.C., no. IMM-6276-05)

Abdi Ahmed, Ilham v. M.C.I. (F.C., no. IMM-3178-12)

Abubakar, Fahmey Abdalla Ali v. M.E.I. (F.C.T.D., no. A-572-92), Wetston, September 9, 1993.

Adjei v. Canada (Minister of Employment and Immigration), [1989] 2 F.C. 680 (C.A.)

Agimelen Oriazouwani, Winifred v. M.C.I. (F.C., no. IMM-6440-10), Shore, July 8, 2011; 2011 FC 827.

Aguilar Soto, Rafael Alberto v. M.C.I. (F.C., no. IMM-1883-10), Shore, November 25, 2010.

Ahmed v. Canada (Minister of Employment and Immigration) (1993), 156 N.R. 221 (F.C.A.)

Ahmed, Ahmed Ibrahim v. M.C.I. (F.C. no. IMM-2187-18), Kane, November 16, 2018; 2018 FC 1157.

Ahmed, Ali v. M.E.I. (F.C.A., no. A-89-92), Marceau, Desjardins, Décary, July 14, 1993.

Ahmed, Ishtiaq v. M.C.I. (F.C.T.D., no. IMM-2931-99), Hansen, March 29, 2000.

Ahoua, Wadjams Jean-Marie v. M.C.I. (F.C., no. IMM-1757-07), Blais, November 27, 2007; 2007 FC 1239.

Ajelal, Mustafa v. M.C.I. (F.C., no. IMM-4522-13), Diner, November 19, 2014; 2014 FC 1093.

Akpojiyovwi, Evelyn Oboaguonona v. M.C.I. (F.C. no. IMM-200-18), Roussel, July 17, 2018; 2018 FC 745.

Alassouli, Yousf v. M.C.I. (F.C., no. IMM-6451-10), de Montigny, August 16, 2011; 2011 FC 998.

Alfaro, Oscar Luis Alfaro v. M.C.I. (F.C., no. IMM-6905-03), O'Keefe, January 20, 2005.

Ali, Chaudhary Liaqat v. M.E.I. (F.C.T.D., no. A-1461-92), Noël, January 20, 1994.

Alvapillai, Ramasethu v. M.C.I. (F.C.T.D., no. IMM-4226-97), Rothstein, August 14, 1998.

Ambrose-Esede, Benedicta Osemen v. M.C.I. (F.C. no. IMM-1685-18),

Russell, December 11, 2018; 2018 FC 1241.

Araya, Carolina Isabel Valenzuela v. M.C.I. (F.C.T.D., no. IMM-3948-97), Gibson, September 4, 1998

Aria, Ashraf v. M.C.I. (F.C., no. IMM-2499-12), de Montigny, April 2, 2013; 2013 FC 324.

Arias Aguilar, Jennifer v. M.C.I. (F.C., no. IMM-1000-05), Rouleau, November 9, 2005; 2005 FC 1519.).

Arias Ultima, Angela Maria v. M.C.I. (F.C., no. IMM-3984-12), Manson, January 25, 2013; 2013 FC 81.

Ascencio Gutierrez, Arnoldo Maximilanov. M.C.I. (F.C., no. IMM-4903-13)

Asfaw, Napoleon v. M.C.I. (F.C.T.D., no. IMM-5552-99), Hugessen, July 18, 2000

Ashraf, Shahenaz v. M.C.I. (F.C., no. IMM-5375-08), O'Reilly, April 19, 2010; 2010 FC 425

Aslam, Muhammad v. M.C.I. (F.C., no. IMM-3264-05), Shore, February 16, 2006; 2006 FC 189

Assadi, Nasser Eddin v. M.C.I. (F.C.T.D., no. IMM-2683-96), Teitelbaum, March 25, 1997.

Ay, Hasan v. M.C.I. (F.C., no. IMM-4149-09), Boivin, June 21, 2010; 2010 FC 671.

Badesha v. Canada (Secretary of State) (1994), 23 Imm. L.R. (2d) 190 (F.C.T.D.).

Badesha, Jagir Singh v. S.S.C. (F.C.T.D., no. A-1544-92), Wetston, January 19, 1994.

Badran, Housam v. M.C.I. (F.C.T.D., no. IMM-2472-95), McKeown, March 29, 1996

Bakos, Robert v. M.C.I. (F.C., no. IMM-2424-15), Manson, February 12, 2016 (amended September 7, 2016); 2016 FC 191

Balasubramaniam, Veergathy v. M.C.I. (F.C.T.D., no. IMM-1902-93), McKeown, October 4, 1994.

Barragan Gonzalez, Julio Angelo v. M.C.I. (F.C., no. IMM-6335-13), Boswell, April 20, 2015; 2015 FC 502.

Bello, Salihou v. M.C.I. (F.C.T.D., no. IMM-1771-96), Pinard, April 11, 1997.

Boakye, Kofi v. M.C.I. (F.C., no. IMM-2361-15), Strickland, December 18, 2015; 2015 FC 1394

5, 1993.

Fernando, Joseph Stanley v. M.E.I. (F.C.T.D., no. 92-A-6986), McKeown, May 19, 1993.

Fosu, Frank Atta v. M.C.I. (F.C., no. IMM-935-08), Zinn, October 8, 2008; 2008 FC 1135.

Gabeyehu, Bruck v. M.C.I. (F.C.T.D., no. IMM-863-95), Reed, November 8, 1995.

Gallo Farias, Alejandrina Dayna v. M.C.I. (F.C., no. IMM-658-08), Kelen, September 16, 2008; 2008 FC 1035.

Garcia Aldana, Paco Jesus v. M.C.I. (F.C., no. IMM-2113-06), Hughes, April 19, 2007.

Gebremichael, Addis v. M.C.I. (F.C., no. IMM-2670-05), Russell, May 1, 2006; 2006 FC 547

Geron, Fernando Bilog v. M.C.I. (F.C.T.D., no. IMM-4951-01), Blanchard, November 22, 2002; 2002 FCT 1204.

Gomez Gonzalez, Veronica v. M.C.I. (F.C., no. IMM-485-11), de Montigny, October 4, 2011

Gomez v. Canada (Minister of Citizenship and Immigration) (F.C., IMM-1412-10), Bédard, October 22, 2010

Gonzalez Camargo, Hernando v. M.C.I. (F.C., no. IMM-38-14), Gleeson, September 2, 2015; 2015 FC 1044.

Gonzalez Torres, Luis Felipe v. M.C.I. (F.C., no. IMM-1351-09), Zinn, March 1, 2010; 2010 FC 234

Gopalapillai, Thinesrupan v. M.C.I. (F.C. no. IMM-3539-18), Grammond, February 26, 2019; 2019 FC 228

Gosal, Pardeep Singh v. M.C.I. (F.C.T.D., no. IMM-2316-97), Reed, March 11, 1998.

Guraya, Balihar Singh v. S.S.C. (F.C.T.D., no. IMM-4058-93), Pinard, July 8, 1994.

Gyawali, Nirmal v. M.C.I. (F.C., no. IMM-926-03), Tremblay-Lamer, September 24, 2003; 2003 FC 1122

Hasa, Ana v. M.C.I. (F.C., no. IMM-3700-17), Strickland, March 7, 2018; 2018 FC 270.

Hashmat, Suhil v. M.C.I. (F.C.T.D., no. IMM-2331-96), Teitelbaum, May 9, 1997.

Hasnain, Khalid v. M.C.I. (F.C.T.D., no. A-962-92), McKeown, December 14, 1995.

Jilani, Zia Uddin Ahmed v. M.C.I. (F.C., no. IMM-711-07), Mosley, December 21, 2007; 2007 FC 1354

John, Shontel Dion v. M.C.I. (F.C., no. IMM-1683-10), Bédard, December 14, 2010; 2010 FC 1283

Kabengele v. M.C.I. (F.C. no., IMM-1422-99), Rouleau, November 16, 2000

Kahlon v. Canada (Solicitor General), (1993), 24 Imm. L.R. (2d) 219 (F.C.T.D.)

Kahlon, Hari Singh v. S.G.C (F.C.T.D., no. IMM-532-93), Gibson, August 5, 1993.

Kaillyapillai, Srivasan v. M.C.I. (F.C.T.D., no. IMM-1263-96), Richard, February 27, 1997.

Kaler, Minder Singh v. M.E.I. (F.C.T.D., no. IMM-794-93), Cullen, February 3, 1994.

Kamana, Jimmy v. M.C.I. (F.C.T.D., no. IMM-5998-98), Tremblay-Lamer, September 24, 1999.

Kanji, Mumtaz Baduraliv.M.C.I. (F.C.T.D., no. IMM-2451-96), Campbell, April 4, 1997.

Karthikesu, Cumariah v. M.E.I. (F.C.T.D., no. IMM-2998-93), Strayer, May 26, 1994.

Kauhonina, Claretha v. M.C.I. (F.C. no. IMM-2459-18), Diner, December 21, 2018; 2018 FC 1300.

Kayumba, Bijou Kamwanga v. M.C.I. (F.C., no. IMM-1920-09), Beaudry, February 10, 2010; 2010 FC 138.

Khan, Naqui Mohd v. M.C.I. (F.C.T.D., no. IMM-4127-01), Rothstein, July 26, 2002.

Khattr, Amani Khzaee v. M.C.I. (F.C. no., IMM-3249-15), Zinn, March 22, 2016; 2016 FC 341.

Kulanthavelu, Gnanasegaram v. M.E.I. (F.C.T.D., no. IMM-57-93), Gibson, December 3, 1993.

Kunin, Aleksandr v. M.C.I. (F.C., no. IMM-5225-09), O'Keefe, November 4, 2010; 2010 FC 1091

Kurtkapan, Osman v. M.C.I. (F.C.T.D., no. IMM-5290-01), Heneghan, October 25, 2002; 2002 FCT 1114

Li, Yi Mei v. M.C.I. (F.C.A., no. A-31-04), Rothstein, Noël, Malone, January 5, 2005; 2005 FCA 1.

Liblizadeh, Hassan v. M.C.I. (F.C.T.D., no. IMM-5062-97), MacKay, July 8, 1998.

Loaiza Brenes, Heyleen v. M.C.I. (F.C., no. IMM-2445-06), Barnes, April 2, 2007; 2007 FC 351.

Lopez Gonzalez, Jaqueline v. M.C.I. (F.C., no. IMM-5321-10), Rennie, May 24, 2011; 2011 FC 592.

Lopez Martinez, Heydi Vanessa v. M.C.I. (F.C., no. IMM-5081-09), Pinard, May 25, 2010; 2010 FC 550.

Lopez, Centeotl Mazadiego v. M.C.I. (F.C., no. IMM-1938-13), Simpson, May 29, 2014; 2014 FC 514

Losowa Osengosengo, Victorine v. M.C.I. (F.C., no. IMM-4132-13), Gagné, March 13, 2014; 2014 FC 244.

Louis, Benito v. M.C.I. (F.C. no. IMM-3068-18), Bell, March 28, 2019; 2019 FC 355

M.C.I. v. Flores Carrillo, Maria del Rosario (F.C.A., no. A-225-07), Létourneau, Nadon, Sharlow, March 12, 2008; 2008 FCA 94.

M.C.I. v. Kadenko, Ninal (F.C.A., no. A-388-95), Hugessen, Décary, Chevalier, October 15, 1996.

M.E.I. v. Satiacum, Robert (F.C.A., no. A-554-87), Urie, Mahoney, MacGuigan, June 16, 1989.

M.E.I. v. Sharbdeen, Mohammed Faroudeen (F.C.A., no. A-488-93), Mahoney, MacGuigan, Linden, March 21, 1994.

M.E.I. v. Villafranca, Ignacio (F.C.A., no. A-69-90), Hugessen, Marceau, Décary, December 18, 1992.

Madoui, Nidhal Abderrah v. M.C.I. (F.C.T.D., no. IMM-660-96), Denault, October 25, 1996

Maldonado v. Canada (Minister of Employment and Immigration), [1980] 2 F.C. 302 (C.A.)

Manoharan, Vanajah v. M.E.I. (F.C.T.D., no. A-1156-92), Rouleau, December 6, 1993.

Maqdassy, Joyce Ruth v. M.C.I. (F.C.T.D., no. IMM-2992-00), Tremblay-Lamer, February 19, 2002; 2002 FCT 182.

Martinez Requena, Ericka Marlene v. M.C.I. (F.C., no. IMM-4725-06), Dawson, September 27, 2007; 2007 FC 968.

Masalov, Sergey v. M.C.I. (F.C., no. IMM-7207-13), Diner, March 4, 2015; 2015 FC 277.

Maximilok, Yuri v. M.C.I. (F.C.T.D., no. IMM-1861-97), Joyal,

August 14, 1998.

Megag, Sahra Abdilahi v. M.E.I. (F.C.T.D., no. A-822-92), Rothstein, December 10, 1993.

Mekideche, Anouar v. M.C.I. (F.C.T.D., no. IMM-2269-96), Wetston, December 9, 1996

Memarpour, Mahdi v. M.C.I. (F.C.T.D., no. IMM-3113-94), Simpson, May 25, 1995

Mendez, Alberto Luis Calderon v. (F.C., no. IMM-1837-04), Teitelbaum, January 27, 2005; 2005 FC 75.

Milian Pelaez, Rogelio v. M.C.I. (F.C., no. IMM-3611-11), de Montigny, March 2, 2012; 2012 FC 285

Mimica, Milanka v. M.C.I. (F.C.T.D., no. IMM-3014-95), Rothstein, June 19, 1996.

Moran Gudiel, Hugo v. M.C.I. (F.C., no. IMM-2054-14), Gascon, July 23, 2015; 2015 FC 902.

Moreb, Sliman v. M.C.I. (F.C., no. IMM-287-05), von Finckenstein, July 5, 2005; 2005 FC 945.

Moreno Maniero, Ronald Antonio v. M.C.I. (F.C., no. IMM-8536-11), Zinn, June 19, 2012; 2012 FC 776.

Mortocian, Alexandru v. M.C.I. (.FC. no., IMM-3837-12), Kane, December 7, 2012; 2012 FC 1447.

Moya, Jaime Olvera v. M.C.I. (F.C.T.D., no. IMM-5436-01), Beaudry, November 6, 2002.

Mudrak, Zsolt Jozsef v. M.C.I. (F.C.A., no. A-147-15), Stratas, Webb, Scott, June 14, 2016; 2016 FCA 178.

Muhammed, Falululla Peer v. M.C.I. (F.C., no. IMM-5122-11), Harrington, February 17, 2012; 2012 FC 226.

Muotoh, Ndukwe Christopher v. M.C.I. (F.C., no. IMM-3330-05)

Murillo Taborda, Lissed v. M.C.I. (F.C., no. IMM-9365-12), Kane, September 17, 2013; 2013 FC 957.

Nadarajah, Sivasothy Nathan v. M.E.I. (F.C.T.D., no. IMM-4215-93), Simpson, July 26, 1994.

Naguleswaran, Pathmasilosini (Naguleswaran) v. M.C.I. (F.C.T.D., no. IMM-1116-94), Muldoon, April 19, 1995.

Natynczyk v. Canada (Minister of Employment and Immigration), (F.C., no. IMM-2025-03)

Rabbani, Sayed Moheyudee v. M.C.I. (F.C.T.D., no. IMM-236-96), Noël, January 16, 1997.

Rahim, Ziany v. *M.C.I.* (F.C., no. IMM-2729-04), Shore, January 18, 2005, 2005 FC 18

Rajagopal, Gnanathas v. M.C.I. (F.C., no. IMM-1350-11), Hughes, November 10, 2011; 2011 FC 1277

Ramanathy, Murugesakumar v. M.C.I. (F.C., no. IMM-1241-13), Mosley, May 27, 2014; 2014 FC 511

Ramirez Martinez, Jorge Armando v. M.C.I. (F.C., no. IMM-1284-09), Snider, June 1, 2010; 2010 FC 600.

Ramirez Rodas, Carlos v. M.C.I. (F.C., no. IMM-6560-13), Zinn, February 27, 2015; 2015 FC 250

Ramirez-Osorio, Alexander v. M.C.I. (F.C., no. IMM-7418-12), Shore, May 3, 2013; 2013 FC 461.

Randhawa, Faheem Anwar v. S.G.C. (F.C.T.D., no. IMM-5621-93), Rouleau, August 12, 1994.

Ranganathan v. Canada (Minister of Citizenship and Immigration), (F.C.A., no. A-348-99), Létourneau, Sexton, Malone, December 21, 2000; [2001] 2 F.C. 164 (C.A.).

Rasaratnam v. Canada (Minister of Employment and Immigration), [1992] 1 F.C. 706 (C.A.)

Ratnam, Selvanayagam v. M.C.I. (F.C.T.D., no. IMM-1881-94), Richard, March 31, 1995.

Reynoso, Edith Isabel Guardian v. M.C.I. (F.C.T.D., no. IMM-2110-94), Muldoon, January 29, 1996.

Rodriguez Capitaine, Rogelio v. M.C.I. (F.C., no. IMM-3449-07), Gauthier, January 24, 2008; 2008 FC 98

Rumb, Serge v. M.E.I. (F.C.T.D., no. IMM-1481-98), Reed, February 12, 1999.

Sabapathy, Thevi v. M.C.I. (F.C.T.D., no. IMM-1507-96), Campbell, March 27, 1997.

Saini v. Canada (Minister of Employment and Immigration) (1993), 151 N.R. 239 (F.C.A.).

Saini v. Canada (Minister of Employment and Immigration) (1993), 158 N.R. 300 (S.C.C.).

Saini v. M.E.I. (S.C.C., no. 23619), Lamer, McLachlin, Major), August 12, 1993.

AKNOWLEDGMENTS

I am generally indebted to my current and former clients from Iran who have successfully defended their refugee claims in Canada.

My gratitude goes to my former students at CDI College, Toronto downtown campus, Herzing College Immigration Consultancy class (whom I lectured when demanded), and Trios College, Kitchener campus, who received and treasured the lectures on immigration and refugee law in Canada.

I would not forget to say, "Thank you," to the help I received from my Iranian friends in Ontario: Aliyeh Pouresmaeili, Hossein Hemati, Javad Kerachian, Marjan Hatamzadeh, Mehnoush Chistan, Mohamad Falsafi, Mohsen Haghparast and Parto Hojjati, – in respect of *Persian/Farsi* interpretation and translation to English – of various documents – and other helps and liaisons. I am particularly thankful to my colleague, Ardavan Rousta, who deputized me when I was not able to represent a client at the RPD.

Thanks to my good friend and personal assistant, "Mr. Billy," who stayed with me through and through and who helped to manage my office emails while I concentrated on writing this book.

And last but not least, to my family (Clarice, Emmerance, Tashany-Idyllia, and Cuteravive). Interestingly, it was while we were on the plane to Hawaii in August 2019 when I first set to compile this book. My family was there with me and gave me the necessary impetus to

putting together the materials contained in this book. To
them, I am eternally grateful.

INTRODUCTION
STATUTORY FRAMEWORK

This book is for those who would like to make a successful refugee claim in Canada, especially those who are persecuted on account of their religion in Iran. It is an introduction to the refugee determination system (RDS) in Canada. Refugee claims may be based on political or religious, sexual orientation or gender-related persecutions. In this book, we will look at religious persecution as the ground of refugee protection and claim in Canada. The principles applicable to religious persecutions can be applied to the other grounds not covered in this book.

Canada protects and grants refugee statuses to people who are fleeing persecution from their country of origin (of citizenship) or of their former habitual residence. Canada is a signatory to the United Nations conventions[1] that variously protect people who are not able to be protected in their own countries of citizenships or of former habitual residence due to political, war, religious, gender or other factors. Article 1

---

[1] Such as the "The Convention Relating to the Status of Refugees" also known as the 1951 Refugee Convention; and the Protocol Relating to the Status of Refugees (also known as 1967 Protocol). It came into force on October 4th, 1967. It had 146 parties. Canada became a signatory on June 4th, 1969.

of the 1951 Refugee Convention (The "UN Refugee Convention") defines a refugee as one:

> ...owing to **well-founded fear** of being persecuted for reasons of **race, religion, nationality, membership of a particular social group or political opinion**, is **outside the country** of his nationality and is unable or, owing to such fear, is **unwilling to avail himself of the protection of that country**; or who, not having a nationality and being outside the country of his former **habitual residence** as a result of such events, is unable or, owing to such fear, is **unwilling to return to it**.[2]

As emphasized above, not all people fleeing their home countries qualify to be refugees. A refugee must have a well-founded fear of persecution in their home country (country of citizenship or of former habitual residence). This fear must be genuine. However, it must not be a proven fear. It must be enough that a person believes that they are in danger of persecution. The fear is such that the Claimant risks being persecuted if returned to their country of citizenship.

Fear alone is not enough; it must be based on five key grounds:[3] Race, religion, nationality (national origin or ancestry), membership in a

---

[2] *Ibid.* (Emphasis added).
[3] It is trite law in Canada to be found a refugee or protected person on only one ground even if more than one grounds equally apply. See definition of trite law under footnote 12.

particular social group; and political opinion. Outside of these itemized grounds (or grounds associated to these), a nation may not have the necessary jurisdiction to grant protection to a refugee Claimant. Moreover, one has to be "outside" of their country of citizenship or of former habitual residence in order to claim for refugee protection. The country of citizenship or former habitual residence must be unwilling or unable to avail the refugee Claimant protection.

Canada has domesticated most UN conventions, including the one that protects refugees. To *domesticate* a convention is to translate it into national law so that in letter as in spirit, the convention is applicable to the local or national environment. *The Immigration Refugee Protection Act* ("IRPA"),[4] and the Immigration and Refugee Protection Regulations,[5] and the *Constitution*[6] and the *Citizenship Act*[7] and its regulations govern immigration, refugees and citizenship matters in Canada.

Once a nation domesticates or contracts or otherwise becomes a signatory to the UN Refugee Convention, it takes on the responsibility of protecting and fulfilling certain obligations for the Claimant. Mandatory

---

[4] (S.C. 2001, c. 27)
[5] (SOR/2002-227)
[6] The *Constitution Act*, 1982
[7] S.C. 1946, c. 15

obligations of the contracting nations include: Exempting refugee Claimants from reciprocity;[8] providing security; transferring marriages and providing free access to courts. Other obligations are: Administrative (paperwork) assistance; travel document assistance and transfer of assets assistance; assimilating and naturalizing refugees; and so on. In dispensing with these obligations, contracting nations must not discriminate, or forcibly return or "refoul" refugees to the country of their danger,[9] and so on.

On June 4th, 1969, Canada signed the UN Refugee Convention, "18 years after it was adopted by the United Nations. Since Canada signed the Refugee Convention, it has gained the enviable reputation of being a world leader in protecting refugees."[10] Because Canada has appended its signature to the UN Refugee

---

[8] Article 7 (2) of Refugee Convention 1951, "After a period of three years' residence, all refugees shall enjoy exemption from legislative reciprocity in the territory of the Contracting States." Legislative Reciprocity has been defined as: "The phrasing of Article 7 (2) constitutes an attempt to restore a balance between those rights and benefits which a State may be prepared to grant to any alien (and where consequently the rule of reciprocity only is a means of achieving equal rights and benefits for one's own nationals abroad); those rights and benefits which are meant to be an exclusive privilege for certain foreign nationals" (Commentary on the Refugee Convention 1951 ARTICLES 2-11, 13-37, published by the Division of International Protection of the United Nations High Commissioner for Refugees, 1997)
[9] See Article 33 of the UN Refugee Convention
[10] Canadian Council for Refugees, "Recognizing successes, acting for change," < https://ccrweb.ca/sites/ccrweb.ca/files/static-files/40thanniversary.htm> (Retrieved: November 22nd, 2019)

Convention that requires that such people be granted a safe haven in Canada, Canada cannot, therefore, return them to the countries to which they claim that they are or will be in danger of being persecuted.

The doctrine that prevents countries like Canada from returning refugees to countries they claim they would face persecution is called *Non-Refoulement*. *Persecution* is generally defined in this book to mean torture or threat of torture, unlawful criminal charges or arrest (with or without a warrant), detentions (with or without trials), and death.

The immigration and refugee system in Canada comprises (1) The Immigration, Refugees and Citizenship Canada (IRCC, formerly Citizenship and Immigration Canada or CIC); (2) The Canada Border Services Agency or CBSA. (The CBSA is part of the Government of Canada's public safety portfolio. It is an agency of Public Safety and Emergency Preparedness Canada (PSEPC)); and (3) the Immigration and Refugee Board of Canada (IRB).

This book does not discuss the IRCC and the CBSA, except to mention that the IRCC deals with all immigration matters, including granting visas and permits, sponsorship applications and other aspects of immigration such as temporary residence, permanent residence, business immigration, express entry or humanitarian and compassionate (H&C) considerations. The responsibility of CBSA includes: Requesting detention reviews, and effecting deportations from Canada, but not adjudicating detention reviews.

The IRB is divided into 4 divisions: The Immigration Division (ID); the Immigration Appeal Division (IAD); the Refugee Protection Division (RPD); and the Refugee Appeal Division (RAD). Special adjudicators called Members make decisions at the IRB. A Claimant at the IRB may be represented by counsel. Counsel means a lawyer. The IRB has extended the meaning of counsel to representatives who are recognized under s.91/2 of the IRPA, and these include Licensed Paralegals and Immigration Consultants.

The meaning of counsel, therefore, denotes representatives who have been licensed either by the Law Society of their respective provincial law regulatory bodies or by the federal Immigration Consultants regulatory body. All paid representatives must be verified by the IRB. They must submit a form called **Counsel** Contact Information and in it provide their membership number. Counsel must also submit an immigration form called Use of a Representative.

The two forms require counsel to provide their membership number, contact details (addresses of their offices, telephone numbers, fax numbers or even email addresses). The Use of the Representative form also requires the Claimant to cancel the representative should that need arise. Once the IRB has received the Counsel Contact Information form and/or the Use of a Representative form, the RPD will then correspondent with counsel as well as the Claimant.

Recent developments in due of the Covid-19 pandemic have led to the formation of an online integrated platform called the Immigration and Refugees Board portal readily available at https://my-case-mon-dossier.irb-cisr.gc.ca/en-US/. Counsel can use this integrated platform to register with the IRB new clients, including processing contact information for both client and counsel.

This author has represented all kinds of Iranian refugee Claimants in Canada. He has been able to win at least 99 percent of the cases with all or nearly all the Members at the RPD in Toronto, and at least with one in Vancouver. Appendix VI[11] showcases some selected successful Notices of Decision from at least every Member who frequently adjudicates cases on religious, sex-

---

[11] See page 524.

related and political persecutions at the RPD.
This is one of the places where the saying, "If
you keep doing the same thing, you'll get the
same results," has a new meaning. If what has
been successful, hitherto, is based on the
principles and jurisprudence shared in this book,
why change it now?

CHAPTER 1
STATUTORY DEFINITION

S ection 96 and subsection 97(1) of *Immigration and Refugee Protection Act* (IRPA)[12] define a Convention Refugee (CR) as a person in need of protection:

Convention Refugee

96 A Convention refugee is a person who, by reason of a well-founded fear of persecution for reasons of race, religion, nationality, membership in a particular social group or political opinion,

(a) is outside each of their countries of nationality and is unable or, by reason of that fear, unwilling to avail themself of the protection of each of those countries; or

(b) not having a country of nationality, is outside the country of their former habitual residence and is unable or, by reason of that fear, unwilling to return to that country.

Person in Need of Protection

97 (1) A person in need of protection is a person in Canada whose removal to their country or countries of nationality or, if they do not have a country of nationality, their country of former habitual residence, would subject them personally

---

[12] S.C. 2001, c. 27

(a) to a danger, believed on substantial grounds to exist, of torture within the meaning of Article 1 of the Convention Against Torture; or

(b) to a risk to their life or to a risk of cruel and unusual treatment or punishment if

(i) the person is unable or, because of that risk, unwilling to avail themself of the protection of that country,

(ii) the risk would be faced by the person in every part of that country and is not faced generally by other individuals in or from that country,

(iii) the risk is not inherent or incidental to lawful sanctions, unless imposed in disregard of accepted international standards, and

(iv) the risk is not caused by the inability of that country to provide adequate health or medical care.

(2) A person in Canada who is a member of a class of persons prescribed by the regulations as being in need of protection is also a person in need of protection.

In Canada, conferring of refugee status or protection is a *trite law*.[13] This means that one ought only to meet the requirement of s. 96 or ss. 97(1) of IRPA. It is common practice in Canadian refugee law that one is usually found under both sections. A refugee is, thus, a person

---

[13] A principle of law so notorious and entrenched that it is commonly known and rarely disputed. See Trite Law Definition < http://www.duhaime.org/LegalDictionary/T/TriteLaw.aspx> (Retrieved: November 24th, 2019)

who has a founded fear of persecution in their country of citizenship or of former habitual residence. This fear must both be *subjective* (it affects them personally) and objective (the State conditions make persecution possible). To make a refugee claim in Canada, the Claimant (the person making a refugee claim) must have left their own country and must be within Canada.[14] The claim can be made at two points:

The claim can be made at the Point of Entry (POE) either at the airport or the border, depending on where the Claimant first enters Canada. This applies to those who are seeking asylum straight upon arrival in Canada, and mostly it concerns those who have no lawful right or authorization to enter into Canada. Those who make claims at the POE are briefly detained by the CBSA officers. They are detained (arrested) because they are inadmissible to Canada. If they decide or show intention to made a refugee claim, they will be issued with removal orders subject to appearing before an

---

[14] This injunction (namely, being out of your country) applies to refugee resettlement programs under the United Nations High Commissioner for Refugees (UNHCR) as well; the Claimant must be out of their countries of citizenship in order to apply to be refugees in Canada. Such a person will become a *Government-Assisted Refugee* (or "GAR"), defined as a person who is outside Canada and has been determined to be a Convention Refugee and who receives financial and other support from the Government of Canada or Province of Quebec for up to one year after their arrival in Canada. GARs are selected from applicants referred by the UNHCR and other referral organizations.

adjudicator at the IRB. At this point, these people are neither refugee Claimants nor refugees; they are considered Foreign Nationals (a Foreign National is legally defined in Canadian as "a person who is not a Canadian citizen or a permanent resident, and includes a stateless person"[15]) who must be subjected to examination by a CBSA officer who may recommend a hearing at the ID. If the foreign national does not show any intention to claim for refugee protection in Canada, a CBSA officer may refer the matter to the ID for an Admissibility Hearing.[16] If the foreign national indicates that they would like to make a refugee claim, the CBSA officer will refer them to an in-land reporting centre to make a refugee claim by submitting the prescribed forms within fifteen (15) days. The claim can also be made *within* Canada. This applies to all those who came to Canada with lawful authorization (Visas) and who subsequently made a refugee claim in Canada. These must report themselves to the In-

---

[15] IRPA, s. 2(1); also see, Glossary, "Foreign National," < https://www.canada.ca/en/services/immigration-citizenship/helpcentre/glossary.html> (retrieved: July 10th, 2020)
[16] An admissibility hearing may be held pursuant to sections 44 and 45 of IRPA to decide if one is allowed to come into or stay in Canada. It applies to both permanent residents and foreign nationals. Admissibility hearings can be started for any of these reasons: Criminal convictions; human or international rights violations; risk to security in Canada health reasons; financial reasons; misrepresentation or not being truthful in immigration applications; failure to comply with IRPA. It also applies to minor children (children 16 years and below) who have travelled alone to Canada.

Land Reporting Centre and make a claim there. In-land reporting is a two-step process. First, the foreign national must attend at the centre with the following documents and forms: All identity documents, such as passports, birth certificates, national identity documents or any such documents. The foreign national must also take to the centre completed immigration and refugee forms, including the following immigration forms: Generic and Schedule A – Background Declaration. The foreign national should also complete the following refugee forms: Basis of Claim or BOC form (formerly the Personal Information Form or PIF) with the narrative attached thereto, and Schedule 12. The BOC form is a very important refugee claim form. The foreign national must also take four (4) passport-photos, and a checklist.

The IRCC officers at the centre will review the BOC narrative and forms and the immigration forms and ascertain that the person has met the criteria for making a refugee claim in Canada. Recently, the IRCC introduced an Integrated Claim Analysis Centre (ICAC) Checklist to assist the IRB-RPD to streamline document collection.[17] Once that has been satisfied, the officer will arrange for an Interview. The purpose of the interview is to determine whether

---

[17] See Appendix V for a redacted sample. This author was one of the first whose clients used this system.

there are any issues, usually security in nature or otherwise that might not qualify the foreign national to making a successful refugee claim in Canada. The officers will also review the foreign national's previous immigration history to making sure that the person is credible or otherwise has misrepresented. Depending on the outcome, the person will be provided with a document called Refugee Protection Claimant's Document or RPCD, which technically entitles the "Claimant" to the Rule of Natural Justice or the Right to be Heard (or due process of law). Even if credibility or misrepresentation issues have been discovered by the officers, the Claimant will still be entitled to procedural fairness so that the Claimant can defend the claim and allegations of misrepresentation. Whether the Minister has elected to Intervene or not, the matter will now be referred to the RPD for adjudication. (Ministerial Intervention means that the Minister of Immigration will be opposing the refugee claim on the basis of credibility findings or other grounds). The Minister's Counsel, as the Minister's representative is referred to, may intervene directly by appearing at the hearing or may only make written submissions without attending at the hearing.

A Claimant is further entitled to some limited access to social, health and employment privileges while she waits for her hearing in Canada. The Notice to Appear for a Hearing, which is a notice provided to the Claimant to appear before an adjudicator to defend the claim, may be given to the Claimant at the Interview or may be mailed later to the Claimant at the address provided in the Generic and the BOC forms. It is important that the Claimant notifies the RPD whenever there is a change of address in order not to miss the hearing.

The limited social, health and employment needs the Claimant is entitled to at this stage are the requirement to attend at a Panel Physician's office and undergo medical examination. A Panel Physician, formerly Designated Medical Doctor, is an IRCC-appointed or designated medical doctor who can perform medical tests and send results directly to IRCC. IRCC does not accept the medical results of any other doctors. Other entitlements are Work Permit, Social Welfare, if needed, and health coverage. Note that the federal government will automatically cover the medical needs of the Claimant's first few months under the Interim Federal Health Program (IFHP). The IFHP, "Provides within Canada, limited, temporary coverage of health-care benefits to resettled refugees, refugee Claimants, and certain others who are not eligible for provincial or territorial health insurance."[18]

---

[18] "Interim Federal Health Program Policy," <

Health Insurance is defined as, "A Canadian provincial or territorial government program that pays for essential health services provided by doctors, hospitals and certain non-physician practitioners. Newcomers must apply to their provincial or territorial health insurance plan to get coverage and a health card."[19] Afterwards, the provincial health system will kick in, depending on the health insurance plan that exists in the province in which the refugee claim was made. For example, if the claim was made in Ontario Province, the province's Ontario Health Insurance Plan or OHIP will subsequently cover the Claimant.[20]

The RPD will provide two dates, one is the actual date of hearing or the Notice to Appear, and the other is reserved for those who may miss the hearing (Show-Cause). The Show-Cause date is not the date for the second chance for those who failed to appear; it is, rather, a date to meet the adjudicator and explain the reasons for failure to appear and whether another hearing should be scheduled. The IRB explains it this

---

https://www.canada.ca/en/immigration-refugees-citizenship/corporate/mandate/policies-operational-instructions-agreements/interim-federal-health-program-policy.html> (Retrieved: November 22nd, 2019)

[19] "Health Insurance," Glossary, *supra*.

[20] For more details on OHIP, see, "Apply for OHIP and get a health card," < https://www.ontario.ca/page/apply-ohip-and-get-health-card#section-0> (Retrieved: November 22nd, 2019)

way:[21]

> The RPD will send you a Notice to Appear by
> mail when your claim is ready to be heard. On
> the Notice to Appear, there are two dates. The
> first date is the date of your hearing. The second
> date on your Notice to Appear is for a special
> hearing. In the event that you do not attend your
> hearing, you must appear at your special hearing
> to explain why you were not able to attend your
> hearing. At the special hearing, the member will
> determine whether your claim should be declared
> abandoned.
>
> Hearings usually take half a day and take place
> in private in order to protect you and your
> family. There is usually a short break about
> halfway through the hearing.
>
> Young children under the age of 12 who are
> accompanied by an adult making a refugee claim
> are not required to appear before the Refugee
> Protection Division unless the presiding member
> requires their attendance. When a member
> determines that it is necessary for a young
> Claimant to attend the hearing, you will be
> informed at the earliest possible opportunity. In
> some situations, older children will need to
> participate in the hearing. If you have concerns
> or questions about your child participating in the
> hearing, contact the RPD before your hearing or
> raise your concerns with the member at the
> hearing.
>
> If the RPD member cannot be in the same
> city as you, your hearing may take place by
> videoconference.

---

[21] IRB, "Claiming refugee protection - 4. Attending your hearing," <
https://irb-cisr.gc.ca/en/applying-refugee-
protection/Pages/index4.aspx> (Retrieved: April 29th, 2020)

It is important to notify counsel way in advance if the Claimant will not attend the hearing at the date scheduled. Counsel then may make an application for a change of hearing date or for an adjournment. As long as this requisition does not prejudice the Minister, is made for a legitimate reason and in good faith and in good time, the Refugee Protection Division (RPD) may consider changing the hearing date to an earliest available future date.

To be granted a refugee status, a Claimant must prove, on a balance of probabilities, that they meet the definition of a refugee or protected person pursuant to section 96 and subsection 97(1) of IRPA. The Balance of Probabilities is a legal standard of proof required to prove that the person is a refugee. The standard is lower than the criminal law threshold which requires the Crown (the Government) to prove a case Beyond a Reasonable Doubt, that is, to only convict an accused where it is very certain that they had committed a crime charged. Therefore, the Board's Member will grant refugee status to a Claimant who, on the balance of probabilities (or the preponderance of evidence), proves or establishes that they are more probable than not to be subjected to persecution if they returned to their country of citizenship or former habitual residence. If it is a scale of 100 percent, the Claimant will succeed in making a refugee claim if they only established about 51 percent.[22]

In subsequent chapters, we will discuss how the Claimant establishes, on the balance of probabilities, that they are a refugee or a person in need of protection in Canada. The BOC will be discussed in great details. It is assumed that the BOC, with its attendant schedule, if applicable, has been completed with the requirement of country-specific condition in place. In this book, Iran is the country of focus.

---

[22] However, as shall be discussed in Chapter 3, under the Refugee Determination System in Canada, one need not establish on the balance of probability to succeed in a refugee claim; one just needs to have a good reason to win. See *Adjei test* under, "Test – Standard of Proof."

CHAPTER 2
BASIS OF CLAIM

The Basis of Claim or BOC is, arguably, the most important document so far as a refugee claim is concerned. It is the basis or the notable information the Claimant provides as the basis of their refugee claim. This information, subject to amendment before the hearing, if necessary, becomes the Claimant's record in the Canadian immigration database. It cannot be easily changed afterwards without inviting allegations of misrepresentation.

The BOC narrative must be thought-through wisely, cogently and accurately.[23] No refugee claim has been successful without a well-written and presented BOC narrative or simply, the "Story." The story must accurately identify the Claimant, including their legal names, dates of birth, country of origin or citizenship, marital status, number of children, if any – this should include their names, ages and marital statuses and so on – educational levels, academic designation/qualification, if applicable, and any pertinent identifying information necessary to establishing a credible claim.

The BOC story must show a relationship

---

[23] See Appendix I, Sample redacted BOC narratives.

between the State and the alleged persecution. Canada cannot protect people who are not in danger of their own government or whose government can protect them if asked. Canada is a signatory to international conventions, but Canada will be declaring war with another sovereign State if it arbitrarily attempts to protect nationals from other sovereign States. The basis for protection is the assumption that the Claimant is either stateless or their own country and government cannot protect them, directly or indirectly. Only State actors and agents can truly persecute the foreign national under the law. However, other non-State actors can be agents of persecution, such as abusive spouses, organized criminal rings, cultural or customary or clan groups, terrorist gangs and etc.

The Meaning of Credibility in Refugee Law

Most, if not, all, refugee claims are won and lost on credibility. Evidence is essential. However, one should look at it from this point of view: How can a total stranger who happen to be hearing the claim believe for certain in your story? How should a Member believe if you are telling the truth or not? The simple answer is: Credibility.

Board Members are humans. They cannot know

what happened to the Claimant just by intuition or guessing. The only thing they have, usually, is the BOC story, the National Documentation Package (NDP),[24] and the evidence submitted, if any, with the claim. They expect that the Claimant's testimony will be consistent with the BOC story submitted. Credibility is synonymous with believability. It is the quality of being trusted and believed. And in relation to the witness' testimony (*viva voce*), credibility relates to the testimony of a witness during a hearing. There are generally five bases for credibility:

First, to be found credible, the Claimant must be trusted. Trust can be illusive in refugee hearing but particular attention to what the Claimant says, how they appear, their voice projection and general demeanor, can go a long way in establishing trust with the adjudicator. Trust is earned. It follows that the Claimant should pay attention to their choice of words, how polite, respectful or careful they are with their general presentation. Once the adjudicator believes and observes that the Claimant is whole and upright, and therefore, candid with overall presentation, the adjudicator will trust the Claimant. Trust is also earned when the Claimant pays particular attention to procedural matters, such as filing the evidence in good time, making necessary changes

---

[24] See Chapter 9

to the BOC story before the hearing,[25] and making necessary applications in good time and in good faith.

Second, credibility is built up through the reliability of what the Claimant says. Reliability means the truthfulness of what is said which is manifested through accuracy and exactitude of the statements made. Reliability is the accuracy of the testimony. It is one's ability to answer questions truthfully and accurately. Only the adjudicator and counsel, if represented, will have access to the BOC narrative. The Claimant will not have access to the BOC narrative at the hearing, but will be expected to answer questions according to the BOC narrative. The Claimant cannot deviate from the story or make arbitrary changes to the original story in the process. She must keep the same tenor and sequence of the story. To be reliable, the Claimant should remember names, places, dates and important landmarks in the story. It should be emphasized that reliability, and thus, credibility, will be impeached where the Claimant is forgetful or negligent in answering questions asked, or is inconsistent with the submitted BOC narrative.

Third, the logical flow of the Claimant's testimony establishes credibility. The story must have a logical trajectory – each paragraph

---

[25] At least more than ten days before the hearing, if necessary.

connecting the next in a logical and seamless flow of ideas and sense. The story should have a sensible start, middle and ending. In terms of a refugee story on religious conversion from Islam, for example, it must establish the following:

(a) That the Claimant was born a Muslim;

(b) That the Claimant converted to another religion other than Islam consciously and deliberately;

(c) That this change of religion came to the attention of the State or state-agents, such as, in the case of Iran, the Iranian Revolutionary Guard Corps (IRGCs),[26] the police, the Intelligence forces, *Sepah*, or *Basij*;

(d) That as a result of the exposure, and how the exposure occurred, the Claimant was or is in danger of being persecuted. Or as in most cases, the Claimant was arrested, interrogated or even tortured, and was made (forced) to sign a commitment (pledge) that they would not be involved with a new religion ever again, and if found to be in breach of the commitment, they would be subjected to worse treatment or even death;

(e) That in some way, this commitment was breached, usually, at the whim of a whistleblower or State informant. Most Claimants, once they become aware of the fact that the State had become aware of the breach, do all and anything to run away from Iran. The Iranian government is known to make people *disappear* who are in violation of security warning. A person who is warned and breaches the commitment is said to have insulted the Islamic Republic and such people could be in danger of being executed for apostasy. Apostasy is considered a capital crime in Iran. It is the public rejection (pouring scorn on Islam

---

[26] Or simply Iranian Revolutionary Guards (IRGs)

and its prophet) and conviction is allegedly punishable by death;[27]

(f) That the Claimant had either attempted to run to another town or province or could not have done so because the State security forces control the entire nation or will be expected to control that area of alternative escape. In other words, the Claimant had no viable Internal Flight Alternative (or IFA);

(g) That the Claimant escaped to Canada and made a refugee claim; and

(h) That the Claimant has continued to follow their newly-founded religion or faith or belief system in Canada.

Fourth, it is the sincerity and personal credibility of the testimony that establish credibility. The message and the medium are the same. The person telling the story cannot be separated from the story. It is, therefore, important that the witness establishes personal credibility by the way they tell their story and answer questions. Generally, the Claimant (witness) must do the following three things:

(a) They must only answer the questions being asked. Failure to follow this rule may force the adjudicator to draw a negative inference , and this might damage credibility beyond repair. If answering through an interpreter, it is vital to keep answers short;
(b) State so if they do not understand the question or ask the adjudicator to restate or rephrase the question; and

(c) Say so if they do not know or cannot remember the

---

[27] See Chapter 9 for a discussion on apostasy.

answer. It is better to not answer a question one does not know or cannot remember than to guess or answer a question one does not know. Credibility means that one is able to say they do not know if they do not know.

Fifth and last, the refugee hearing process is an inquisitorial process. This means that the adjudicator conducts the hearing like an inquiry. The hearing only becomes adversarial when the Minister decides to intervene. Otherwise, both the Claimant and her counsel must be prepared to follow the guideline and process as determined by the adjudicator.

The adjudicator sets the tone and trajectory of how the hearing is to be conducted. All that both the Claimant and counsel should do is to be prepared. Because the IRB sets the direction of how the hearing should be conducted, the adjudicator has freedom (or discretion) and ample opportunity to observe both how the Claimant answers questions and also, how she behaves during the hearing. This is called observing the personal demeanor and emotional disposition of the witness (Claimant). This will generally involve the following three aspects:

(a) How and what the Claimant wears. It is always better to be dressed modestly and avoiding both over- and underdressing. The best precaution is to error on the side of decency and morality, rather than being overtly extravagant and casual. The Claimant must observe basic hygiene, dress modestly, comb hair well and wear clothes that are well-pressed and in good taste. It is advisable to avoid outrageous colours – navy blue, black, dark grey suites or pants are ideal for men. For woman, closed shoes, long dresses or skirts and less tight clothing is advisable. Both men and women should avoid wearing expensive jewelry and heavily-scented perfumes.[28]

(b) Eye contact with the adjudicator;

(c) And a strong voice that can be heard but that is not excessive and irritating to the adjudicator. If there is an interpreter, the Claimant (witness) should speak in short sentences and allow the interpreter to finish the interpretation before saying another word. It is good policy to allow the interpreter to finish talking before the witness can say another word. It is equally important to allow the adjudicator to finish the sentence before the witness can answer. Speaking through the microphone with a firm voice is also advisable for the purposes of recording. The microphone only picks the Claimant's voice. It does not record the Claimant's demeanor, non-verbal gestures, and etc.

In the next seven chapters, we will provide a compilation of caselaw, policy, judicial determinations and jurisprudence already prepared by the IRB. The aim of the ensuing seven chapters, therefore, is to expose the Claimant to ready materials and reasonings of the IRB so that the Claimant is prepared to defend the claim. The materials, for the most part, have been uprooted in their entirety and only minimal

---

[28] Most Boards and Courts in Ontario facilitate a scent-free atmosphere.

modifications and changes have been made, and only for relevance, emphasis and contextual analysis.

CHAPTER 3
FOUNDED FEAR OF
PERSECUTION

C anada has established a strong legal regime for dealing with the subject of Founded Fear of Persecution. What follows in this Chapter is uprooted, in whole or in part, from Canadian Immigration and Refugee Board (IRB) website.[29]

Under the refugee determination system (RDS), for a claim to be accepted, on the question of law and fact, it must meet the following threshold:

It must meet the definition of a Convention Refugee (CR). The definition of a CR is forward-looking – meaning that not only the Claimant had a fear of persecution in the past, but that, that fear still remains and will continue in the future. The Standard of Proof still remains, "on the balance of probabilities." However, under the RDS, that standard is lower than the civil standard of proof. The Claimant need only to prove that he or she is more likely than not to be persecuted. In short, the Claimant has to state that there exist good reasons why they will be

---

[29] Immigration and Refugee Board of Canada [IRB], "Chapter 5 - Well-Founded Fear," https://irb-cisr.gc.ca/en/legal-policy/legal-concepts/Pages/RefDef05.aspx (Retrieved: August 20th, 2019)

persecuted.

Meaning of Subjective Fear

Generally, to satisfy an adjudicator under the RDS in refugee claim, a Claimant must establish a "subjective fear" or fear that is as a result of the Claimant's experience with the object of their persecution. In other words, fear that is real to the Claimant personally.

Subjective fear must be supported by "objective elements." That is, fear that is personal to the Claimant must have an objective, country-specific basis. The country must be such that it has a government (or State) policy, or practice or philosophy that causes people to be persecuted if they violate it. For example, in Iran, it is the policy of the Islamic Republic that people who change religion, if they were born Muslims, will be subjected to persecution – arrest, torture, imprisonment and even execution. If someone is then found to have been converted from Islam to, say, Christianity (subjective element), the Islamic Republic can then enforce its laws (objective element) and may arrest, torture or execute such a person.

Subjective fear is similarly established when a Claimant decided to flee from persecution soon as it had happened or showed potential signs of happening. In other words, the Claimant must not have delayed in either leaving the country of persecution or in making a refugee claim as soon as practicable when they arrived in a safe country. The adjudicator will have to determine whether the Claimant had sought for refugee protection in other safe countries where they first arrived. In Canada, generally, the Claimant must make a refugee claim within three months of arrival.[30] The sooner they make such refugee claim within that three months window the better. This suggestion is derived from the author's experience with the Canadian RDS.

The Claimant must also establish that if they return to their country of danger or persecution, which is usually either their country of citizenship or of former habitual residence, they will be arrested or executed. In law, this is routinely referred to as Re-Availment of Protection.[31] For example, Iranian nationals who have fled their country for fear of persecution or who have, upon arrival in Canada, changed religion, may claim Re-Availment of Protection in Canada. This is because Iran is known to send informants who report their own nationals back to Iran. Upon arrival at the POE, these people may be arrested, tortured, imprisoned or

---

[30] Determination usually is done on a case-by-case basis.
[31] See Chapter 6.

executed in Iran.

Similarly,[32] there are situations where the Claimant initial action of fleeing was not motivated by any fear of persecution. However, upon arrival in the new country, they have engaged or participated in activities that their nations might view as inimical to their values or practice. In Canadian RDS, Claimants can ask for protection even if, at first, there was no subjective fear of persecution, but at the time of the claim, or shortly thereafter, they would be in danger of returning to their countries of citizenship or of former habitual residence. This is referred to as *"Sur place claim."*[33] And it arises where even when the motivation for refugee claim indicates the absence of subjective fear, but the reality would portend danger.

Convention Refugee is Forward-Looking

The definition of CR is forward-looking. In a claim for refugee protection, the issue is not whether the Claimant had good reason to fear persecution in the past, but whether, at the time the claim is being assessed, the Claimant has

---

[32] Materials in the ensuing sections are retrieved from the IRB website.
[33] Chapter 6, *supra.*

good grounds for fearing persecution or in the future.

Claimants must establish that they have a subjective fear of persecution and also that the fear is well-founded in an objective sense. That is, subjective fear is justified in light of the objective situation. When evaluating conditions in the Claimant's country of origin, the RPD is also required to consider evidence of the conditions as they exist at the time of the hearing.

Claimants do not have to establish that they have been persecuted in the past. Even if they can do so, past persecution is insufficient of itself to establish a fear of future persecution. Nonetheless, past persecution remains a relevant factor because evidence relating to it (or to a fear of past persecution) can properly be the foundation for present fear. In *Natynczyk*,[34] the Court remarked that even though the test for a well-founded fear was forward-looking, in cases where incidents of past persecution were alleged, the RPD had an obligation to assess those incidents because "evidence of past persecution is one of the most effective means of showing that a fear of future

---

[34] *Natynczyk v. Canada (Minister of Employment and Immigration)*, (F.C., no. IMM-2025-03), O'Keefe, June 25, 2004, at para. 71

persecution is objectively well-founded."[35] Where a Claimant is able to establish a pattern of long-standing persecution, there may be reason to believe that the pattern will continue.

Evidence about persecution faced by similarly-situated people will often be compelling because it tends to show that a Claimant would face the same risks. However, that does not change the fact that it is still the Claimant who must face a serious possibility of persecution.

Legal Test

Claimants must establish the factual elements of their claim on a balance of probabilities, but they do not have to prove that persecution would be more likely than not. The evidence must show only that there are "good grounds" for fearing persecution. The test, which has become known as the *Adjei Test*, was set out as:

Is there a reasonable chance that persecution would take place were the applicant returned to his country of origin?

In *Li*,[36] the Federal Court of Appeal cautioned against confusing the "standard of proof" and

---

[35] *Ibid.*
[36] *Li, Yi Mei v. M.C.I.* (F.C.A., no. A-31-04), Rothstein, Noël, Malone, January 5, 2005; 2005 FCA 1.

the "legal test to be met." The standard of proof refers to the standard the panel will apply when assessing the evidence adduced for the purpose of making factual findings, whereas the legal test is the test for the likelihood of persecution which a Claimant must establish in order to obtain Convention refugee status.

Courts have used various terms to describe this test – "good grounds," "reasonable chance," and "reasonable" or even "serious" possibility, as opposed to a "mere" possibility. The test does not require a probability of persecution and asking Claimants to establish that they "would" be persecuted in the future. Such a test has been held to be the wrong test. However, in one case, the Court held that the RPD did not err when it stated that there was insufficient evidence that the Claimant would face a serious possibility of persecution, as the word "would" has "both a degree of certainty in some contexts and a degree of likelihood in other contexts". In the Court's view, the Member was speaking of the reasonable likelihood, not the absolute certainty.

The test for the well-foundedness of a fear of persecution was further clarified in *Ponniah*,[37] where Desjardins J.A. stated:

---

[37] *Ponniah, Manoharan v. M.E.I.* (F.C.A., no. A-345-89), Heald, Hugessen, Desjardins, May 16, 1991. Reported: *Ponniah v. Canada*

> "Good grounds" or "reasonable chance" is
> defined in *Adjei* as occupying the field between
> upper and lower limits; it is less than a 50 per
> cent chance (i.e., a probability), but more than a
> minimal or mere possibility. There is no
> intermediate ground: what falls between the two
> limits is "good grounds."[38]

In *Ioda*,[39] the Court referred to the test set out in *Adjei*[40] and *Ponniah*[41] and rejected the argument that when the Refugee Division based its negative decision on there being a "mere risk" of persecution it was equivalent to finding a "mere possibility." In the Court's view, "risk" conveyed a higher threshold of probability. The Court found in *Rajagopal*[42] that the Officer misstated the test when he concluded that the Claimant "would not be at particular risk."[43]

(Minister of Employment and Immigration) (1991), 13 Imm. L.R. (2d) 241 (F.C.A.), at 245

[38] *Ibid.*

[39] *Ioda, Routa v. M.E.I.* (F.C.T.D., no. 92-A-6604), Dubé, June 18, 1993. Reported: *Ioda v. Canada (Minister of Employment and Immigration)* (1993), 21 Imm. L.R. (2d) 294 (F.C.T.D.)

[40] *Adjei v. Canada (Minister of Employment and Immigration)*, [1989] 2 F.C. 680 (C.A.), at 682. For a case where the Court does an in-depth analysis of the RPD's language and finds that it incorrectly required the Claimant to prove persecution on a balance of probabilities, see *Ramanathy, Murugesakumar v. M.C.I.* (F.C., no. IMM-1241-13), Mosley, May 27, 2014; 2014 FC 511

[41] *Ponniah, supra.*

[42] *Rajagopal, Gnanathas v. M.C.I.* (F.C., no. IMM-1350-11), Hughes, November 10, 2011; 2011 FC 1277, at para. 11

[43] *Ibid.*

In *Sivaraththinam*[44] the Claimant alleged that all he
was required to establish was that there was more
than a minimal possibility that he would be
persecuted upon return to Sri Lanka. Justice
Annis undertook a detailed examination of the
wording of the legal test for section 96 of IRPA.
According to his interpretation of *Adjei*, the
Court of Appeal was not proposing either "more
than a mere possibility" or "not more than a 50
percent chance" as the test for determining a
well-founded fear under section 96. In his view,
the Court was looking for a compromise
standard between the two extremities, neither of
which it suggested should apply. Justice Annis
concluded that *Adjei* established the proper
expression of the standard to determine a well-
founded fear as a "reasonable chance",
"reasonable possibility", "serious possibility", or
"good grounds". He went on to express his own
preference:

> Returning to the issue of appropriate
> qualifiers of possibilities, chances, etc., I am
> of the view that any test not containing the
> term "reasonable" as a limitation should be
> shunned. This would leave the appropriate
> standard to be either a "reasonable chance"
> or a "reasonable possibility", as there is no

---

[44] *Sivaraththinam, Mayooran v. M.C.I.* (F.C., no. IMM-13174-12),
Annis, February 20, 2014; 2014 FC 162

distinction between a chance or a
possibility.[45]

The Court also cautions that if the tribunal sets
out a multiplicity of misstated tests in its reasons,
then later stating the test correctly elsewhere in
the reasons will not cure those errors and the
decision may not be saved.

With regard to the standard of proof used to
assess evidence, the Federal Court has held that
certain phrasing in CRDD[46] reasons, such as "we
are not convinced" or "the Claimant did not
persuade the panel" implied overly exacting
standards of proof.

Failure to Seek Protection in Other Countries

A Claimant's behaviour after leaving his or her
country, but before arriving in Canada, may also
be taken into consideration in determining
whether the subjective component of a well-
founded fear has been established. Failure to
seek the protection of another country which is
also a signatory to the Convention may be a
significant factor to consider but is not in itself
determinative. Voluntarily leaving a country

---

[45] *Sivaraththinam*, at para. 49
[46] Convention Refugee Determination Division (Immigration and Refugee Board of Canada)

where the Claimant could safely live is another example of behaviour that can cast doubt on a Claimant's subjective fear.

There is no provision in the Convention that obliges refugee Claimants to seek asylum in the first country they reach. However, there is a presumption that persons fleeing persecution will seek protection at the first opportunity, which would normally be in the first country they reach. Case law states that a negative inference can be drawn from a Claimant's failure to claim in a safe third country, but it also clearly states that this failure cannot be determinative. The Claimant's explanation must be considered in order to determine whether the Claimant's behaviour can fairly be considered to be evidence of a lack of subjective fear.

For example, some jurisprudence has suggested that where the Claimant had a legal status in the third country, and was, therefore, not at immediate risk of removal, it is not reasonable to draw a negative inference from the Claimant's failure to claim in that country.

Another important consideration is the age of the Claimant. In *Pulido Ruiz*,[47] the Court noted that:

> [I]t goes without saying that a child does not have the same capacities as an adult. Even though the IRB seemed to have considered [the applicant's] age in its decision, it found that he should have behaved like an adult and claimed asylum at the earliest opportunity. However, [he] was barely 15 years old. It seems unlikely to us that an adolescent would know the complexities and subtleties of the administrative apparatus with respect to asylum and be able to gauge the rough waters of the immigration process in the United States without an adult's help. Imposing such a burden on an adolescent seems unreasonable to us.[48]

Whether or not a country is a signatory to the Convention is relevant to determining whether it is reasonable to expect the Claimant to have sought protection there. It is clearly a factor for decision-makers to consider.

---

[47] *Pulido Ruiz, Cristian Danilo v. M.C.I.* (F.C., no. IMM-2819-11), Scott, February 24, 2012; 2012 FC 258. See also *Manage, Pierrette v. M.C.I.* (F.C., no. IMM-4966-13), Kane, April 17, 2014; 2014 FC 374, where the RPD had found that the applicants' failure to seek asylum in Kenya and Germany, while in transit to Canada, demonstrated a lack of subjective fear. The Court held that this finding was not reasonable based on the applicants' circumstances and youth. The RPD unreasonably expected the applicants to appreciate that their failure to seek asylum in the very first country they landed would jeopardize their claim and undermine their subjective fear of persecution.

[48] *Ibid.*

The significance of the failure to claim and the
resulting conclusion of an absence of subjective
fear is highlighted by the case of *Memarpour*[49]
where, despite finding that the Claimants had
been denied a fair hearing, Madame Justice
Simpson declined to send the case back for
rehearing. She made this rather exceptional ruling
because she had no doubt that the RPD would
again reject the claim, based on the Claimant's
conduct which indicated a total lack of a
subjective fear of persecution. In the ten-year
period after he left Iran the Claimant studied and
worked in several countries but never sought
asylum in any of them. His testimony that he was
deterred from claiming by the prospect of line-
ups at embassies showed how little importance
he attached to the issue of protection. Moreover,
he travelled extensively on false documents,
apparently little worried by the prospect of being
discovered and deported to Iran.

In cases concerning Claimants who do not claim
in a third country, their reasons for not claiming
are rarely as easy to dismiss as a reluctance to
wait in line. There are many cases of Claimants
whose intention it is to claim refuge in Canada,
and who simply transit through other countries
on their way. Some Claimants say that they were

---

[49] *Memarpour, Mahdiv.M.C.I.* (F.C.T.D., no. IMM-3113-94), Simpson,
May 25, 1995, at para. 23-24

not aware that they could ask for asylum in the other country. Others choose not to claim in the third country because they have been warned that they have little chance of success there. A reviewing court will normally uphold a decision that considers whether the explanation is reasonable in light of the circumstances of the Claimant, including whether they have engaged in other conduct that tends to support or undermine the subjective fear element. The following are examples that illustrate how the various factors have been weighed.

- *In transit*

  The Court has frequently held that a short stay in a safe third country *en-route* to Canada is not necessarily considered a sufficiently material sojourn to create an expectation that the Claimant would claim refugee status during that stay.

  A failure to make a refugee claim in a third country may raise doubt that a refugee Claimant has a subjective fear. However, where a Claimant had always planned to come to Canada, and merely was in transit during a stopover in a third country, the Court has held that such a situation does not undermine the subjective fear of persecution.

- *Family in Canada*

   Failure to make a refugee claim in an *en-route* country because the Claimant would rather make the claim in Canada because he or she has family here may be a valid reason for not making the claim at the first opportunity.

- *Ignorance of the Process*

   In *Perez*, the Court upheld the Board's finding that the Claimant who spent five years in the United States before claiming refugee protection in Canada did not provide convincing evidence of his subjective fear. His testimony that he was unaware he could claim asylum in the United States was found implausible in light of his repeated attempts to apply to stay under another United States program which offered temporary protection.

   Similarly, in *Idahosa*,[50] the Court found that it was reasonable for the RAD to conclude that the appellant would have some understanding that she could claim

---

[50] *Idahosa, Musili Amoke v. M.C.I.* (F.C. no. IMM-1124-18), Favel, March 29, 2019; 2019 FC 384 at para. 31.

refugee status in the United States in light of the contradictory evidence she gave. On the one hand, she stated she left the United States to come to Canada due to her concerns about changes in American refugee policies. On the other hand, she denied knowing she could file a refugee claim in the United States.

In the case of *Bello*,[51] the Claimant from Cameroon lived in France for seven years, travelled in adjoining countries and lived in the United States for another six months, without ever claiming refugee status. The Board found this to be inconsistent with a subjective fear of persecution. It noted that all the countries in question were either signatories to the 1951 Convention or to the 1967 Protocol. The reason given by the Claimant for not seeking protection was that France supported the Cameroonian government, and as for the neighbouring countries, he did not know about claiming refugee status. The Court held that it was open to the Board to disbelieve the Claimant had a subjective fear of persecution, given the delay in claiming refugee status. It noted that the RPD's conclusion was also

---

[51] *Bello, Salihou v. M.C.I.* (F.C.T.D., no. IMM-1771-96), Pinard, April 11, 1997.

influenced by the Claimant having returned twice to Cameroon.

- *Little Hope of Success*

In *Madoui*,[52] an Algerian Claimant failed to claim during 19 months in Italy. He had been told by friends that he had little, if any, chance of obtaining refugee status in Italy. Despite statistics in evidence showing that similar claims were rarely accepted, the Board was not satisfied that the subjective component had been met and the Court saw no error in the Board's assessment.

In *Mekideche*,[53] when the Board asked why the Claimant did not claim refugee status during his two years in Italy, he testified that it was because he believed that Algerian refugees would be denied and returned to Algeria. This belief was based on news reports that other European countries were not receptive to Algerian refugees. Noting that he travelled throughout Europe with false

---

[52] *Madoui, Nidhal Abderrahv.M.C.I.* (F.C.T.D., no. IMM-660-96), Denault, October 25, 1996
[53] *Mekideche, Anouarv. M.C.I.* (F.C.T.D., no. IMM-2269-96), Wetston, December 9, 1996

documentation before arriving in Canada,
the Board stated that this was a risk that a
person who feared persecution would not
take. The Court found no error in the
Board's conclusion that these two issues
showed an absence of a subjective fear of
persecution.

In another case, a young Pakistani
Claimant who arrived in the United States
came to Canada after just nine days. He
feared that he would not be considered for
asylum because of the negative
atmosphere towards persons from his part
of the world following the September 11
attack. The Court held that the
circumstances were comparable to those
in *El Naem*[54] and that the Board had erred
in drawing an unreasonable inference that
there was no subjective basis to the claim.

In *Liblizadeh*,[55] the Court quashed the
decision of the Board when it found that
there was no evidence before the panel
that the Claimant could realistically have
applied for refugee status in Turkey, even
though he was there seven months, and in

[54] *El-Naem, Faisalv. M.C.I.* (F.C.T.D., no. IMM-1723-96), Gibson,
February 17, 1997. Reported: *El-Naem v. Canada (Minister of Citizenship
and Immigration)* (1997), 37 Imm. L.R. (2d) 304 (F.C.T.D.)
[55] *Liblizadeh, Hassanv.M.C.I.* (F.C.T.D., no. IMM-5062-97), MacKay,
July 8, 1998

the United States, where he was only in transit.

A few cases have pointed out that failure to claim in a third country may not be indicative of a lack of subjective fear in situations *where a person is not anticipating a return to his or her country.*[56] These were the circumstances in *Yoganathan.*[57] Mr. Justice Gibson followed the same reasoning as the Court of Appeal in *Hue.*[58] Both cases involved seamen. Justice Gibson held that the CRDD erred in concluding that the Claimant did not have a subjective fear of persecution as he had failed to claim refugee status at the first opportunity in other signatory countries: "The [Claimant] had his 'sailor's papers' and 'a ship to sail on'. In the circumstances, he did not have to

---

[56] Emphasis added.

[57] *Yoganathan, Kandasamy v. M.C.I.* (F.C.T.D., no. IMM-3588-97), Gibson, April 20, 1998, at para. 8

[58] *Hue, Marcel Simon Chang Tak v. M.E.I.* (F.C.A., no. A-196-87), Marceau, Teitelbaum, Walsh, March 8, 1988; *Heer, Karnail Singh v. M.E.I.* (F.C.A., no. A-474-87), Heald, Marceau, Lacombe, April 13, 1988 and *Huerta, Martha Laura Sanchez v. M.E.I.* (F.C.A., no. A-448-91), Hugessen, Desjardins, Létourneau, March 17, 1993. Reported: *Huerta v. Canada (Minister of Employment and Immigration)* (1993), 157 N.R. 225 (F.C.A.). In *Andrade Ramos, Norberto v. M.C.I.* (F.C. no., IMM-1867-10), Russell, January 10, 2011; 2011 FC 15 at para. 28, the Court reiterated this principle as follows: "[…] the RPD's conclusion that the Applicants' failure to claim asylum at the earliest opportunity (that is, in the U.S.) indicates their lack of subjective fear is contrary to Federal Court of Appeal jurisprudence, which says that a board may consider this factor in assessing subjective fear, provided it is not the only evidence upon which the board relies. See Hue […]"

seek protection. He was safe from persecution in Sri Lanka."

Leaving a country which has provided refuge and where a Claimant has no fear of persecution is generally considered to be behaviour indicative of a lack of subjective fear. In *Shahpari*,[59] the Court suggested, in *obiter*, that:

> Applicants should also remember that actions they themselves take which are intended to result in their not being able to return to a country which has already granted them Convention refugee status may well evidence an absence of the subjective fear of persecution in their original country from which they purport to be seeking refuge.[60]

In *Geron*,[61] the Board concluded that the Claimants, citizens of the Philippines, were not credible and lacked subjective fear, as evidenced by the long delay before they claimed refugee status and the fact that they had valid residence permits for Italy but allowed them to lapse during the 18 months they remained in Canada prior to making their claims. The Court held that the Board had not erred in failing to consider the objective basis of the claim; it could be dismissed

---

[59] *Shahpari, Khadijeh v. M.C.I.* (F.C.T.D., no. IMM-2327-97), Rothstein, April 3, 1998, at para.14
[60] *Ibid.*
[61] *Geron, Fernando Bilog v. M.C.I.* (F.C.T.D., no. IMM-4951-01), Blanchard, November 22, 2002; 2002 FCT 1204

in the absence of any credible evidence to support the Claimants' subjective fear.

Even where the refuge is not necessarily a permanent one, questions about the Claimant's fear will usually be raised whenever a safe haven is abandoned in order to claim refugee status in Canada. In *Bains*, a Claimant from India who applied for asylum in England, left after waiting five or six years without an answer. He explained that he had heard that the British authorities were removing Claimants awaiting status, though he produced no evidence of this. The Court noted that the British authorities had clearly told the Claimant that he would not be deported before a decision on his status had been made. The Court considered that the CRDD was justified in verifying the reason the Claimant gave for leaving England and that it was reasonable to conclude that the Claimant's decision to leave did not demonstrate a fear of being returned to India.

Delay in Making a Claim Upon Arrival in Canada

Mr. Justice Shore summarized the basic principles related to delay in claiming once in Canada:

There is a well-established principle to the effect
that any person having a well-founded fear of
persecution should claim refugee protection in
Canada as soon as he or she arrives in the
country, if that is his or her intent. On this point,
the Federal Court of Appeal has already
concluded that any delay in claiming refugee
protection is an important factor which the
Board may take into consideration in its analysis.
Such a delay indicates a lack of a subjective fear
of persecution, since there is a presumption to
the effect that a person having a well-founded
fear of persecution will claim refugee protection
at the first opportunity. Accordingly, in
conducting its assessment, the Board is entitled
to take into consideration the applicant's delay in
claiming refugee protection.[62]

There is case law dealing with the issue of timing;
namely whether the proper reference point is
always the date of arrival in Canada. The Court
in *Gabeyehu*[63] stated otherwise. The Court noted
as a general proposition that "[d]elay in making a
claim can only be relevant from the date as of
which [a Claimant] begins to fear persecution."[64]
It is the same principle applied to a *sur
place* claim in *Tang*.[65]

[62] *Idahosa, Musili Amoke v. M.C.I.* (F.C. no. IMM-1124-18), Favel,
March 29, 2019; 2019 FC 384 at para. 31.
[63] *Gabeyehu, Bruck v. M.C.I.* (F.C.T.D., no. IMM-863-95), Reed,
November 8, 1995, at para. 7
[64] *Ibid.*
[65] *Tang, Xiaoming v. M.C.I.* (F.C.T.D., no. IMM-3650-99), Reed, June
21, 2000, at para. 6. "His claim is a *sur place* claim and, therefore, the
date as of which he became aware that he would allegedly face
persecution on return to China is the relevant date, not the date on

Because delay is relevant only after the Claimant has a reason to fear persecution, *it has been argued that negative inferences cannot be drawn when persons who have legal status in Canada fail to claim.*[66] In *Gyawali*,[67] Madame Justice Tremblay-Lamer agreed that there exist situations in which negative inferences may not be drawn from a failure to apply for refugee status immediately upon arrival. She found that a valid status in Canada could constitute a good reason for not claiming refugee protection. The Court drew a parallel between the sailor on the ship whose contract expired, leaving him nowhere to go but home, and the Claimant, who had a student visa and had also made an application for permanent residency in Canada. Until he could no longer pay for his studies, he had no reason to fear having to return to his country. Both the sailor and the student had left their countries fearing persecution, but having found a safe place to stay, they felt no immediate need to apply for refugee status. As soon as they found themselves at risk of being forced to return home, they filed claims for refugee protection.

---

which he arrived in Canada."
[66] Emphasis added.
[67] *Gyawali, Nirmal v. M.C.I.* (F.C., no. IMM-926-03), Tremblay-Lamer, September 24, 2003; 2003 FC 1122

In several cases, the Court has upheld RPD decisions in which possession of a valid but temporary status was not found to be an acceptable reason to delay claiming protection. Madame Justice Tremblay-Lamer, the year before her ruling in *Gyawali*,[68] held that it was open to the Board to reject a claim based largely on a two-year delay in claiming refugee status. The Claimant in that case was on a student visa in Canada. On the advice of a consultant, he applied for permanent residence and claimed refugee status only after his permanent residence application was unsuccessful. Other cases of persons in status were similarly rejected in 2005 and 2007. In 2009, Mr. Justice de Montigny wrote:

> It is trite law that a delay in submitting a refugee protection claim, while not decisive, remains a relevant element that the tribunal may take into account in assessing both the statements and the actions and deeds of a Claimant: *Huerta* [citation omitted]. The Claimant knew upon his arrival in Canada that he was only authorized to stay in Canada for a specific and limited period of time. Under these circumstances, it was reasonable to expect that he would regularize his status as soon as possible if he truly feared for his life and physical integrity in India.[69]

---

[68] See footnote 67, *supra*.

[69] *Nijjer, Yadhwinder Singh v. M.C.I.* (F.C., no. IMM-340-09), de Montigny, December 9, 2009; 2009 FC 1259, at para. 24. In *Peti, Qamile, v. M.C.I.* (F.C., no. IMM-1764-11), Scott, January 19, 2012; 2012 FC 82, the Claimant, who was found to be not credible by the RPD, had a valid visa and waited six months before filing her claim.

Apart from persons who do not feel the need to claim immediately, there are Claimants who have no knowledge of the refugee process or their eligibility to claim protection. In the absence of any adverse credibility finding, the explanation that a Claimant did not know that she could claim refugee status based on spousal abuse has successfully been used to refute findings that lengthy delays in claiming were due to an absence of subjective fear.

In *Ahshraf*,[70] the Court found that the RPD's finding that the Claimant's five-year delay in filing her claim showed her fear was not genuine was unreasonable as there was evidence that while her husband was in Canada she had been entirely under his influence and never left the house alone.

In a case where the Claimant did not claim refugee status for four years because he wanted to know what was needed to claim, his explanation was not accepted. The Board interpreted the fact that he renewed his visa twice without ever making inquiries about claiming refugee status as evidence that he had

---

The Court found the Minister's contention that "possession of a visa does not rebut the presumption that a true refugee would claim protection at the first opportunity" to be a sound argument.
[70] *Ashraf, Shahenaz v. M.C.I.* (F.C., no. IMM-5375-08), O'Reilly, April 19, 2010; 2010 FC 425

no subjective fear. The Court saw nothing unreasonable about that conclusion.

Depending on the advice or help of others has also been held to be an unsatisfactory reason to delay claiming. For example, in *Singh*,[71] the Claimant waited almost one and a half years after he arrived in Canada before filing his refugee claim. The RPD did not accept the Claimant's explanation that he had asked the gurdwara management to help him file for political asylum but that whenever he asked them about his immigration status, he received no satisfactory response. The Court dismissed the judicial review on the grounds of delay, *saying it was not reasonable that someone fearing for his life would not take any action himself.*[72] When the Claimant had not received any help for almost a year and a half, he should have taken the initiative and inquired about his rights and obligations under the Canadian immigration system.

For practical reasons, however, many Iranian nationals who come to Canada for the first time

---

[71] *Singh, Nirmal v. M.C.I.* (F.C., no. IMM-7334-05), Teitelbaum, June 13, 2006, 2006 FC 743. In *Ismayilov, Anar v. M.C.I.* (F.C., no. IMM-7263-14), Mactavish, August 26, 2015; 2015 FC 1013, the Claimant had explained to the RPD that he had delayed claiming because his lawyer had advised him to wait until his wife and child arrived in Canada so that they could make their claims as a family. The Court noted that the RPD had an obligation to consider this evidence before it could conclude that the delay in claiming indicated a lack of subjective fear
[72] Emphasis added.

may face delay in making a refugee claim in Canada due to a number of reasons. One of the three commonest reasons why they delay within Canada is because they have valid visas. The second is that they are not aware of how the RDS works. And the third is because of language barrier. Those who delay because they have valid visas, or because they do not know how the RDS works, or because of language barriers, should mention so in their BOC narratives. Most Claimants do not speak English or French as their first language. However, this should not be an excuse for not making a claim in good time. Failure to make a claim in good time without adequate explanation, may affect the Claimant's overall credibility, and may allow the Member to draw a negative inference for lack of subjective fear of persecution.[73]

---

[73] See Chapter 5, page 106, footnote 119.

CHAPTER 4
OBJECTIVE BASIS

The materials covered in this chapter are imported directly, with only minor modification where necessary for clarity and emphasis, from the IRB document entitled, "Chapter 5 - Well-Founded Fear."[74] A Claimant's subjective fear of persecution must have an objective basis. The subjective component relates to the existence of a fear of persecution in the mind of the refugee. The objective component requires that the refugee's fear be evaluated objectively to determine if there is a valid basis for that fear.

Claimants may have a subjective fear that they will be persecuted if returned to their country, but that fear must be assessed objectively in light of the situation in that country in order to determine whether the fear is well founded.

Both subjective fear and the objective basis for it are crucial elements in the definition of a Convention refugee. In *Kamana*,[75] Madam Justice Tremblay-Lamer held that the panel's finding

---

[74] IRB, "Chapter 5 - Well-Founded Fear," <https://irb-cisr.gc.ca/en/legal-policy/legal-concepts/Pages/RefDef05.aspx> (Retrieved: April 30th, 2020)
[75] *Kamana, Jimmy v. M.C.I.* (F.C.T.D., no. IMM-5998-98), Tremblay-Lamer, September 24, 1999.

that the Claimant had not credibly established the subjective element was reasonable and that:

> The lack of evidence going to the subjective
> element of the claim is a fatal flaw which in and
> of itself warrants dismissal of the claim, since
> both elements of the refugee definition –
> subjective and objective – must be met.[76]

The same reasoning was repeated by Madam Justice Tremblay-Lamer shortly afterwards in *Tabet-Zatla*,[77] a case which was followed by a number of judges at the Trial Division. In 2002, Justice Tremblay-Lamer was faced with a challenge to her holding in the *Maqdassy* case.[78] The applicant relied on *Yusuf*,[79] an earlier decision by the Federal Court of Appeal which had found that the soundness of rejecting a claim because of the absence of subjective fear in the presence of an objective basis for the fear was "doubtful." In *Yusuf*, Hugessen J.A. stated:

> I find it hard to see in what circumstances it
> could be said that a person who, we must not
> forget, is by definition claiming refugee status
> could be right in fearing persecution and still be

---

[76] *Ibid.*

[77] *Tabet-Zatla, Mohamed* v. *M.C.I.* (F.C.T.D., no. IMM-6291-98), Tremblay-Lamer, November 2, 1999.

[78] *Maqdassy, Joyce Ruth v. M.C.I.* (F.C.T.D., no. IMM-2992-00), Tremblay-Lamer, February 19, 2002; 2002 FCT 182.

[79] *Yusuf v. Canada (Minister of Employment and Immigration)*, [1992] 1 F.C. 629 (C.A.), at 632.

rejected because it is said that fear does not actually exist in his conscience.[80]

The applicant in *Maqdassy*[81] relied on this to argue that it might not be necessary to establish a subjective fear of persecution where an objective basis for the fear had been shown to exist. Justice Tremblay-Lamer disagreed, noting that *Yusuf*[82] had been decided prior to *Ward*,[83] in which the Supreme Court made it clear that *both*[84] components of the test were required. In *Geron*,[85] a case decided several months later, Mr. Justice Blanchard also referred to *Ward* as authority for finding that the lack of evidence going to the subjective element of the claim was a "fatal flaw". Mr. Justice Harrington too, cited *Ward* when he held in *Nazir*[86] that it was not necessary for him to rule on other issues in that case because "even if there were grounds for an objective fear, there must also be a subjective fear of persecution."

---

[80] *Ibid.*

[81] *Maqdassy, supra.*

[82] See *Yusuf, supra.*

[83] See *Canada (Attorney General) v. Ward,* [1993] 2 S.C.R. 689, 103 D.L.R. (4th) 1, 20 Imm. L.R. (2d) 85, at 723.

[84] Emphasis added.

[85] *Geron, Fernando Bilog v. M.C.I.* (F.C.T.D., no. IMM-4951-01), Blanchard, November 22, 2002; 2002 FCT 1204.

[86] *Nazir, Qaiser Mahmood v. M.C.I.* (F.C., no. IMM-3857-04), Harrington, February 3, 2005; 2005 FC 168 at para. 4.

Subjective Fear and Credibility

As mentioned in *Yusuf*, children or persons suffering from mental disability may be incapable of experiencing fear. The *Patel*[87] case concerns a minor but notes that either age or disability may cause a Claimant to be incapable of articulating his or her subjective fear in a rational manner. If a Claimant is not competent and the evidence establishes an objective basis for fear of persecution, the person acting as the Claimant's designated representative may establish a subjective fear. However, the claim must be evaluated from the perspective of the minor. In some cases, it may be possible for the RPD to infer the subjective fear from the evidence. As the Court points out in *Patel*, it is rare that a Claimant who has good reason to be afraid will not be – unless the Claimant is incompetent, exceptionally committed to a cause, or perhaps just foolhardy.

Judicial reviews are seldom about such cases. Far more often, they concern Claimants who have not met their burden of establishing the subjective component of a well-founded fear because of a credibility issue.

---

[87] *Canada (Minister of Citizenship and Immigration) v. Patel, Dhruv Navichandra* (F.C., no. IMM-2482-07), Lagacé, June 17, 2008; 2008 FC 747.

The relationship between subjective fear and credibility has been analyzed from various perspectives and the Federal Court and Federal Court of Appeal have provided a number of observations on this subject, including the following:

- MacGuigan, J. in *Shanmugarajah*: "(…) it is almost always foolhardy for a Board in a refugee case, where there is no general issue as to credibility, to make the assertion that the Claimants had no subjective element in their fear (…)"[88]

- Cullen, J. in *Parada*[89] held that if a Claimant testifies that he fears for his life and there is evidence to reasonably support those fears, it is improper for the Refugee Division to reject that testimony out of hand without making a negative finding of credibility.

- Teitelbaum, J. in *Assadi* wrote: "Failure to immediately seek protection can impugn the Claimant's credibility, including his or her testimony about events in his country of origin."[90]

---

[88] *Shanmugarajah, Appiah v. M.E.I.* (F.C.A., no. A-609-91), Stone, MacGuigan, Henry, June 22, 1992. This principle has been applied in many cases since. See for example *Ramirez-Osorio, Alexander v. M.C.I.* (F.C., no. IMM-7418-12), Shore, May 3, 2013; 2013 FC 461.
[89] *Parada, Felix Balmore v. M.C.I.* (F.C.T.D., no. A-938-92), Cullen, March 6, 1995, at para. 16.
[90] *Assadi, Nasser Eddin v. M.C.I.* (F.C.T.D., no. IMM-2683-96), Teitelbaum, March 25, 1997. at para. 14.

- Joyal, J. in several cases, including *Parmar*,[91] stated that the subjective component of the well-founded fear test depended solely on the Claimant's credibility.

- Cullen, J. in *Dirie*: "Once the objective grounds for the Claimant's fear are present, it is very likely that a subjective fear is also present unless the Board questions the Claimant's credibility."[92]

- Lemieux, J. in *Hatami*[93] held that the Board had no evidentiary basis on which to conclude that the Claimant did not have a genuine subjective fear of persecution when her subjective fear was clearly established in her PIF and the Board had found her evidence credible.

- Beaudry, J. in *Herrera*[94] first cites *Ward* to say that the determination of the existence of a subjective fear is based on the Claimant's credibility. Then, he agrees with the respondent that the absence of subjective fear "may be fatal to a refugee claim, beyond the simple negative inference of credibility."

- Blais, J. in *Ahoua*: "The Minister properly pointed out that a negative finding regarding subjective

---

[91] *Parmar, Satnam Singh v. M.C.I.* (F.C.T.D., no. IMM-838-97), Joyal, January 21, 1998; *Chudinov, Nickolai v. M.C.I.* (F.C.T.D., no. IMM-2419-97), Joyal, August 14, 1998; and *Maximilok, Yuri v. M.C.I.* (F.C.T.D., no. IMM-1861-97), Joyal, August 14, 1998.
[92] *Dirie, Abdulle Milgo v. M.C.I.* (F.C.T.D., no. IMM-5428-97), Cullen, October 6, 1998.
[93] *Hatami, Arezo v. M.C.I.* (F.C.T.D., no. IMM-2418-98), Lemieux, March 23, 2000, at para. 25.
[94] *Herrera, William Alexander Cruz v. M.C.I.* (F.C., IMM-782-07), Beaudry, October 1, 2007, at para. 23

fear may render the assessment of the objective aspect of the complaint superfluous and may in itself warrant the dismissal of the claim."[95]

• Mactavish, J. in *Hidalgo Tranquino*: "Having accepted Ms. Hidalgo's evidence as truthful, including the explanation that she provided for her failure to claim elsewhere, it was simply unreasonable for the Board to dismiss her claim for protection under section 96 on the basis that she lacked subjective fear."[96]

• Bédard, J. in *Gomez*, after stating that a finding of a lack of subjective fear is determinative only for a section 96 claim, adds that "subjective fear may sometimes be relevant when assessing the truth of the allegations of a person who claims to be a person in need of protection (...)"[97]

• O'Keefe, J. in *Kunin*: "A finding that a Claimant lacks a subjective fear of persecution necessarily impugns any Claimant's credibility."[98] The Court

---

[95] *Ahoua, Wadjams Jean-Marie v. M.C.I.* (F.C., no. IMM-1757-07), Blais, November 27, 2007; 2007 FC 1239, at para. 16.
[96] *Hidalgo Tranquino, Claudia Isabel v. M.C.I.* (F.C., no. IMM-86-10), Mactavish, July 29, 2010; 2010 FC 793, at para. 8.
[97] *Gomez v. Canada (Minister of Citizenship and Immigration)* (F.C., IMM-1412-10), Bédard, October 22, 2010, at para. 34.
[98] *Kunin, Aleksandr v. M.C.I.* (F.C., no. IMM-5225-09), O'Keefe, November 4, 2010; 2010 FC 1091, at para. 20. Also see *Louis, Benito v. M.C.I.* (F.C. no. IMM-3068-18), Bell, March 28, 2019; 2019 FC 355 where the Court rejected the argument that the RPD erred by importing a subjective fear component into its section 97 analysis. The Court noted that the RPD never used the term "subjective fear" and "although the RPD's analysis is similar to that which would be employed by a panel considering a Convention refugee's claim of

does add a caveat to the effect that this finding may only impugn one aspect of the Claimant's credibility and does not equate to a finding that the Claimant is less than credible in all aspects of the claim and thus an analysis of the claim under IRPA s. 97 may still be required.

When the RPD concludes that a Claimant who alleges having a fear is not credible concerning the existence of subjective fear, it almost always does so on the basis of some behaviour of the Claimant which it considers to be inconsistent with that allegation. Case law has confirmed that there are certain ways that persons *fearful of serious harm can normally be expected to act.*[99] As the Court stated in *Aslam,*[100] the RPD would expect that individuals who fear for their personal safety and their life would not only flee at their earliest opportunity but would seek refugee protection as soon as they are beyond the reach of their persecutors and it is reasonable to do so.

Consequently, staying any longer than necessary in a country where a Claimant fears persecution, voluntarily returning to that country, passing through other countries without asking for protection or failing to make a claim for protection immediately upon arrival in Canada

---

subjective fear, it used this information in its assessment of Mr. Louis' credibility..."

[99] Emphasis added.

[100] *Aslam, Muhammad v. M.C.I.* (F.C., no. IMM-3264-05), Shore, February 16, 2006; 2006 FC 189, at para. 28.

are all behaviours which, in numerous cases, have been found to be indicative of a lack of subjective fear. *However, none of these behaviours mandates the rejection of a claim to Convention refugee status without further examination.*[101] The Board may be justified in drawing a negative inference when Claimants are unable to provide satisfactory explanations for conduct that seems incompatible with their alleged fear.

In addition to seeking protection in a timely manner, there are other types of conduct normally associated with being fearful. If a Claimant provides credible evidence demonstrating efforts to avoid detection, such as *going into hiding,*[102] this evidence is considered to support the existence of subjective fear. Conversely, adverse inferences may be drawn when Claimants fail to vary their routine or to take other precautions against falling victim to the persecution they claim to fear.

---

[101] Emphasis added.
[102] *Aslam, supra.*

CHAPTER 5
IMPACT OF DELAY

L ike in Chapter 4 of this book, the materials covered in this chapter are imported directly, with only minor modification where necessary for clarity and emphasis, from the IRB document entitled, "Chapter 5 - Well-Founded Fear."[103]

When Claimants do not take steps to seek protection promptly, decision-makers often conclude that their behaviour shows a lack of subjective fear. *Case law has been consistent in saying that delay in making a claim to refugee status is not in itself determinative.*[104] Three often-cited Federal Court of Appeal decisions acknowledged that delay is, nonetheless, a relevant, and potentially important consideration. In *Huerta*, Mr. Justice Létourneau wrote:

> The delay in making a claim to refugee status is not a decisive factor in itself. It is, however, a relevant element which the tribunal may take into account in assessing both the statements and the actions and deeds of a Claimant.[105]

---

[103] IRB, "Chapter 5 - Well-Founded Fear," <https://irb-cisr.gc.ca/en/legal-policy/legal-concepts/Pages/RefDef05.aspx> (Retrieved: April 30th, 2020)
[104] Emphasis added.
[105] *Huerta v. Canada (Minister of Employment and Immigration)* (1993), 157 N.R. 225 (F.C.A.) at 227.

As Madam Justice Simpson explained in *Cruz*, the reason why delay is an important factor in the assessment of a refugee claim is because it addresses the existence of a subjective fear, which is an essential element of a Convention refugee claim.

Although not generally a determinative factor in a refugee claim, there are circumstances in which delay can assume a decisive role. A claim to be a Convention refugee may be rejected when delay is accepted as evidence that establishes, on a balance of probabilities, that the Claimant lacks subjective fear. Such a determination would be made on the basis of a *Claimant's failure to provide good reasons for the delay*.[106] Mr. Justice Crampton remarked that, "it is [...] well established that, in the absence of a satisfactory explanation for the delay, the delay can be fatal to such claim, even where the credibility of an applicant's claim has not otherwise been challenged."[107]

The RPD must weigh the evidence and it may reject an explanation for the delay if it finds it inadequate or implausible on reasonable grounds.

---

[106] Emphasis added.

[107] *Velez, Liliana v. M.C.I.* (F.C., no. IMM-5660-09), Crampton, September 15, 2010; 2010 FC 923, at para. 28. The converse of the same principle was expressed in *Abawaji, Abdulwahid Haji Hassen v. M.C.I.* (F.C., no. IMM-6276-05), Mosley, September 6, 2006; 2006 FC 1065; at para. 16: 'Delay in making a claim for refugee protection should not be fatal to the claim where it is supported by a reasonable explanation."

It is essential that decision-makers clearly express their findings on the credibility of a Claimant's explanation for behaving in a particular manner. When the Board does not accept an explanation as valid, the Member is obliged to give reasons. In *Martinez Requena*,[108] the Board asked the Claimant to explain why she had returned to Bolivia, and then simply concluded that she had no subjective fear of persecution. Madam Justice Dawson held that the Board could not make that finding unless it found the evidence to be incredible - which it had not done.

The length of the delay is often a factor taken into consideration[109] but it is not in and of itself determinative. While short delays may tend to be more easily explained, even very long delays cannot be assumed to indicate a lack of subjective fear. They must be examined in light of the circumstances and the explanations offered by the Claimant. Madam Justice Bédard reviewed a decision where the RPD had found a six-year delay in claiming to be incompatible with

---

[108] *Martinez Requena, Ericka Marlene v. M.C.I.* (F.C., no. IMM-4725-06), Dawson, September 27, 2007; 2007 FC 968.

[109] In *Salguero, Erbin Salomon Rosales v. M.C.I.* (F.C., no. IMM-4402-04), Mactavish, May 18, 2005; 2005 FC 716, the Court distinguishes the Claimants' 16-year residence in the U.S. from the "short stays" en route to Canada referred to in para. 37 of *Mendez, Alberto Luis Calderon v.* (F.C., no. IMM-1837-04), Teitelbaum, January 27, 2005; 2005 FC 75.

the attitude of a person who feared for her life. However, the Claimant was a minor when she arrived to live with some relatives in Canada and the Court held:

> [...] There is a presumption that a person having a well-founded fear of persecution will claim refugee protection at the earliest opportunity. If they do not, the legitimacy of the subjective fear that they allege is called into question (*Singh citation omitted*). This presumption makes sense in the context of an adult refugee who, upon entering Canada, is expected to be aware that in order to stay in Canada indefinitely, he or she will need to regularize their status. *However, the mere existence of delay in claiming cannot always be construed as indicating an absence of subjective fear. The delay, and even more importantly, the reasons for the delay, must be assessed in the context of the specific circumstances of each case.*[110]

Canadian case law has consistently stressed that the assessment of the credibility and reasonableness of explanations must be done in light of the particular circumstances of the Claimant. In the case of *El-Naem*,[111] the Court found that the 19-year-old Syrian Claimant's explanation for spending a year in Greece without claiming was not unreasonable "considering all of his circumstances." The

---

[110] *John, Shontel Dion v. M.C.I.* (F.C., no. IMM-1683-10), Bédard, December 14, 2010; 2010 FC 1283 at para. 23 [Emphasis added].
[111] *El-Naem, Faisalv. M.C.I.* (F.C.T.D., no. IMM-1723-96), Gibson, February 17, 1997. Reported: *El-Naem v. Canada (Minister of Citizenship and Immigration)* (1997), 37 Imm. L.R. (2d) 304 (F.C.T.D.).

young man testified that he had heard that refugee protection in Greece was problematic and he feared deportation to Syria if he exposed his illegal status. He was alone in Greece, anxious to join a brother in Canada who had successfully claimed refugee status. However, he first had to accumulate the money he needed to travel.

In a similar vein, case law has also pointed out the need to closely assess the reasons *a Claimant engages in behaviour that would normally be seen as incompatible with having a fear.*[112] In one case where the RPD found that the Claimant had no subjective fear because he continued to put himself at risk by returning home to protect his mother against her abusive husband, the Court observed that bonds of family loyalty may lead a person to engage in dangerous conduct that otherwise could be viewed as conduct inconsistent with a lack of subjective fear.

Psychological reports[113] may provide useful insight into the reasons for a Claimant's behaviour, and thus whether or not a particular way of behaving can be taken to be indicative of an absence of fear. In *Diluna*,[114] the Trial Division held, *in obiter*,

---

[112] Emphasis added.
[113] *El-Naem, supra.*
[114] *Diluna, Roselene Edyr Soares v. M.E.I.* (F.C.T.D., no. IMM-3201-94),

that the Refugee Division should have considered a *psychiatric assessment*[115] that supported the Claimant's assertion that she delayed seeking refugee status due to post-traumatic stress syndrome.

Not all expert reports, however, are probative regarding the issue of subjective fear. In one case,[116] the Court noted that though there was a psychological report, *it provided no explanation justifying the Claimant's 14-month delay in claiming protection in Canada.*[117]

In another case in which the Claimant had voluntarily given up protection in the U.K.,[118] it was argued that her mental disorders would have affected the rationality of her decision to give up protection. The Court rejected that argument because the psychiatric report submitted was dated more than two years after she left the U.K. and did not establish that the Claimant was suffering from any mental disorder at the time she gave up protection.

Gibson, March 14, 1995. Reported: *Diluna v. Canada (Minister of Employment and Immigration)* (1995), 29 Imm. L.R. (2d) 156 (F.C.T.D.), at 162.

[115] Emphasis added.

[116] *Espinosa, Roberto Pablo Hernandez v. M.C.I.* (F.C., no. IMM-5667-02), Rouleau, November 12, 2003; 2003 FC 1324, at para. 19.

[117] Emphasis added.

[118] *Sabapathy, Thevi v. M.C.I.* (F.C.T.D., no. IMM-1507-96), Campbell, March 27, 1997.

Delay in Leaving the Country of Persecution

Mr. Justice Shore stated in *Rahim* that, "[T]he time it takes an applicant to leave his or her country of origin can be taken into account in determining whether that person had a subjective fear of persecution."[119]

Delay in leaving the country if a Claimant alleges he or she had reason to fear persecution there normally calls into question the credibility of the fear.[120] In *Zuniga*,[121] the Claimant alleged that he feared for his life and that of his family, and yet his wife and children, who already had visas, did not leave the country at the first opportunity. Nor did he himself follow as soon as he could. The whole family left Honduras five months after the principal Claimant was issued his United States visa. The Court did not accept his

---

[119] *Rahim, Ziany* v. *M.C.I.* (F.C., no. IMM-2729-04), Shore, January 18, 2005, 2005 FC 18 at para. 11.
[120] See Chapter 3, page 88, footnote 72.
[121] *Zuniga, Alexis Ramon Garciav. S.C.C.* (F.C.T.D., no. IMM-118-94), Teitelbaum, July 4, 1994 at para. 49 – 50. See also *Singh, Sebastian Swatandra v. M.C.I.* (F.C.T.D., no. IMM-3840-97), Nadon, December 7, 1998 where the Court upheld the negative finding of the CRDD based on the view that the male Claimant had not made a serious attempt to leave Fiji between 1987 and 1995, conduct which undermined his subjective fear of persecution.

explanation that he remained to arrange his papers and pay taxes, as reasonable.

The failure to leave in a timely manner must be assessed in light of all the circumstances.[122] In *Gebremichael*[123] the *Claimants remained in hiding in their country for a month, despite having acquired visas for the United States.*[124] The Board drew an adverse inference concerning their subjective fear, a conclusion which the Court upheld as reasonable and clearly explained. It is interesting to note, however, that as a preface to its analysis of the issue, *the Court wrote that delay in fleeing a country could normally be justified if the Claimant was in hiding at that time.*[125]

When a claim is based on a number of discriminatory or harassing incidents which culminate in an event which forces a person to

---

[122] As noted in *Bibby-Jacobs, supra,* footnote 56,it was not appropriate for the RPD to expect that "if the risk were of a level of severity that could be described as persecution, the Claimant [a young woman subject to sexual harassment at the hands of her powerful employer] would have left her job." In the same vein is the case of a Claimant who was subject to domestic abuse but had returned to her husband after several earlier trips to Canada. See *Abdi Ahmed, Ilham v. M.C.I.* (F.C., no. IMM-3178-12), O'Reilly, December 18, 2012; 2012 FC 1494, where the Court found that the RPD failed to take into account the Claimant's personal circumstances and apply the IRB's Guidelines on Women Refugee Claimants Fearing Gender Related Persecution (Guideline 4) when evaluating her testimony regarding why she stayed with and returned to her husband.

[123] *Gebremichael, Addis v. M.C.I.* (F.C., no. IMM-2670-05), Russell, May 1, 2006; 2006 FC 547, at para. 44.

[124] Emphasis added.

[125] *Gebremichael, supra.*

leave his country, the Federal Court has warned that it is problematic to consider delay to be indicative of an absence of subjective fear.

In *Voyvodov*,[126] the first of the two Claimants left Bulgaria after being beaten by skinheads. His partner stayed and endured other incidents of violence and discrimination. The Refugee Division considered that the first Claimant had failed to meet his burden because he had experienced only one incident. It then went on to express its concern about the second Claimant having delayed his departure from the country. The Court observed:

> [...] The tribunal appears to place the applicants in an impossible position. It implies that it does not believe Mr. Galev's claim of persecution because he only experienced one alleged attack due to his sexual orientation. On the other hand, it finds that Mr. Voyvodov is not credible because he delayed seeking international protection after being initially attacked.[127]

The Court was similarly critical of the RPD's conclusion in *Shah*,[128] describing the Claimant as

---

[126] *Voyvodov, Bogdan Atanassov v. M.C.I.* (F.C.T.D., no. IMM-5601-98), Lutfy, September 13, 1999, at para. 10.
[127] *Ibid.*
[128] *Shah, Mahmood Ali v. M.C.I.* (F.C., no. IMM-4425-02), Blanchard, September 30, 2003; 2003 FC 1121, at para. 23.

being "between a rock and a hard place." The RPD rejected the claim essentially because the Claimant waited a year and a half rather than fleeing when his troubles first started. The Court found the RPD's conclusion unreasonable in view of the Claimant's explanation that the threats had become progressively more serious, that he moved from home the same evening his life was threatened, and left the country the next month.

The analytical flaw was more fully explained by Justice Heneghan in *Ibrahimov*:

> [...] If a person's claim is actually based on several incidents which occur over time, the cumulative effects of which may amount to persecution, then looking to the beginning of such discriminatory or harassing treatment and comparing that to the date on which a person leaves the country to justify rejection of the claim on the basis of delay, undermines the very idea of cumulative persecution.[129]

Cumulative persecution should be considered in context. It happens when there have been several incidents of persecution. The RPD should consider the last incident in the series of incidents that triggered the escape to Canada.

---

[129] *Ibrahimov, Fikrat v. M.C.I.* (F.C., no. IMM-4258-02), Heneghan, October 10, 2003; 2003 FC 1185., at para. 19. This reasoning was more recently followed in *Ramirez Rodas, Carlos v. M.C.I.* (F.C., no. IMM-6560-13), Zinn, February 27, 2015; 2015 FC 250, at para. 31. A number of incidents over a period of a few months culminated in an event which convinced the Claimants they had to leave.

CHAPTER 6
RE-AVAILMENT AND REFUGEE SUR PLACE

As noted in chapters 4 and 5 of this book, the materials covered in this chapter are imported directly, with only minor modification where necessary for clarity and emphasis, from the IRB document entitled, "Chapter 5 - Well-Founded Fear."[130]

Re-availment refers to voluntarily returning to the country of origin and availing oneself of the protection of that country.[131] The issue of re-availment arises in two contexts: 1) the assessment of subjective fear in the determination of the refugee claim, and 2) the assessment of a cessation application made by the Minister under IRPA.[132]

Return to the country of nationality is the kind of re-availment that is most often discussed in the case law. Citing several cases in *Kabengele,*[133] Mr. Justice Rouleau stated:

---

[130] IRB, "Chapter 5 - Well-Founded Fear," <https://irb-cisr.gc.ca/en/legal-policy/legal-concepts/Pages/RefDef05.aspx> (Retrieved: April 30th, 2020)
[131] See IRPA, s. 108(1)(a)
[132] *Ibid.* s. 108(2)
[133] *Kabengele v. M.C.I.* (F.C. no., IMM-1422-99), Rouleau, November

> It is quite proper for the Refugee Division to take the plaintiff's actions into account in assessing his subjective fear. It is reasonable for it to conclude that the fact he returned to the country where he feared persecution makes the existence of such a fear unlikely (*citations omitted*).[134]

However, the Court has cautioned that the mere fact of returning to a country of nationality is not determinative of whether a refugee Claimant possesses a subjective fear, or has ceased to be a Convention refugee. The Court gave the examples of evidence of a Claimant's belief that country conditions have changed or evidence of a Claimant's temporary visit while he or she remained in hiding, that would be evidence inconsistent with a finding of a lack of subjective fear.[135]

16, 2000, at para. 41.

[134] *Ibid.*

[135] *Martinez Requena, supra*, footnote 64, at para. 7. In *Milian Pelaez, Rogelio v. M.C.I.* (F.C., no. IMM-3611-11), de Montigny, March 2, 2012; 2012 FC 285, the Court noted that the RPD held against the applicant his return to Guatemala, the place where the people he feared could be found, without considering that he had apparently relocated 100 km away from the place where he had had problems and had changed his profession. In *Ascencio Gutierrez, Arnoldo Maximilanov. M.C.I.* (F.C., no. IMM-4903-13), O'Keefe, March 3, 2015; 2015 FC 266, the Court disagreed with the RPD's finding that two one-month returns to Mexico City (not to the Claimant's home state) to renew his student visa amounted to re-availment. In *Yuan, Xin v. M.C.I.* (F.C., no. IMM-5365-14), Boswell, July 28, 2015; 2015 FC 923, the RPD allowed the Minister's application for cessation because the refugee had returned to his country of origin for one month. The Court found the decision to be unreasonable because

The credibility assessment of the reasons Claimants give for returning to their country is important. If they clearly state that they did not intend to re-avail themselves of the protection of their country and assert not having lost their subjective fear, *absent an adverse finding of credibility, the RPD would err in finding that the Claimants had re-availed themselves of protection and did not have a subjective fear.*[136]

In *Kanji,*[137] the Board made no express finding that it disbelieved the Claimant's evidence and it gave no reasons for doing so. The Court held that the Claimant's clear statement that she did not re-avail herself of the protection of India, nor lose her subjective fear contradicted and negated any possible finding to the contrary on the basis of the purely circumstantial evidence of her returns to India.

In *Caballero,*[138] where the Claimant testified that he went back to Honduras intending to stay a

---

the refugee had returned to arrange his mother's funeral and during his stay had remained in hiding and had avoided the actual funeral out of fear that his persecutors (the Chinese PSB) would find him there.

[136] Emphasis added.

[137] *Kanji, Mumtaz Baduraliv.M.C.I.* (F.C.T.D., no. IMM-2451-96), Campbell, April 4, 1997.

[138] *Caballero, Fausto Ramon Reyes v. M.E.I.* (F.C.A., no. A-266-91), Marceau (dissenting), Desjardins, Létourneau, May 13, 1993. In *Duarte, Augustina Castelanos v. M.C.I.* (F.C.T.D., no. IMM-6616-02),

year in order to sell his land, the Court agreed with the Refugee Division that his behaviour was inconsistent with a well-founded fear of persecution.

Even where the motivation for returning may be seen as quite compelling, a consideration of all the circumstances may result in a negative inference as to the existence of subjective fear.

In *Arayo*,[139] the principal Claimant had returned to Chile and remained there for some nine weeks while she obtained the permission of the father of her child to remove the child from Chile. While the evidence regarding re-availment clearly indicated that it was for the sole purpose of allowing the mother to bring her son to Canada with her, the evidence did not go so far as to establish that other arrangements could not have been made so that the two Claimants could have left Chile together when the mother first left.

In *Prapaharan*,[140] where the Claimants alleged they had suffered persecutory treatment before the first time they left Sri Lanka as well as after their

---

Kelen, August 21, 2003; 2003 FCT 988 the Board and the Court took a similar view of the Claimant's return to Cuba to transfer ownership of her house to prevent the government from confiscating it.

[139] *Araya, Carolina Isabel Valenzuela v. M.C.I.* (F.C.T.D., no. IMM-3948-97), Gibson, September 4, 1998.

[140] *Prapaharan, Sittampalam v. M.C.I,* (F.C. no. IMM-3667-00), McKeown, March 30, 2001; 2001 FCT 272 at para. 17.

return there, with the main claims pre-dating the Claimants' return, the Court states that "subsequent persecution after re-availment does not preclude a person from making a claim for refugee status without being faced with the re-availment argument." However, in *Gopalapillai*[141] the Claimant had returned to Sri Lanka and, after his return, had been arrested, questioned and beaten more than once. The Court held that "to the extent that the RPD considered that re-availment in 2008 was a bar to the claim, without considering subsequent events…this would be unreasonable."

Claimants may exhibit an apparent absence of subjective fear not only in physically returning to their home country, but also in actions such as obtaining or renewing a passport or travel document,[142] and leaving or emigrating through lawful channels.[143] The evidence is all assessed in

---

[141] *Gopalapillai, Thinesrupan v. M.C.I.* (F.C. no. IMM-3539-18), Grammond, February 26, 2019; 2019 FC 228 at paras 17-19.

[142] In *Maldonado v. Canada (Minister of Employment and Immigration)*, [1980] 2 F.C. 302 (C.A.), at 304, the Court pointed out that the Immigration Appeal Board had ignored the fact that the Claimant was able to obtain his passport (and exit papers) through his brother's contacts with the government.

[143] *Orelien v. Canada (Minister of Employment and Immigration)*, [1992] 1 F.C. 592 (C.A.), at 611. Though the Court acknowledged that applying for immigrant visas might possibly be relevant to deciding whether a person really had a fear of persecution, it remarked that a desire to emigrate and a fear of persecution could hardly be considered mutually exclusive.

the same way: the surrounding circumstances and the credibility of the Claimant's explanations determine whether it can reasonably be concluded that they indicate the absence of the subjective component of a well-founded fear of persecution.

In *Vaitialingam*,[144] although the Claimant argued that she did not intend to remain in Sri Lanka, the Court was satisfied that it was reasonable for the Board to conclude that the Claimant did not harbour a genuine fear of persecution in Sri Lanka because she had voluntarily made two trips back to her country. The Board also considered that the Claimant's renewal of her Sri Lankan passport for the purpose of travelling there indicated her willingness to entrust her welfare to the state of Sri Lanka.

In *Chandrakumar*,[145] the Court held that the Board erred in drawing the inference that the applicant re-availed himself of his country's protection from the mere fact that he renewed his passport. More evidence was required, particularly concerning the Claimant's motivations in renewing his passport, namely whether his intention was to re-avail himself of Sri Lanka's protection.

---

[144] *Vaitialingam v. M.C.I.* (F.C., no. IMM-9445-03), O'Keefe, October 20, 2004, 2004 FCT 1459, at para. 27.
[145] *Chandrakumar v. M.E.I.* (F.C.T.D., no. A-1649-92), Pinard, May 16, 1997, at para. 6.

REFUGEE PROTECTION IN CANADA

The Federal Court has held that *it is an error to find a lack of subjective fear when the Claimant was removed to his or her country, and thus did not return voluntarily.*[146] In *Kurtkapan*,[147] the Court found the Board's conclusion that the Claimant lacked a subjective basis for a fear of persecution "perverse, capricious and unreasonable" because it ignored the fact that he was deported to Turkey and did not return there voluntarily. This author has recently represented a client who had made several trips to Iran after making a refugee claim in Canada. The claim was successful because the Claimant utilized disguises and avoided coming in contact with his persecutors.[148]

Sur Place Claims and Well-Founded Fear

A *Refugee Sur Place* is defined as, "A person who was not a refugee when he left his country, but who becomes a refugee at a later date.[149] It is proper for the RPD, when considering the

---

[146] Emphasis added.

[147] *Kurtkapan, Osman v. M.C.I.* (F.C.T.D., no. IMM-5290-01), Heneghan, October 25, 2002; 2002 FCT 1114, at para. 31.

[148] See selected redacted sample BOC narrative of Bismarck on page 395.

[149] UNHCR *Handbook on Procedures and Criteria for Determining Refugee Status*, Geneva, September 1979, paragraphs 94-96

subjective element, to look at the fact that the Claimant took allegedly self-endangering actions after making his or her claim, and to inquire into the Claimant's motivation.[150] However, the case law is consistent that if dealing with a *sur place* claim, even when the motivation indicates the absence of subjective fear, the analysis cannot end there.[151]

Mr. Justice Hugessen affirmed the relevance of motive in assessing the subjective component of a well-founded fear in cases where the Claimants themselves were responsible for creating the circumstances leading to their *sur place* claims, but he also warned that the objective component nonetheless had to be assessed. In *Asfaw,*[152] he stated:

---

[150] *Herrera, Juan Blas Perez de Corcho v. M.E.I.* (F.C.T.D., no. A-615-92), Noël, October 19, 1993, at para. 10. The Court upheld the Board's conclusion that the Claimant had no subjective fear and was not a *bona fide* refugee because the basis for his alleged fear, namely speaking out against the Cuban regime after claiming refugee status in Canada, was a self-serving act intended to facilitate his refugee claim.

[151] In *Ngongo, Ngongo v M.C.I.* (F.C.T.D., no. IMM-6717-98), Tremblay-Lamer, October 25, 1999, at para. 23, from Justice Tremblay-Lamer's remarks concerning sur place claims, it is clear that the objective basis of the risk must be assessed even where a Claimant's behaviour may have been opportunistic: [...] The only relevant question is whether activities abroad might give rise to a negative reaction on the part of the authorities and thus a reasonable chance of persecution in the event of return.

[152] *Asfaw, Napoleon v. M.C.I.* (F.C.T.D., no. IMM-5552-99), Hugessen, July 18, 2000, at para. 4.

In my view, it has been the law for a very long
time that a Convention refugee Claimant must
demonstrate both an objective and a subjective
basis for his fear of persecution. It is my view
that the case will be rare where there is an
objective fear but not a subjective fear, but such
cases may exist. In my view, it is certainly
relevant to examine the motives underlying a
Claimant's participation in demonstrations such
as this one in order to determine whether or not
that Claimant does have a subjective fear. The
Board's examination of the motives was
therefore not an irrelevant matter and the
determination which they reached on that subject
was one which was open to them on the
evidence. It would I agree have been an error if
the Board had stopped its examination at that
point and had not also looked at whether or not
the Claimant had an objective fear but, they did
not commit that error. The Board looked at the
evidence with respect to the objective basis for
the applicant's fear of return and found it not to
be well-founded. That was a determination which
was equally open to the Board on the evidence
before it and I can take no issue with it.[153]

In a similar case,[154] decided on the same date, he
stated:

The argument is that it was irrelevant for the
Board to examine the applicant's motives in
acting as she did. In the view which I and other
members of this Court have previously

---

[153] *Ibid.*
[154] *Zewedu, Haimanot v. M.C.I.* (F.C.T.D., no. IMM-5564-99),
Hugessen, July 18, 2000, at para. 5.

expressed, it is not irrelevant. The matter of
motive goes to the genuineness or otherwise of
the applicant's expressed subjective fear of
persecution. That said, however, there is and
must always be an intimate interplay between the
subjective and objective elements of the fear of
persecution which is central to the definition of
Convention refugee and, I have previously
expressed the view that it would be an error for a
Board to rely exclusively on its view that a
Claimant did not have a subjective fear of
persecution without also examining the objective
basis for that fear. The Board in this case,
however, did not commit an error of that sort.[155]

In *Ejtehadian*,[156] the Court stated that it is
necessary to consider the credible evidence of
the Claimant's activities while in Canada
independently from his motives for conversion,
and assess the risk of persecution on return.
Iranian religious converts who continue to
practice their new religions (Christianity or Erfan
Halgheh) in Canada may invoke *refugee sur place*.
The Iranian Islamic government routinely sends
out informants to track and collect evidence
against its nationals in Canada who attend
churches or religious functions.

---

[155] *Ibid.*
[156] *Ejtehadian, Mostafa v. M.C.I.* (F.C., no. IMM-2930-06), Blanchard,
February 12, 2007; 2007 FC 158, at para. 11.

CHAPTER 7
STATE PROTECTION

Materials covered in this chapter are taken, with modification where necessary, from the IRB's document dubbed, "Chapter 6 - State Protection."[157] *State Protection* means that the Claimant's nation of citizenship or former habitual residence is able to protect them or avail them the necessary protection from persecution. It is at the core of CR and the RDS, and the Claimant must subscribe to this objective element of founded fear of persecution. State Protection or the State's ability to protect the Claimant, is, therefore, "...a crucial element in determining whether the fear of persecution is well founded, and as such, is not an independent element of the definition."[158]

Contextual Consideration of State Protection

The issue of State Protection was extensively canvassed by the Supreme Court of Canada in *Ward*.[159] State protection must be considered

---

[157] IRB, "Chapter 6 - State protection," < https://irb-cisr.gc.ca/en/legal-policy/legal-concepts/Pages/RefDef06.aspx> (Retrieved: November 27th, 2019).
[158] *Ibid.*
[159] *Canada (Attorney General) v. Ward*, [1993] 2 S.C.R. 689, 103 D.L.R.

in context. The *contextual approach* was explained by the Court in *Gonzalez Torres*[160] as follows:

> ...State Protection cannot be determined in a vacuum. When undertaking a contextual approach in determining whether the refugee Claimant has rebutted the presumption of State Protection, many factors ought to be considered, including the following:

a. The nature of the human rights violation;
b. The profile of the alleged human rights abuser;
c. The efforts that the victim took to seek protection from authorities;
d. The response of the authorities to request for their assistance, and
e. The available documentary evidence.

Thus, in claims involving religion, the State must not have sanctioned such a religion or recognized it under law. The religion itself must be banned or its adherents ostracized. In Iran, for example, Christianity is not allowed where a person was born a Muslim then later converts to Christianity. Christianity, in Iran, is, therefore, profiled as statutorily banned except in exceptional circumstances where the State has given limited rights to those who were born in

---

(4th) 1, 20 Imm. L.R. (2d) 85
[160] *Gonzalez Torres, Luis Felipe v. M.C.I.* (F.C., no. IMM-1351-09), Zinn, March 1, 2010; 2010 FC 234

Christian families. These are the religious minority in Iran.

The presumption of State Protection to Christian converts in Iran, is, therefore, rebutted. The same State that is mandated to guarantee people's religious freedoms is the same actor that persecutes those who convert from Islam to Christianity.[161] For religious persecutions in Iran, the response of the authorities to requests for their assistance may not be a necessary factor in claiming for refugee protection in Canada. This is, similarly, a rebuttable presumption as it is the Iranian authorities who are known to arrest and torture those it finds have converted to a proscribed religion in Iran. Available evidence for Christian converts in Iran may be in the form of summons issued against the Christian converts. However, many Claimants may not need to provide any documentary proof because there is usually no procedural fairness or due process to those accused of converting. Most Claimants escape from Iran before they receive summons.

The definition of State Protection must be had in reference to the following:

---

[161] This applies to converts to Interuniversalism or Erfan Halgheh propagated and founded by Mohammed Ali Taheri in Iran; to Bahai' Faith; and to Gonabadi Dervishes.

Surrogate Protection

The responsibility to provide international protection only becomes engaged when national or State Protection is unavailable to the Claimant (international protection as a surrogate).

Multiple Nationalities

In the case of multiple nationalities (citizenship), the Claimant is normally expected to make inquiries or applications to ascertain whether or not he or she might avail him or herself of the protection of all the countries of nationality. The Claimant need not literally approach the other states for protection unless there is a reasonable expectation that protection will be forthcoming.

Timing of Analysis

The State's ability to protect, whether one is speaking of the Claimant being "unable" or "unwilling", must be considered at the stage of the analysis when one is examining whether the Claimant's fear is well founded. The test is in part objective; if a State is able to protect the Claimant, then his or her fear is not, objectively speaking, well-founded.

> It is clear that the lynch-pin of the analysis is the state's inability to protect: it is a crucial element in determining whether the Claimant's fear is well-founded, and thereby

> *the objective reasonableness of his or her unwillingness to seek the protection of his or her state of nationality.[162]*

Some jurisprudence suggests that the Board should assess the subjective fear of the Claimant before addressing the objective basis of his fear, including the availability of State protection. For example, in *Troya Jimenez;* *Pikulin*,[163] and *Moreno*,[164] where the Court said that "the State Protection issue should not be a means of avoiding a clear determination concerning the subjective fear of persecution". In *Lopez*,[165] the Court allowed that "there is nothing wrong in doubting the truth of certain facts, which might otherwise suggest credibility concerns, but nevertheless *treating them as true* for the purpose of considering State Protection" [emphasis added]. A Claimant who is not at risk does not need State Protection and, therefore, the issue need not be addressed.[166]

Unable or Unwilling

---

[162] *Ward, supra*, footnote 26, at 712 and 722 [Emphasis added].

[163] *Troya Jimenez, Jose Walter v. M.C.I.* (F.C., no. IMM-128-10), *Mainville*, July 7, 2010; 2010 FC 727; and *Pikulin, Alexandr v. M.C.I.* (F.C., no. IMM-5787-09), Martineau, October 1, 2010; 2010 FC 979.

[164] *Velasco Moreno, Sebastian v. M.C.I.* (F.C., no. IMM-454-10), Lutfy, October 5, 2010; 2010 FC 993.

[165] *Lopez, Centeotl Mazadiego v. M.C.I.* (F.C., no. IMM-1938-13), Simpson, May 29, 2014; 2014 FC 514

[166] *Muotoh, Ndukwe Christopher v. M.C.I.* (F.C., no. IMM-3330-05)

Unable or Unwilling to avail oneself of State Protection creates a blurred distinction but is necessary for the determination of State complicity. The Convention refugee definition refers to inability or unwillingness to avail of State Protection, however, the distinction between "unable" (physically or literally unable) and "unwilling" (not wanting) has become blurred. Whether the Claimant is "unwilling" or "unable" to avail him- or herself of the protection of a country of nationality, State complicity in the persecution is irrelevant. The distinction between these two branches of the CR definition resides in the party's precluding resort to State Protection: in the case of "inability," protection is denied to the Claimant, whereas when the Claimant is "unwilling," he or she opts not to approach the state by reasons of his or her fear on an enumerated basis. In either case, the state's involvement, in the persecution is not a necessary consideration. This factor is relevant, rather in the determination of whether a fear of persecution exists.[167]

Presumptions

There are two presumptions at play in refugee determination:

Presumption 1:

---

[167] *Ward, supra*, footnote 26, at 720-721

If the fear of persecution is credible (the Court uses the word "legitimate")[168] and there is an absence of State Protection, it is not a great leap "… to presume that persecution will be likely, and the fear well-founded."[169] Having stablished the existence of a fear and a state's inability to assuage those fears, it is not assuming too much to say that the fear is well-founded. Of course, the persecution must be real - the presumption cannot be built on fictional events - but the well-foundedness of the fear can be established through the use of such a presumption:

> The presumption goes to the heart of the inquiry, which is whether there is a likelihood of persecution…nothing wrong with this, if the Board is satisfied that there is a legitimate fear, and an established inability of the state to assuage those fears through effective protection. The presumption is not a great leap.[170]

Presumption 2:

Except in situations where the State is in a state of complete breakdown, States must be presumed capable of protecting their citizens. This presumption can be rebutted by "clear and convincing" evidence of the State's inability to

---

[168] See *Ward, supra,* footnote 26, at 722.
[169] *Ibid.*
[170] *Ibid.*

protect.[171] The danger that [presumption one] will operate too broadly is tempered by a requirement that clear and convincing proof of a state's inability to protect must be advanced. In *Hinzman*,[172] the Federal Court of Appeal held that the presumption of State Protection described in *Ward* applies equally to cases where the State is alleged to be the agent of persecution. However, where agents of the State are themselves the source of persecution, the presumption of State Protection can be rebutted without exhausting all avenues of recourse in the country.[173]

Nexus

In *Badran*,[174] the Court indicated that the "law does not require that the inability to protect be connected to a Convention reason." Conversely, one may argue that even though the source of the persecution is not grounded in a Convention

---

[171] *Ward, supra*, footnote 26, at 724-726.

[172] *Hinzman, Jeremy v. M.C.I.* and *Hughey, Brandon David v. M.C.I.* (F.C.A, nos. A-182-06; A-185-06)

[173] *Chaves, Alejandro Jose Martinez v. M.C.I.* (F.C., no. IMM-603-04), Tremblay-Lamer, February 8, 2005; 2005 FC 193. See also *Lopez Gonzalez, Jaqueline v. M.C.I.* (F.C., no. IMM-5321-10), Rennie, May 24, 2011; 2011 FC 592, where the Court noted at paragraph 12 that "[T]he case law shows that an applicant must include proof that they have exhausted all recourse available, except in exceptional circumstances where it would be unreasonable for them to do so, such as when the persecutor is an agent of the state, because of police corruption …. or where it would otherwise be futile."

[174] *Badran, Housam v. M.C.I.* (F.C.T.D., no. IMM-2472-95), McKeown, March 29, 1996, at 3-4.

reason, a State's failure to act (protect), if motivated by a Convention ground, can establish the nexus to the definition, i.e., the failure to protect for a Convention reason can in itself amount to persecutory treatment.

Burden of Proof

In *Flores Carrillo*,[175] the Federal Court of Appeal stated that there are three different factual realities and legal concepts which should not be confused. They are the burden of proof, the standard of proof and the evidentiary burden to rebut the presumption of State Protection.

In answering the certified question, the Court summarized the law as follows:

> A refugee who claims that the State Protection is inadequate or non-existent bears the evidentiary burden of adducing evidence to that effect and the legal burden of persuading the trier of fact that his or her claim in this respect is founded. The standard of proof applicable is the *balance of probabilities* and there is no requirement of a higher degree of probability than what that standard usually requires. As for the quality of the evidence required to rebut the presumption of State Protection, the presumption is rebutted by clear and convincing evidence that the State

---

[175] *M.C.I. v. Flores Carrillo, Maria del Rosario* (F.C.A., no. A-225-07), Létourneau, Nadon, Sharlow, March 12, 2008; 2008 FCA 94.

Protection is inadequate or non-existent
(emphasis added).[176]

Burden of Proof and Obligation to
Approach the State

The burden or onus of showing the absence of
State Protection is on the Claimant, not the
Board. This however, does not relieve the RPD
of its obligation to provide clear and adequate
reasons indicating why the onus was not met. A
Claimant is required to approach his or her state
for protection in situations in which protection
might reasonably be forthcoming. The Claimant
will not meet the definition of "Convention
refugee" where it is objectively unreasonable for
the Claimant not to have sought the protection
of his home authorities: otherwise, the Claimant
need not literally approach the state.

In other words, the Claimant must show that it
was reasonable for him or her not to seek State
Protection. However, a Claimant is not required
to risk his or her life seeking ineffective
protection of a State, merely to demonstrate that
ineffectiveness.

The Trial Division in *Peralta*[177] stated that a
Claimant is not required to show that he or she

---

[176] *Ibid.*
[177] *Peralta, Gloria Del Carmen v. M.C.I.* (F.C.T.D., no. IMM-5451-01),
Heneghan, September 20, 2002; 2002 FCT 989. See also *Sanchez,
Leonardo Gonzalez v. M.C.I.* (F.C., no. IMM-3154-03), Mactavish, May

has exhausted all avenues of protection. Rather, the Claimant has to show that he or she has taken all steps reasonable in the circumstances, taking into account the context of the country of origin in general, the steps taken and the Claimant's interactions with the authorities. In determining if the Claimant took reasonable steps, the Board is required to consider the Claimant's personal circumstances and characteristics as well as previous efforts to access State Protection. Where the Claimant left his or her country several years prior to claiming, the country conditions evidence may take on greater importance than the Claimant's efforts to seek protection. The obligation of minors to approach the State for protection requires special consideration. For example, the Court has

---

18, 2004; 2004 FC 731 and the discussion under section 6.1.8. and the discussion under section 6.1.8. In *Garcia Aldana, Paco Jesus v. M.C.I.* (F.C., no. IMM-2113-06), Hughes, April 19, 2007; 2007 FC 423, v. M.C.I. (F.C. no. IMM-2113-06), Hughes, April 19, 2007; 2007 FC 423, the Court noted that the Board must assess the steps actually taken by the Claimant in the context of country conditions and consider the interaction that the Claimant did have with the police authorities; and in *Prieto Velasco, Augosto Pedro v. M.C.I.* (F.C., no. IMM-3900-06), Shore, February 8, 2007; 2007 FC 133, the Court noted that the RPD failed to consider the fact that the Claimants' situation worsened after they filed a complaint with the police. The same point was made in *Aguilar Soto, Rafael Alberto v. M.C.I.* (F.C., no. IMM-1883-10), Shore, November 25, 2010; 2010 FC 1183. In *Moreno Maniero, Ronald Antonio v. M.C.I.* (F.C., no. IMM-8536-11), Zinn, June 19, 2012; 2012 FC 776, the Court held that the RPD erred in holding that the applicant must exhaust every possible avenue of state protection – the test is that all "reasonable" efforts must be made.

cautioned about faulting a sexually molested child with not approaching the State for protection when the parents themselves do not do so.

More Than One Authority in the Country

The Court of Appeal in Canada in *Zalzali*[178] recognized that there may be several established authorities in a country which are each able to provide protection in the part of the country controlled by them. The "country", the "national government", the "legitimate government", the "nominal government" will probably vary depending on the circumstances and the evidence and it would be presumptuous to attempt to give a general definition. There may be several established authorities in the same country which are each able to provide protection in the part of the territory controlled by them, protection which may be adequate though not necessarily perfect.

In *Chebli-Haj-Hassam*,[179] the Court of Appeal answered a certified question on this matter as follows:

---

[178] *Zalzali v. Canada (Minister of Employment and Immigration)*, [1991] 3 F.C. 605 (C.A.).

[179] *Chebli-Haj-Hassam, Atef v. M.C.I.* (F.C.A., no. A-191-95), Marceau, MacGuigan, Décary, May 28, 1996. Reported: *Chebli-Haj-Hassam v. Canada (Minister of Citizenship and Immigration)* (1996), 36 Imm. L.R.

In the circumstances where there is a legitimate
government supported by the forces of another
government and there is no difference in interest
between the two governments in relation to a
refugee Claimant, the protection given to the
Claimant is adequate to establish an internal
refuge.[180]

Standard of Proof

The lack of State Protection is proven on a
balance of probabilities. The requirement set out
in *Ward* that the Claimant's evidence to rebut the
presumption must be "clear and convincing"
does not mean a higher degree of probability
than the normal standard of "more likely than
not." As explained by Létourneau, J. in *Flores
Carrillo*:

The *Ward* case does not require a higher
probability than what is normally required on the

(2d) 112 (F.C.A.). See also *Isufi, Arlind v. M.C.I.* (F.C., no. IMM-5631-
02), Tremblay-Lamer, July 15, 2003; 2003 FC 880, where the Court
considered the situation of a Claimant from Kosovo and had this to
say: "In the case at bar, there is no difference in interest between the
UN forces and the government of the Federal Republic of
Yugoslavia. As such, the Board did not commit an error in
determining that state protection was available to the applicant
through non-state actors. ... The presence of UN forces is not
evidence of a breakdown of the state apparatus in Yugoslavia or
Kosovo. The UN forces and security police in Kosovo work in
conjunction with the local Kosovo police service to maintain
order.".."
[180] *Ibid.*

> balance of probabilities standard to meet the
> legal burden...I fully agree with the finding of
> the judge that La Forest J. in *Ward* was referring
> to the quality of the evidence necessary to rebut
> the presumption and not to a higher standard of
> proof.

That a person "might" receive State Protection is not the proper test. While no state offers perfect protection, and there will always be instances of persons who were not able to obtain adequate or any protection, the level necessary to show "adequate" State Protection is a level where it is more likely than not that the individual will be protected.[181]

Rebutting the Presumption of Protection

In this section, there are two concepts that are discussed: the evidentiary burden, and the standard of protection a Claimant must establish.

The Evidentiary Burden of "Clear and Convincing"

---

[181] *Salamanca, Miguel Angel Sandoval v. M.C.I.* (F.C., no. IMM-6737-11), Zinn, June 19, 2012; 2012 FC 780. Note that while the Court in Salamanca uses the phrase "far more likely than not" (in paragraph 17), a number of subsequent cases have referred to the phrase but have omitted the word "far". For example, see *Bakos, Robert v. M.C.I.* (F.C., no. IMM-2424-15), Manson, February 12, 2016 (amended September 7, 2016); 2016 FC 191, which says that Salamanca suggests that adequate state protection means that it is more likely than not that the applicant will be protected (see paragraph 30).

Rebutting the presumption refers to the ability of a Claimant to establish that State Protection is not forthcoming in his or her case. This is an evidentiary burden and as noted above, the question is whether there is sufficient "clear and "convincing" evidence of the state's failure to protect. Absent an admission by the state that it is unable to protect (as was the case in *Ward*), a Claimant can establish, with "clear and convincing evidence," that State Protection would not be reasonably forthcoming (thus rebutting the presumption) where:

a. there is a complete breakdown of state apparatus;
b. there is evidence "…similarly situated individuals [were] let down by the State Protection arrangements…;"
c. there is evidence "…of past personal incidents in which State Protection did not materialize."

The Supreme Court in *Ward* refers to the Federal Court of Appeal decision in *Satiacum*[182] and quotes with approval the following statement:

> In the absence of exceptional circumstances established by the Claimant, it seems to me that in a Convention refugee hearing, as in an extradition hearing, Canadian tribunals have to assume a fair and independent judicial process in the foreign country. In the case of a non-

---

[182] *M.E.I. v. Satiacum, Robert* (F.C.A., no. A-554-87), Urie, Mahoney, MacGuigan, June 16, 1989. Reported: *Canada (Minister of Employment and Immigration) v. Satiacum* (1989), 99 N.R. 171 (F.C.A.).

democratic State, contrary evidence might be readily forthcoming, but in relation to a democracy like the United States contrary evidence might have to go to the extent of substantially impeaching, for example, the jury selection process in the relevant part of the country, or the independence or fair-mindedness of the judiciary itself.[183]

In *Kadenko*,[184] the Court of Appeal noted that the burden of proof to establish absence of State Protection is "directly proportional to the level of democracy in the state in question ..."

In *Alassouli*,[185] the Court held that:

---

[183] *Ward, supra*, footnote 26, at 725 (quoting from *Satiacum*, at 176).
[184] *M.C.I. v. Kadenko, Ninal* (F.C.A., no. A-388-95), Hugessen, Décary, Chevalier, October 15, 1996. Reported: *Canada (Minister of Citizenship and Immigration) v. Kadenko* (1996), 143 D.L.R. (4th) 532 (F.C.A.), (application for leave to appeal dismissed by the S.C.C. on May 8, 1997). In *Diaz De Leon, Andromeda v. M.C.I.* (F.C., no. IMM-6429-06), Frenette, December 12, 2007; 2007 FC 1307, the Court noted that in the case of a developing democracy (in this case Mexico), where corruption and drug trafficking are prevalent, the presumption of state protection can be more easily overcome, particularly if, as in this case, those whose job was to protect could not protect themselves. In *Rodriguez Capitaine, Rogelio v. M.C.I.* (F.C., no. IMM-3449-07), Gauthier, January 24, 2008; 2008 FC 98, the Court, in paragraphs 20-22, discusses the notion of "democracy spectrum" raised in *Hinzman, supra*. It appears to apply not only to exhausting recourses, but also to determining the extent of the evidence needed to displace the presumption and whether it would be unreasonable not to seek protection.
[185] *Alassouli, Yousf v. M.C.I.* (F.C., no. IMM-6451-10), de Montigny, August 16, 2011; 2011 FC 998. See also *Ahmed, Ahmed Ibrahim v. M.C.I.* (F.C. no. IMM-2187-18), Kane, November 16, 2018; 2018 FC 1157 at paragraph 52 where, in the context of a claim against Iraq, the Court stated that "the RAD's conclusions do not reflect the principle that democracy alone may not be an indicator of state protection, nor do they sufficiently account for the Applicant's

... democracy should not be used as a proxy for State Protection. There is obviously a strong relationship between the citizens' participation in the institutions of the state on the one hand, and the effectiveness and fairness of the state's apparatus to protect them. There is no automatic equation between the two, and an assessment of State Protection must always rest on a more nuanced analysis, taking into account the particular circumstances of a Claimant, as well as the state involved.

In *Shaka*,[186] the Court clarified that the question as to whether the presumption has been rebutted is a factual question and that the test is the same for all countries. What varies is the amount of evidence necessary to rebut the presumption:

The newness or the age of the democracy are not necessarily demonstrative of whether the state is truly democratic. More scrutiny may be required of countries that are in transition, but there is no automatic presumption or lesser threshold as

---

particular circumstances."

[186] *Shaka, Abdul Shema v. M.C.I.* (F.C., no. IMM-4141-11), Rennie, February 21, 2012; 2012 FC 235. Some cases appear to treat the presumption as being different depending on the level of democracy; however, the presumption as set out by the SCC in Ward was a presumption that applied to all countries. What was recognized was that the presumption could be rebutted differently depending on the level of democracy in the state in question. Cases such as *Sow, Harouna Sibo v. M.C.I.*, no. IMM-5287-10, Rennie, June 6, 2011; 2011 FC 646, and *Masalov, Sergey v. M.C.I.* (F.C., no. IMM-7207-13), Diner, February 4, 2015; 2015 FC 277, which refer to the notion that the presumption varies with the nature of democracy in a country should be read with caution in this regard.

contended. The test is the same, for all countries.
*What may vary is the amount of evidence required to
rebut the presumption* (emphasis added).

In *Hinzman*,[187] the Federal Court of Appeal noted
that a Claimant coming from a democratic
country (like the US) will have a heavy burden
when attempting to show that he or she should
not have been required to exhaust all of the
recourses available domestically before claiming
protection elsewhere. However, democracy alone
does not guarantee effective State Protection, it
is merely an indicator of the likely effectiveness
of a state institution. The RPD is required to do
more than determine whether a country has a
democratic political system and must assess the
quality of the institutions that provide State
Protection.

Another case that refers to the need for a
contextual analysis is *Loaiza*,[188] where the Court
noted that the analysis must begin with an
assessment of the *personal circumstances* of the
Claimant and the degree of the individual risk
faced. The Court noted that in some countries
there may be only a weak correlation between the
existence of a constitutional democracy and a
willingness of the state to take effective measures
against spousal abuse. Moreover, the Board must

---

[187] *Hinzman, supra.*
[188] *Loaiza Brenes, Heyleen v. M.C.I.* (F.C., no. IMM-2445-06), Barnes,
April 2, 2007; 2007 FC 351.

REFUGEE PROTECTION IN CANADA

proceed with a fulsome and contextualized analysis of each Claimant's particular situation and that it is not enough to state broadly that there are free and general elections, and that legislation has been enacted to ensure basic standards of human rights.

Standard of Protection

Over the years, there has been much discussion and confusion about what the standard of protection should be. The argument has boiled down to either requiring that the protection offered be adequate or that it be more than that, namely effective. To the extent that establishing that the protection offered be effective has been understood in some cases as shifting the burden to the Board, the Court of Appeal in *Mudrak*[189] stated that this inference is wrong.

As noted by the Court, the cases that have faulted the Board for not analyzing the operational adequacy of protection were not shifting the burden to the Board but were simply finding that the Board's decisions could not stand because they ignored relevant evidence or because the syllogism was flawed, which were legitimate grounds to intervene.

---

[189] *Mudrak, Zsolt Jozsef v. M.C.I.* (F.C.A., no. A-147-15), Stratas, Webb, Scott, June 14, 2016; 2016 FCA 178.

The Court in *Mudrak* was of the view that the question that was certified by the Federal Court, namely: "Whether the RPD commits a reviewable error if it fails to determine whether protection measures introduced in a democratic state to protect minorities have been demonstrated to provide operational adequacy of State Protection in order to conclude that adequate State Protection exists?"[190] was based on a misunderstanding of the jurisprudence and did not arise on the record. Also, the question was theoretical and not of general importance and therefore did not need to be answered.

The standard of adequate protection has been further qualified by the notion that the degree of protection required is not perfection, but adequacy. In *Villafranca*,[191] the Federal Court of Appeal stated:

> No government that makes any claim to democratic values or protection of human rights can guarantee the protection of all of its citizens at all times. Thus, it is not enough for a Claimant merely to show that his government has not always been effective at protecting persons in his particular situation. Terrorism in the name of one warped ideology or another is a scourge afflicting many societies today; its victims, however much they may merit our sympathy, do not become

---

[190] *Mudrak, ibid.*
[191] *Zalzali, supra,* at 614. *M.E.I. v. Villafranca, Ignacio* (F.C.A., no. A-69-90), Hugessen, Marceau, Décary, December 18, 1992.

Convention refugees simply because their
governments have been unable to suppress the
evil. ... where a state is in effective control of its
territory, has military, police and civil authority in
place, and makes serious efforts to protect its
citizens from terrorist activities, the mere fact
that it is not always successful at doing so will
not be enough to justify a claim that the victims
of terrorism are unable to avail themselves of
such protection.[192]

---

[192] *Villafranca, ibid.* In *Lopez Gonzalez, Jaqueline v. M.C.I.* (F.C., no.
IMM-5321-10), Rennie, May 24, 2011; 2011 FC 592, the Court noted
that the "test of police protection is… adequacy; *Carillo* [sic] at para
32. The test is not that of successful arrest, detention and
conviction… A failure of state protection cannot be founded,
therefore, on a failure to bring a perpetrator to justice." Much the
same point was made in *Salvagno, Sergio Santiago Raymond v. M.C.I.*
(F.C., no. IMM-5848-10), *Pinard*, May 26, 2011; 2011 FC 595. In two
earlier cases involving Costa Rica, the Court followed Villafranca and
noted that the absence of a witness protection program did not
render the Board's decision on protection unreasonable, and that a
duty to provide personal protection to every person who files a
police complaint is unreasonable by the standards of any country:
Alfaro, Oscar Luis Alfaro v. M.C.I. (F.C., no. IMM-6905-03), O'Keefe,
January 20, 2005; 2005 FC 92 and *Arias Aguilar, Jennifer v. M.C.I.*
(F.C., no. IMM-1000-05), Rouleau, November 9, 2005; 2005 FC
1519.).

Also, the Federal Court stated in *Gomez Gonzalez, Veronica v. M.C.I.*
(F.C., no. IMM-485-11), de Montigny, October 4, 2011; 2011 FC
1132: "As stated by this Court on a number of occasions, it is
difficult to criticize the state authorities for their failure to act when
the Applicants do not give them a reasonable opportunity to protect
them." In other words, the authorities should be given the
information that is necessary in order to react adequately.

In *Boston, Edwin v. M.C.I.* (F.C., no. IMM-6554-06), Snider,
December 4, 2007; 2007 FC 1271, the Court noted that Villafranca is
not inconsistent with Ward. The Court noted that "[a]bsent
evidence to the contrary, a state that can provide adequate protection

In summary, according to the Federal Court of Appeal in *Mudrak*, the law on State Protection is settled law and the apparent debate about whether protection has to be effective rather than adequate is based on a misunderstanding of the jurisprudence. It would appear that the evidence relating to measures taken by the state (also referred in some cases as "serious efforts") to protect its citizens and the efficacy of those measures (sometimes referred to as "operational adequacy" or "effectiveness at the operational level") are evidentiary issues, not legal tests that need to be assessed in each individual case. In this regard, the Court notes that each case will turn on its own facts.[193]

In an earlier case, *Gonzalez Camargo*,[194] the Federal Court had expressed similar thinking as follows:

---

to all of its citizens who may be subject to persecution by the NPA [guerilla group operating in the Philippines], can also reasonably be found to be able to protect an individual who has suffered at the hands of the same organization. Thus, the Board did not err by focusing its examination on the level of protection vis-à-vis the NPA available for all citizens in the Philippines."

[193] What is becoming clear from the case law is that it is an error to stop the analysis of state protection at the "serious efforts" level without also examining the operational adequacy of those efforts. See for example, *Boakye, Kofi v. M.C.I.* (F.C., no. IMM-2361-15), Strickland, December 18, 2015; 2015 FC 1394; *Hasa, Ana v. M.C.I.* (F.C., no. IMM-3700-17), Strickland, March 7, 2018; 2018 FC 270.
[194] *Gonzalez Camargo, Hernando v. M.C.I.* (F.C., no. IMM-38-14), Gleeson, September 2, 2015; 2015 FC 1044.

The Board correctly identifies the principles
underpinning State Protection as set out
in *Ward* and *Hinzman* including the Claimant's
burden of providing clear and convincing
evidence of the state's inability to protect its
citizens and the requirement that Claimants must
approach the state for protection in situations
where that protection might be reasonably
forthcoming. In my opinion, however, the Board
failed to correctly recognize that the assessment
of the adequacy of State Protection involves
more than a consideration of state efforts. This
caused the Board to focus on state efforts and
not consider the operational adequacy of State
Protection for the applicants and individuals in
like circumstances; the proper test when
considering the question of adequate State
Protection.

In *Moran*,[195] the Court explained it as follows:

I pause to note that counsel for [the applicant]
appears to try to distinguish between what is
"adequate" protection and what is protection
"effective at an operational level". There is
indeed a line of jurisprudence from this Court
suggesting that "adequate" may be different from
"effective"; however, these cases do not dispute
that the protection needs to yield actual results...
*A protection that is adequate is a protection that works at
the operational level.* Adequacy of State Protection
has been held to mean that the RPD has to
consider the state's capacity to implement

---

[195] *Moran Gudiel, Hugo v. M.C.I.* (F.C., no. IMM-2054-14), Gascon,
July 23, 2015; 2015 FC 902.

measures at the operational or practical level for the persons concerned.

The following appear to be the evidentiary factors that need to be considered in order to determine whether the presumption of State Protection has been rebutted:

- The efforts made by the Claimant to obtain protection, including:
- o reports made to the authorities
- o whether sufficient details were provided
- o follow-up efforts
- o whether other agencies besides the police were approached
- Measures taken by the state and the efficacy of those measures, including:
- o applicable laws in place
- o mechanisms to protect (police, other agencies)
- o enforcement efforts
- o tangible results
- Evidence of similarly situated individuals
- Particular circumstances of the Claimant and profile, addressing the basis of the claim (e.g., gender, and etc.), not just generalities.

Source of Protection

As part of the assessment of what constitutes clear and convincing evidence of the State's failure to protect, the question has arisen as to who exactly a Claimant is required to approach for protection. In other words, what avenues of protection is a Claimant required to exhaust before claiming international protection? At issue is whether State Protection is to be provided by the **police** (the State organ entrusted with the role of protecting a country's citizens) or whether other agencies play a role that the tribunal needs to consider. What those governmental and non-governmental agencies might be will depend on the country in question. A number of Federal Court decisions state that it is the police force that has the primary responsibility to protect a nation's citizens and is in possession of enforcement powers commensurate with this mandate. Therefore, alternative institutions do not constitute avenues of protection *per se*.

Stateless Claimants

As to whether stateless Claimants need to avail themselves of State Protection, the UNHCR *Handbook*, in paragraph 101 states that "…[i]n the case of a stateless refugee, the question of 'availment of protection' of the country of his former habitual residence does not, of course, arise…" In the very early case of *El Khatib*,[196] Mr. Justice McKeown agreed with this approach and stated:

> … the discussion and conclusions reached
> in *Ward* apply only to citizens of a state, and not
> to stateless people. In my view the distinction
> between paragraphs 2(1)(a)(i) and 2(1)(a)(ii) of

---

[196] *El Khatib, Naif v. M.C.I.* (F.C.T.D., no. IMM-5182-93), McKeown, September 27, 1994.

the *Act* is that the stateless person is not expected
to avail himself of State Protection when there is
no duty on the state to provide such protection.

However, more recent case law has interpreted
the law differently. For example, starting
with *Nizar*[197] where the Court was of the view
that, even though states owe no duty of
protection to non-nationals, "it is relevant for a
stateless person, who has a country of former
habitual residence, to demonstrate that *de
facto* [sic] protection within that state, as a result
of being resident there is not likely to exist." The
Court reasoned that this was relevant to the well-
foundedness of the Claimant's fear.

The Federal Court of Appeal in *Thabet*,[198] in the
context of discussing whether a stateless
Claimant who has more than one country of
former habitual residence must establish the
claim with respect to one, some or all of the
countries, had this to say about the issue of State
Protection:

> ... The definition takes into account the inherent
> difference between those persons who are
> nationals of a state, and therefore are owed
> protection, and those persons who are stateless
> and without recourse to State Protection.

---

[197] *Nizar v. M.C.I.* (F.C.T.D., no. A-1-92), Reed, January 10, 1996, at
5.
[198] *Thabet, Marwan Youssef v. M.C.I.* (F.C.A., no. A-20-96), Linden,
McDonald, Henry, May 11, 1998. Reported: *Thabet v. Canada (Minister
of Citizenship and Immigration)*, [1998] 4 F.C. 21 (C.A.).

Because of this distinction one cannot treat the
two groups identically, even though one should
seek to be as consistent as possible. (At 17).

... If it is likely that a person would be able to
return to a country of former habitual residence
where he or she would be safe from persecution,
that person is not a refugee. This means that the
Claimant would bear the burden ... of showing
on the balance of probabilities that he or she is
unable or unwilling to return to any country of
former habitual residence. (At 28).

In *Popov*,[199] the Claimants argued that as stateless
individuals, they were not subject to the
presumption of State Protection and in support
of their argument relied on *Thabet*.[200] The Court
rejected the argument and held that, although it
is true that in *Thabet*, the Federal Court of Appeal
creates a distinction between stateless individuals
and those who do have a state, one must read
further. The Court answered the certified
question before it as follows:

In order to be found to be a Convention refugee,
a stateless person must show that, on a balance
of probabilities he or she would suffer
persecution in **any** country of former habitual
residence, and that he or she cannot return
to **any** of his or her countries of former habitual
residence. (*Thabet* at paragraph 30) [emphasis

---

[199] *Popov, Alexander v. M.C.I.* (F.C. no., IMM-841-09, Beaudry,
September 10, 2009; 2009 FC 898.
[200] *Thabet, supra.*

added] [43] *Thabet* clearly set outs that it is not sufficient to simply be unable to return to all countries of former habitual residence - the individual must prove that they will suffer persecution in one of those countries. [44] In this case, [the Claimants], being stateless individuals, must establish that they would suffer persecution in either Russia or the United States – their countries of former habitual residence and that they cannot return to the other. Although it is clear they cannot return to Russia, they have made their claim against the United States and as such must prove that they would suffer persecution in that country.

In order to do so, they must prove not only a subjective fear but also an objective fear. This requires that they rebut the presumption of State Protection and are "required to prove that they exhausted all the domestic avenues available to them before without success before claiming refugee status in Canada."[201] The RPD has been correct in finding that the stateless Applicants must have exhausted all domestic avenues in order to establish that they have a well-founded fear of persecution in one of their countries of former habitual residence. And more recently, in *Khattr*,[202] the court agreed with *Popov*[203] that the presumption of State Protection applies to stateless individuals.

---

[201] *Hinzman, Jeremy v. M.C.I.* (F.C.A, nos. A-182-06, at paragraph 46
[202] *Khattr, Amani Khzaee v. M.C.I.* (F.C. no., IMM-3249-15), Zinn, March 22, 2016; 2016 FC 341.
[203] See *Popov, supra.*

CHAPTER 8
INTERNAL FLIGHT ALTERNATIVE

I n terms of Internal Flight Alternative (or IFA), there is a wealth of resources produced by the IRB. In this chapter, IRB's document entitled, "Chapter 8 - Internal Flight Alternative," is reproduced, with necessary modifications.[204]

IFA sets limitation on conferring refugee status when a Claimant's risk of persecution is confined to a specific area of their country. It arises when a Claimant who otherwise meets all the elements of the Convention refugee definition in their home country but is still not a Convention refugee because that Claimant has an IFA elsewhere in that country. Therefore, among other things, the Claimant must satisfy a refugee panel that they had no IFA in their country of citizenship or the former place of their habitual residence.

The Two-Prong Test

In the following sections, the author will draw upon the available materials prepared by the IRB,[205] and only make slight modification for

---

[204] See https://irb-cisr.gc.ca/en/legal-policy/legal-concepts/Pages/RefDef08.aspx (retrieved: March 30th, 2020)
[205] *Ibid.*

emphasis where applicable. The question of whether an IFA exists is an integral part of the Convention refugee definition.[206] The key concepts concerning IFA come from two cases: *Rasaratnam*[207] and *Thirunavukkarasu*.[208] From these cases it is clear that the test to be applied in determining whether there is an IFA is two-pronged:

1.   "… the Board must be satisfied on a balance of probabilities that there is no serious possibility of the Claimant being persecuted in the part of the country to which it finds an IFA exists."[209]

2.   Moreover, conditions in the part of the country considered to be an IFA must be such that it would not be unreasonable, in all the circumstances, including those particular to the Claimant, for him to seek refuge there.[210]

Both prongs must be satisfied for a finding that the Claimant has an IFA.

The Court of Appeal in *Kanagaratnam*, was of the view that the determination of whether a Claimant has a well-founded fear of persecution in his or her home area of the country is not a prerequisite to the consideration of an IFA. At

---

[206] *Rasaratnam v. Canada (Minister of Employment and Immigration)*, [1992] 1 F.C. 706 (C.A.), at 710.
[207] *Ibid.*
[208] *Thirunavukkarasu v. Canada (Minister of Employment and Immigration)*, [1994] 1 F.C. 589 (C.A.).
[209] *Rasaratnam, supra*, at 710.
[210] *Ibid.*, at 709 and 711

the same time, if a Claimant fails to meet elements of the definition in the home area, it is open to the tribunal not to proceed to do an IFA analysis.[211] In other words, if the Claimant fails to establish a subjective fear,[212] it is not necessary to make an IFA analysis. A Claimant must first establish a subjective fear for an IFA analysis to be performed.

The concept of an IFA does not require that the safe haven be in another city or province of the state of origin so long as it is truly an area in which the Claimant can seek refuge from the experienced persecution.[213] In other words, *an IFA can still exist in the same country, province or town in which the Claimant has experienced persecution. Therefore, the Claimant must satisfy the panel that there is no IFA in their country, province or town even before the Claimant looks to other countries for safety. At the same time, an IFA may still exist where the risks in the proposed IFA are risks faced by all inhabitants.[214] In short, the risks must not be of general nature but specific*

[211] *Hernandez Cardozo, Eduardo v. M.C.I.* (F.C., no. IMM-5095-11), Shore, February 9, 2012; 2012 FC 190.
[212] See chapters 3 and 4
[213] *Jilani, Zia Uddin Ahmed v. M.C.I.* (F.C., no. IMM-711-07), Mosley, December 21, 2007; 2007 FC 1354
[214] In *Muhammed, Falululla Peer v. M.C.I.* (F.C., no. IMM-5122-11), Harrington, February 17, 2012; 2012 FC 226, the risks in the proposed IFA area included unexploded landmines and infrastructural issues affecting millions of Sri Lankans of all backgrounds.

to the Claimant's case. If everyone is exposed and suffers from the similar dangers in that area, an IFA analysis will fail.[215]

A finding of IFA must be based on a distinct evaluation of a region for that purpose taking into account the Claimant's identity. It cannot be inferred from earlier findings of fact unconnected to the issue of an IFA.[216] The relationship between IFA, change of circumstances and the applicability of "compelling reasons" was considered by the Court,[217] which concluded that where an IFA applies to a Claimant, that person is not and never could have been a Convention refugee. Accordingly, he or she could not cease to be a Convention refugee on the basis of a change of circumstances. In other words, if a Claimant had an IFA, they could not become a refugee. And if that Claimant became a refugee because he had no IFA and then at some point after the claim is successful and an IFA becomes available in their home country, that refugee Claimant cannot have their refugee status revoked.

---

[215] Emphasis added.

[216] *Selvakumaran, Sivachelam v. M.C.I* (F.C.T.D., no. IMM-5103-01), Mckeown, May 31, 2002

[217] *Singh, Gurmeet v. M.C.I.* (F.C.T.D., no. IMM-75-95), Richard, July 4, 1995. Reported: *Singh, (Gurmeet) v. Canada (Minister of Citizenship and Immigration)* (1995), 30 Imm. L.R. (2d) 226 (F.C.T.D.), at 4. See also, *Sangha, Karamjit Singh v. M.C.I.* (F.C.T.D., no. IMM-1555-98), Reed, October 28, 1998

With respect to whether an "external flight alternative" might exist in the European Union for Claimants who might have experienced persecution in one of the member states, the closest to a determination that this concept may not be applicable in Canadian law can be inferred from the *Mortocian*[218] case. The Court was considering the RPD's determination, which it found reasonable, that the Romanian Claimant of Roma ethnicity was not a Convention refugee or a person in need of protection because what he faced was discrimination not amounting to persecution. The issue of an external flight alternative in the EU was addressed as follows:

> [15] Regarding discrimination in employment, the Applicant submits that the Board, in essence, relied on an External Flight Alternative, suggesting that the Applicant could be employed elsewhere in the European Union. In addition, the Applicant submits that the Board failed to consider that the Applicant would be forced to work at menial jobs and or at a lesser wage in Romania and that this constitutes persecution.
>
> [16] With respect to the notion of an External Flight Alternative, I agree with the Applicant that there is no such requirement. An Applicant need not demonstrate that they are unable to go to any country where they may have the right to work in order to establish that they satisfy the

---

[218] *Mortocian, Alexandru v. M.C.I.* (.FC. no., IMM-3837-12), Kane, December 7, 2012; 2012 FC 1447

Convention refugee definition. Despite the increased mobility within the European Union [EU], those who work in other countries do not enjoy all the privileges of nationals and while they may be permitted to work, the periods of employment are limited. The European Union is a union of several distinct countries and is not one country. Whether this argument is cast as an Internal Flight Alternative within the EU or an External Flight Alternative beyond the country of origin, there is no requirement on an Applicant to exhaust employment opportunities in other countries.

Notice and Burden of Proof

With respect to notice, the issue of IFA must be raised by the panel or the Minister (before or during the hearing). The Act does not automatically put Claimants on notice that IFA is an issue in the claim. The principles regarding fair notice [giving proper notice as] expressed in *Rasaratnam* and *Thirunavukkarasu* are still relevant under the Act.[219] The notice must be clear and sufficient.[220]

It is a breach of natural justice to tell the Claimant that IFA is not an issue and then, later, make a contrary finding on that issue.[221] *Extensive*

---

[219] See *Thevarajah, Anton Felix v. M.C.I.* (F.C., no. IMM-695-04), Mosley, November 24, 2004; 2004 FC 1654

[220] *Ay, Hasan v. M.C.I.* (F.C., no. IMM-4149-09), Boivin, June 21, 2010; 2010 FC 671

[221] *Moya, Jaime Olvera v. M.C.I.* (F.C.T.D., no. IMM-5436-01),

questioning[222] during the hearing (by the Board or by counsel) on the subject of IFA can be sufficient notice.[223]

With respect to burden of proof, once the issue is raised, the onus is on the Claimant to show that he or she does not have an IFA. Even though the burden of proof rests on the Claimant, the Board cannot base a finding that there is an IFA, in the absence of sufficient evidence, solely on the basis that the Claimant has not fulfilled the onus of proof.[224] There is no onus on a Claimant to personally test the viability of an IFA before seeking protection in Canada.[225] While in earlier jurisprudence there was inconsistency about whether a specific location

---

Beaudry, November 6, 2002.

[222] Emphasis added.

[223] *Hasnain, Khalid v. M.C.I.* (F.C.T.D., no. A-962-92), McKeown, December 14, 1995. In *Scott, Dailon Ronald v. M.C.I.* (F.C., no. IMM-2691-12), Gagné, September 10, 2012; 2012 FC 1066, the questioning by counsel and the oral and written arguments were held to be adequate notice that IFA was an issue in the case.

[224] *Chauhdry, Mukhtar Ahmed v. M.C.I.* (F.C.T.D., no. IMM-3951-97), Wetston, August 17, 1998.

[225] *Alvapillai, Ramasethu v. M.C.I.* (F.C.T.D., no. IMM-4226-97), Rothstein, August 14, 1998. In *Estrado Lugo, Regina v. M.C.I.* (F.C., no. IMM-1166-09), O'Keefe, February 18, 2010; 2010 FC 170, the Court noted that there was no obligation on the Claimants to have already sought state protection in the proposed IFA location. See also *Ramirez Martinez, Jorge Armando v. M.C.I.* (F.C., no. IMM-1284-09), Snider, June 1, 2010; 2010 FC 600, where the Court, quoting Alvapillai, held that it is an error to require that the IFA be tested before seeking refugee protection in Canada.

or region must be identified as the potential IFA,[226] more recent case law suggest that the RPD must identify the specific IFA locations.[227] The outcome of any one particular

---

[226] In *Rabbani, Sayed Moheyudee v. M.C.I.* (F.C.T.D., no. IMM-236-96), Noël, January 16, 1997, the Court said that the CRDD must identify a specific geographic location; but in *Singh, Ranjit v. M.C.I.* (F.C.T.D., no. A-605-92), Reed, July 23, 1996, the Court rejected the Claimant's argument that the CRDD should identify a place within the country as an IFA, especially in a country as large as India. In *Vidal, Daniel Fernando v. M.E.I.* (F.C.T.D., no. A-644-92), Gibson, May 15, 1997 no notice was given at outset of hearing, but counsel presented evidence on IFA. The Court found no prejudice was suffered by the Claimant as a result of the failure to give notice. Similarly, in *Gosal, Pardeep Singh v. M.C.I.* (F.C.T.D., no. IMM-2316-97), Reed, March 11, 1998, the Court found that one need not identify a specific location within the country for an IFA analysis. Rabbani was distinguished on its facts as in that case the country concerned was Afghanistan and control over areas considered safe tended to shift. In *Moreb, Sliman v. M.C.I.* (F.C., no. IMM-287-05), von Finckenstein, July 5, 2005; 2005 FC 945, the Court found the RPD to have erred when it referred to Jerusalem and Nazareth as the only possible IFA locations and then went on to consider Tel-Aviv-Yafo as an IFA. The Court offered that the panel could have raised the issue of IFA generally without referring to any specific location.

[227] Utoh, *Helen v. M.C.I.* (F.C., no. IMM-6120-11), Rennie, April 10, 2012; 2012 FC 399. This case relied on the checklist of legal criteria for determining whether an IFA exists set out in *Gallo Farias, Alejandrina Dayna v. M.C.I.* (F.C., no. IMM-658-08), Kelen, September 16, 2008; 2008 FC 1035, where the first criteria is set out as follows: "If IFA will be an issue, the Refugee Board must give notice to the refugee Claimant prior to the hearing (Rasaratnam ..., Thirunavukkarasu) and identify a specific IFA location(s) within the refugee Claimant's country of origin (Rabbani ..., Camargo ...)" In *Ahmed, Ishtiaq v. M.C.I.* (F.C.T.D., no. IMM-2931-99), Hansen, March 29, 2000, the Court found the CRDD had erred in considering Islamabad and Karachi as possible IFAs when the Claimant only had notice that Lahore was being considered as a possible IFA. In *Lopez Martinez, Heydi Vanessa v. M.C.I.* (F.C., no. IMM-5081-09), Pinard, May 25, 2010; 2010 FC 550, the Court, at paragraph 23, noted: "...I do not propose that the Board is under an obligation to provide justification for selecting the city it did

judicial review application involving this issue may hinge on how clearly the Claimant was questioned regarding the IFA issue and how clearly the panel explains its findings.

Interpretation and Application of the Two-Pronged Test

The abundance of case law on the topic of IFA basically concerns the interpretation and application of the two-pronged test. Some factors are relevant to both prongs of the test, some are relevant to one or the other prong.

Fear of Persecution

On the issue of whether there is a serious possibility of persecution in the potential IFA, the considerations are basically the same as when making this determination with respect to the Claimant's home area of the country. However, there are some specific points concerning this issue and IFA that are noteworthy:

a.   In determining whether there is an objective basis for fearing persecution in the IFA, RPD must consider the personal circumstances of the

---

initially…" (Emphasis added). But note that the Board did have to explain why the proposed IFA was safe given that the agent of harm was active there.

Claimant, and not just general evidence concerning other persons who live there.[228]

b.   RPD must consider the circumstances of those persons in IFA who are situated similarly to the Claimant.[229]

---

[228] See for example: *Abubakar, Fahmey Abdalla Ali v. M.E.I.* (F.C.T.D., no. A-572-92), Wetston, September 9, 1993, at 3-5; *Pathmakanthan, Indradevi v. M.E.I.* (F.C.T.D., no. IMM-2367-93), Denault, November 2, 1993. Reported: *Pathmakanthan v. Canada (Minister of Employment and Immigration)* (1993), 23 Imm. L.R. (2d) 76 (F.C.T.D.), at 79-80; *Kaler, Minder Singh v. M.E.I.* (F.C.T.D., no. IMM-794-93), Cullen, February 3, 1994, at 9; *Dhillon, Harbhagwant Singh v. S.S.C.* (F.C.T.D., no. IMM-3256-93), Rouleau, March 17, 1994, at 3; *Jeyachandran, Senthan v. S.G.C.* (F.C.T.D., no. IMM-799-94), McKeown, March 30, 1995; *Ratnam, Selvanayagam v. M.C.I.* (F.C.T.D., no. IMM-1881-94), Richard, March 31, 1995. However, it is an error to interpret the first prong of the test as requiring that all similar persons would be persecuted in the IFA area. In *Aria, Ashraf v. M.C.I.* (F.C., no. IMM-2499-12), de Montigny, April 2, 2013; 2013 FC 324, the RPD erred when it stated that it was "not credible that all young women are subject to forced marriages which are not forced by their own families". A serious possibility of persecution does not mean that "all young women" would be subject to forced marriages with warlords. In *Ambrose-Esede, Benedicta Osemen v. M.C.I.* (F.C. no. IMM-1685-18), Russell, December 11, 2018; 2018 FC 1241, the Court quashed an RPD decision in which the RPD had concluded there was a viable IFA. The Court held that the fact the Claimant was a lawyer and her name, along with her contact information, would appear on the Nigerian Bar Association's members' portal would make her easy to locate in the IFA location.
[229] *Kahlon, Hari Singh v. S.G.C* (F.C.T.D., no. IMM-532-93), Gibson, August 5, 1993. Reported: *Kahlon v. Canada (Solicitor General),* (1993), 24 Imm. L.R. (2d) 219 (F.C.T.D.), at 222-224; *Manoharan, Vanajah v. M.E.I.* (F.C.T.D., no. A-1156-92), Rouleau, December 6, 1993, at 7-8; *Naguleswaran, Pathmasilosini (Naguleswaran) v. M.C.I.* (F.C.T.D., no. IMM-1116-94), Muldoon, April 19, 1995, at 6 (however, caution is suggested concerning interpretation of the phrase, "…solid proof of personal persecution (either individually or collectively)…" given case law indicating there is no need for past persecution, individually or collectively, e.g. see *Salibian v. Canada (Minister of Employment and Immigration),* [1990] 3 F.C. 250 (C.A.)).

c. In assessing the particular circumstances of the Claimant, the RPD may consider the condition of family members who have sought refuge in the IFA.[230]

d. The nature and the agents of the persecution feared ought to suggest that the persecution would be confined to particular areas of the country.[231] In a case where the agents of persecution were the local police, the Court found that if the Claimant was of no interest to the central authorities, the Claimant may be able to relocate to other areas.[232] The fact that the

---

[230] See for example *Ali, Chaudhary Liaqat v. M.E.I.* (F.C.T.D., no. A-1461-92), Noël, January 20, 1994, at 5-6.

[231] *Ahmed, Ali v. M.E.I.* (F.C.A., no. A-89-92), Marceau, Desjardins, Décary, July 14, 1993. Reported: *Ahmed v. Canada (Minister of Employment and Immigration)* (1993), 156 N.R. 221 (F.C.A.), at 223-224. See also for example: *M.E.I. v. Sharbdeen, Mohammed Faroudeen* (F.C.A., no. A-488-93), Mahoney, MacGuigan, Linden, March 21, 1994. Reported: *Canada (Minister of Employment and Immigration) v. Sharbdeen* (1994), 23 Imm. L.R. (2d) 300 (F.C.A.) (although this issue appears to be considered under reasonableness); *Nadarajah, Sivasothy Nathan v. M.E.I.* (F.C.T.D., no. IMM-4215-93), Simpson, July 26, 1994; *Randhawa, Faheem Anwar v. S.G.C.* (F.C.T.D., no. IMM-5621-93), Rouleau, August 12, 1994; *Zetino, Rudys Francisco Mendoza v. M.C.I.* (F.C.T.D., no. IMM-6173-93), Cullen, October 13, 1994. Reported: *Zetino v. Canada (Minister of Citizenship and Immigration)* (1994), 25 Imm. L.R. (2d) 300 (F.C.T.D.) (although this issue may be considered under reasonableness); See also *Khan, Naqui Mohd v. M.C.I.* (F.C.T.D., no. IMM-4127-01), Rothstein, July 26, 2002, where the court found that the localized nature of the Claimants activities and the region's legal system supported the panel's finding of an IFA outside of that region. In *Siddiq, Dawood v. M.C.I.* (F.C., no. IMM-1684-03), Harrington, March 31, 2004; 2004 FC 490, the Court found that a failure to address the question of persecution by national authorities when considering an internal flight alternative is a reviewable error.

[232] *Singh, Harminder v. M.C.I.* (F.C`. no. IMM-4333-13), Gleason, March 20, 2014; 2014 FC 269.

agents of persecution are the central authority in
the country does not necessarily prevent a
finding that there is an IFA.[233]
e.   If an individual had to remain in hiding to
avoid problems, this would not be evidence of an

---

[233] *Saini, Makhan Singh v. M.E.I.* (F.C.A., no. A-750-91), Mahoney,
Stone, Linden, March 22, 1993. Reported: *Saini v. Canada (Minister of
Employment and Immigration)* (1993), 151 N.R. 239 (F.C.A.), leave to
appeal to the S.C.C. denied: *Saini v. M.E.I.* (S.C.C., no. 23619),
Lamer, McLachlin, Major), August 12, 1993. Reported: *Saini v.
Canada (Minister of Employment and Immigration)* (1993), 158 N.R. 300
(S.C.C.). See also for example: *Sidhu, Jadgish Singh v. M.E.I.* (F.C.T.D.,
no. 92-A-6540), Muldoon, May 31, 1993; *Badesha, Jagir Singh v. S.S.C.*
(F.C.T.D., no. A-1544-92), Wetston, January 19, 1994. Reported:
Badesha v. Canada (Secretary of State) (1994), 23 Imm. L.R. (2d) 190
(F.C.T.D.); *Uppal, Jatinder Singh v. S.S.C.* (F.C.T.D., no. A-17-93),
Wetston, January 19, 1994, affirmed: *Uppal, Jatinder Singh v. M.C.I.*
(F.C.A., no. A-42-94), Isaac, Hugessen, Décary, November 1, 1994;
Kaler, *supra*, at 9; *Karthikesu, Cumariah v. M.E.I.* (F.C.T.D., no. IMM-
2998-93), Strayer, May 26, 1994; *Guraya, Balihar Singh v. S.S.C.*
(F.C.T.D., no. IMM-4058-93), Pinard, July 8, 1994; *Balasubramaniam,
Veergathy v. M.C.I.* (F.C.T.D., no. IMM-1902-93), McKeown,
October 4, 1994; *Dhillon, Inderjit Kaur v. M.C.I.* (F.C.T.D., no. IMM-
2652-94), McKeown, February 1, 1995; *Zamora Huerta, Erika Angelina
v. M.C.I.* (F.C., no. IMM-1985-07), Blanchard, May 8, 2008; 2008 FC
586; and *Fosu, Frank Atta v. M.C.I.* (F.C., no. IMM-935-08), Zinn,
October 8, 2008; 2008 FC 1135. In *Idris, Omer Mahmoud Hussein v.
M.C.I.* (F.C. no. IMM-2321-18), Brown, January 9, 2019; 2019 FC 24
the Court held that an IFA was viable despite the fact the Claimant
had been targeted by the Sudanese security forces. He was targeted
to spy on the customers in his shop and now that the shop was
closed, there was no reason for the security forces to be interested in
him.

In *Sharbdeen, supra*, in quashing the CRDD decision, the Court cited
Saini and stated that in order to find a viable IFA in a part of the
country controlled by the same army who was persecuting the
Claimant, it would require an evidentiary basis. *Saini* has been
distinguished in *Singh, Sucha v. M.E.I.* (F.C.T.D., no. 93-A-91), Dubé,
June 23, 1993, where the Court held that the CRDD's conclusion
that an IFA existed because there was not a nation-wide campaign
against the Claimant's ethnic group did not satisfy the criteria for
finding an IFA as established in *Rasaratnam, supra*.

IFA.[234] Similarly, if a person has to hide their
sexual orientation in order to be safe, the IFA is
not available.[235]

f.   The presence of close relatives in the putative
IFA, and the duration of previous residence and
past employment there, may have a bearing on
"whether or not it is 'objectively reasonable' for
the Claimant to live in … [the IFA] without fear
of persecution", rather than being matters merely
of personal comfort or convenience.[236]

g.   There is some lack of clarity concerning how
the concept of cumulative harassment or
cumulative grounds applies in the consideration
of IFA.[237] In *Karthikesu*, the Court appears to find

---

[234] *Murillo Taborda, Lissed v. M.C.I.* (F.C., no. IMM-9365-12), Kane,
September 17, 2013; 2013 FC 957; *Zaytoun, Hussein v. M.C.I.* (F.C.,
no. IMM-1769-14), Mactavish, October 2, 2014; 2014 FC 939; and
Ehondor, Tosan Erhun v. M.C.I. (F.C., no. IMM-2372-17), Brown,
December 14, 2017; 2017 FC 1143.

[235] *Fosu, Frank Atta v. M.C.I.* (F.C., no. IMM-935-08), Zinn, October
8, 2008; 2008 FC 1135. The Fosu decision was cited with approval in
Akpojiyovwi, Evelyn Oboaguonona v. M.C.I. (F.C. no. IMM-200-18),
Roussel, July 17, 2018; 2018 FC 745 at paragraph 9. Also, it is not
reasonable for the Board to suggest that the Claimant should avoid
contact with family member in the IFA to avoid the risk of being
located: *I.M.P.P. v. M.C.I.* (F.C., no. IMM-4049-09), Mosley, March
9, 2010; 2010 FC 259.

[236] *Kulanthavelu, Gnanasegaram v. M.E.I.* (F.C.T.D., no. IMM-57-93),
Gibson, December 3, 1993, at 5-6. In *Losowa Osengosengo, Victorine v.
M.C.I.* (F.C., no. IMM-4132-13), Gagné, March 13, 2014; 2014 FC
244, the Court found that it was unreasonable for the RPD to find
that the Claimant, a nun, could find an IFA in Kinshasa where she
had family and could make a living as a teacher. The Court found
that it was legitimate for the Claimant, as a nun, to insist upon living
among her congregation as her religious duty. Evidence that she
could seek refuge with her family members should not have been
determinative for the Board.

[237] *Karthikesu, Cumariah v. M.E.I.* (F.C.T.D., no. IMM-2998-93),

that experiences in the non-IFA area do not form part of a cumulative assessment when considering the IFA area. In *Balasubramaniam*, however, the Court suggests that depending on the tribunal's other findings "… it [the tribunal] may or may not have to consider the question of the cumulative effect of all the incidents that occurred to the applicant at the hands of the Sri Lankan armed forces to determine whether these, together with the likelihood of continuing harassment at the hands of the authorities, might constitute persecution on a cumulative basis."(Emphasis added). This statement seems to suggest that experiences in the non-IFA area can form part of a cumulative assessment when considering the IFA area.

h.　　Large urban areas cannot be assumed to be an IFA by virtue of their population size alone.[238]

i.　　The fact that a putative location was "far away", would not, without more, constitute a viable IFA.[239]

Reasonable in All the Circumstances

The second prong of the IFA test may be stated as follows: would it be unduly harsh to expect the Claimant to move to another, less hostile part

---

Strayer, May 26, 1994, *Balasubramaniam, Veergathy v. M.C.I.* (F.C.T.D., no. IMM-1902-93), McKeown, October 4, 1994.

[238] *Reynoso, Edith Isabel Guardian v. M.C.I.* (F.C.T.D., no. IMM-2110-94), Muldoon, January 29, 1996; *Sanno, Aminata v. M.C.I.* (F.C.T.D., no. IMM-2124-95), Tremblay-Lamer, April 25, 1996.

[239] *Cadena Ramirez, Francisco José v. M.C.I.* (F.C., no. IMM-5911-09), Rennie, December 20, 2010; 2010 FC 1276.

of the country before seeking refugee status abroad?[240]

The test is an objective one: is it objectively reasonable to expect the Claimant to seek safety in a different part of the country? *Thirunavukkarasu*[241] sets a very high threshold for what makes an IFA unreasonable in all the circumstances. The hardship associated with dislocation and relocation is not the kind of undue hardship that renders an IFA unreasonable. The standard is high and requires proof of adverse conditions which would jeopardize the life and safety of the Claimant in travelling to and in living in the IFA location.[242]

An IFA cannot be speculative or theoretical only; it must be a realistic, attainable option. The Claimant cannot be required to encounter great

---

[240] *Thirunavukkarasu, supra.*

[241] *Ibid.*

[242] *Ranganathan v. Canada (Minister of Citizenship and Immigration),* (F.C.A., no. A-348-99), Létourneau, Sexton, Malone, December 21, 2000; [2001] 2 F.C. 164 (C.A.). In *Sikiratu Iyile, Sandra v. M.C.I.* (F.C., no. IMM-6609-10), Harrington, July 25, 2011; 2011 FC 928, the Court rejected the Claimant's argument that it would be inhumane to send her back to Lagos, to return her to a life of begging and prostitution. The Court noted this is a situation in which any young uneducated female might find herself in a big city. It does not give rise to a refugee claim. It agreed with the RPD that although she professed that she had no knowledge of help available in Lagos from NGOs, she now had the knowledge and these organizations can help to find her shelter and employment.

CHARLES MWEWA

physical danger or to undergo undue hardship in travelling there or staying there.[243] However, it is not enough for the Claimant to say that he or she does not like the weather there, or that he or she has no friends or relatives there, or that he or she may not be able to find suitable work there.[244]

A distinction must be maintained between the reasonableness of an IFA and humanitarian and compassionate considerations. The fact that a Claimant might be better off in Canada, physically, economically and emotionally than in a safe place in his own country is *not* a factor to consider in assessing the reasonableness of the IFA.[245]

Regarding the issue of "reasonable in all the circumstances," the Court of Appeal has stated that the circumstances must be relevant to the

---

[243] Thirunavukkarasu, supra, footnote 3. In applying the principle set out in Thirunavukkarasu that the IFA must be an area that is realistically attainable, the Court in *Playasova, Liudmila Fedor v. M.C.I.* (F.C., no. IMM-3931-02), Martineau, July 18, 2003; 2003 FC 901 stated that the failure of the RPD to consider that the Claimant could only relocate to the IFA if she had the means to pay bribes to obtain a Propiska was an error. In *Dubravac, Petar v. M.C.I.* (F.C.T.D., no. IMM-839-94), Rothstein, February 1, 1995. Reported: *Dubravac v. Canada (Minister of Citizenship and Immigration)* (1995), 29 Imm. L.R. (2d) 55 (F.C.T.D.), where the Claimant's hometown had been surrounded by opposing Serbian forces, the Court commented that they "would not be required to go from their hometown to the safe zone of Croatia, but ... from wherever they were relanded upon being sent back."
[244] *Thirunavukkarasu, supra.*
[245] *Ranganathan, supra.*

IFA question. They cannot be catalogued in the abstract. They will vary from case to case.[246]

The Federal Court has provided the following general guidance:

a. The test is a flexible one that takes into account the particular situation of the Claimant and the particular country involved.[247] The evidence, before the Refugee Division, of circumstances in the IFA must be more than general information and must be relevant to the Claimant's specific circumstances.[248]

---

[246] *Sharbdeen, supra.*

[247] See for example: *Thirunavukkarasu, supra.*; *Rasaratnam, supra.*; *Fernando, Joseph Stanley v. M.E.I.* (F.C.T.D., no. 92-A-6986), McKeown, May 19, 1993; *Abubakar, supra.*; *Megag, Sahra Abdilahi v. M.E.I.* (F.C.T.D., no. A-822-92), Rothstein, December 10, 1993; *Chkiaou, Dimitri v. M.C.I.* (F.C.T.D., no., IMM-266-94), Cullen, March 7, 1995; and *Sanno, supra.* In *Yoganathan, Kandasamy v. M.C.I.* (F.C.T.D., no. IMM-3588-97), Gibson, April 20, 1998, the Court noted that, in assessing the reasonableness of the IFA, the CRDD must look at the personal circumstances of the Claimant and it is insufficient to simply assess whether the Claimant fits the "most at risk profile." In *Cartagena, Wilber Orlando v. M.C.I.* (F.C., no. IMM-961-06), Mosley, March 4, 2008; 2008 FC 289, the Court noted that the Board failed to take into account the Claimant's vulnerable mind-set; and in *Calderon, Sonia Blancas v. M.C.I.* (F.C., no. IMM-5367-08), Near, March 8, 2010; 2010 FC 263, the Court noted that it was unduly harsh and unreasonable for the RPD to hold that the Claimant had a viable IFA as long as she never attempted to re-secure custody of her young children from her abusive ex-husband.

[248] See for example: *Singh, Sucha v. M.E.I.* (F.C.T.D., no. 93-A-91), Dubé, June 23, 1993; *Kahlon; supra.*; *Dhaliwal, Jasbir Singh v. M.E.I.* (F.C.T.D., no. 93-A-364), MacKay, August 9, 1993; *Singh, Swarn v. M.E.I.* (F.C.T.D., no. A-1409-92), Rothstein, May 4, 1994. In *Thevasagayam, Ebenezer Thevaraj v. M.C.I.* (F.C.T.D., no. IMM-252-97), Tremblay-Lamer, October 23, 1997, the evidence of past detention

b. *Psychological evidence*[249] is central to the question of whether an IFA is reasonable and cannot be disregarded.[250]

c. The regional conditions which would make an IFA reasonable must be considered.[251]

---

and torture of the Claimant in relation to a Colombo bombing cast doubt on the reasonableness of an IFA. In *Premanathan, Gopalasamy v. M.C.I.* (F.C.T.D., no. IMM-4423-96), Simpson, August 29, 1997, it was noted that random roundups and routine reporting requirements do not make IFA unreasonable. In *Kaillyapillai, Srivasan v. M.C.I.* (F.C.T.D., no. IMM-1263-96), Richard, February 27, 1997, the Court found no IFA in Colombo for a Claimant who had been arrested, beaten and released and told to leave Colombo. In *Masalov, Sergey v. M.C.I.* (F.C., no. IMM-7207-13), Diner, March 4, 2015; 2015 FC 277, the Court found that it was unreasonable to expect the applicants to relocate to the proposed IFA. The principal applicant had attempted to relocate to Kazan but could only obtain temporary residence for three or four days because he was unable to obtain a Propiska registration. The documentary evidence listed the cascading effects of an inability to register and how it operates as an invitation for harassment by the authorities. Also, expecting an elderly couple to endure persistent police harassment is unreasonable, as it implicates their safety within the IFA.

[249] Emphasis added.

[250] Cartagena, supra. See also *Okafor, Sara v. M.C.I.* (F.C., no. IMM-6848-10), Beaudry, August 17, 2011; 2011 FC 1002. In *Kauhonina, Claretha v. M.C.I.* (F.C. no. IMM-2459-18), Diner, December 21, 2018; 2018 FC 1300 the Court quashed an RPD decision wherein it found there to be a viable IFA in Namibia for the Claimant. The Court held that the Board did not engage with the psychiatric report which set out her mental health issues and treatment she had been receiving at a major hospital in Toronto over two years. The Board also did not acknowledge her profile as a single mother of two young children.

[251] In *Idrees, Muhammad v. M.C.I.* (F.C., no. IMM-4136-13), Diner, December 10, 2014; 2014 FC 1194, the Court found that the RPD failed to consider the applicant's risk of ethnic violence in determining whether it was reasonable for him, an ethnic Pashtun, to seek refuge in Karachi. In *Chand, Mool v. M.C.I.* (F.C., no. IMM-61-14), Rennie, February 19, 2015; 2015 FC 212, the RPD was faulted

d.   The presence or absence of family in the IFA is a factor in assessing reasonableness,[252] especially in the case of Claimants who are minor.[253] However, the absence of relatives in an IFA would have to jeopardize the safety of a Claimant before that factor would make an IFA unreasonable.[254]

e.   A destroyed infrastructure and economy in the IFA, and the stability or instability of the government that is in place there, are relevant factors.[255] Instability alone is not the test of

---

with ignoring evidence of acts of violence and forced conversions against Hindus in finding that it was reasonable for the Claimants to relocate to Karachi. In two cases involving Colombians and the finding that Bogota would constitute a safe IFA, the Court stated that the RPD ignored evidence that internally displaced persons (IDP) in Colombia lead a fragile and vulnerable existence and that they face life in overcrowded slums where they experience violations of their fundamental human rights. See *Arias Ultima, Angela Maria v. M.C.I.* (F.C., no. IMM-3984-12), Manson, January 25, 2013; 2013 FC 81; and *Barragan Gonzalez, Julio Angelo v. M.C.I.* (F.C., no. IMM-6335-13), Boswell, April 20, 2015; 2015 FC 502.

[252] *Ranganathan, supra.*

[253] The absence of family in an IFA is relevant to determining the unreasonableness of requiring a child to live there. *Elmi, Mahamud Hussein v. M.E.I.* (F.C.T.D., no. IMM-580-98), McKeown, March 12, 1999. Similarly, in *Hassan, Liban v. M.E.I.* (F.C.T.D., no. IMM-3634-98), Campbell, April 14, 1999, the Court found that in the case of a minor, an IFA cannot be reasonable unless proper settlement arrangements are made.

[254] *Ranganathan, supra.* As the Court put it: "The absence of relatives in a safe place, whether taken alone or in conjunction with other factors, can only amount to such condition if it meets that threshold, that is to say if it establishes that, as a result, a Claimant's life or safety would be jeopardized. This is in sharp contrast with undue hardship resulting from loss of employment, loss of status, reduction in quality of life, loss of aspirations, loss of beloved ones and frustration of one's wishes and expectations."

[255] *Farrah, Sahra Said v. M.E.I.* (F.C.T.D., no. A-694-92), Reed,

reasonableness,[256] nor is a disintegrating infrastructure.[257]

f.   An IFA is not reasonable if it requires the perpetuation of human rights abuses.[258]

October 5, 1993, at 3. Regarding stability, see also *Tawfik, Taha Mohammed v. M.E.I.* (F.C.T.D., no. 93-A-311), MacKay, August 23, 1993. Reported: *Tawfik v. Canada (Minister of Employment and Immigration)* (1993), 26 Imm. L.R. (2d) 148 (F.C.T.D.).

[256] *Megag, supra.* This case was relied on in *Muhammed, Falululla, Peer v. M.C.I.* (F.C. no., IMM-5122-11), Harrington, February 17, 2012; 2012 FC 226. The Court noted that [I]t was submitted that it would be unreasonable to have Mr. Peer Muhammed relocate in the east because, although not as ravaged as other parts of the country in the civil war, there are unexploded landmines and the infrastructure leaves much to be desired. However, this is a situation facing millions of Sri Lankans, Sinhalese and Tamils alike, be they Buddhist, Hindu, Christian or Muslim."

[257] *Rumb, Serge v. M.E.I.* (F.C.T.D., no. IMM-1481-98), Reed, February 12, 1999. The Court held that, "[I]nsofar as the IFA is concerned, a disintegrating infrastructure is not equivalent to a dessert, or to a battle zone. In the first place, one must be careful when comparing the infrastructures of countries that the standard of our own is not held up as the required standard. There are many countries where telephones do not work well or all the time, where the roads are very, very poor, where electricity only works at certain times. These conditions are not such however, that a person can say they cannot live in that country because it is not practical (reasonable) to do so. The Board was not in error in failing to assess the deteriorating infrastructure as a reason the applicant could not live in Kinshasa or elsewhere in the Congo."

[258] *Mimica, Milanka v. M.C.I.* (F.C.T.D., no. IMM-3014-95), Rothstein, June 19, 1996, the Claimant could only find accommodation in the IFA, the Serbian controlled part of Bosnia, if the current Muslim residents of the area were forcibly expelled because of their religion/ethnicity to make room for returning Serbian refugees. The Court held that making accommodation available to the Claimant would be as a result of human rights abuses to other residents and that this could not be the basis of a finding of a viable internal flight alternative.

g.   Hardship in accessing the IFA must be assessed.[259]

h.   In gender-based claims, the Board must have regard to section C4 of the Gender Guidelines.[260]

---

[259] In *Hashmat, Suhil v. M.C.I.* (F.C.T.D., no. IMM-2331-96), Teitelbaum, May 9, 1997, the Claimant could only access the IFA in northern Afghanistan by going through the neighbouring state of Uzbekistan. The Court found it unreasonable for the panel to conclude, without any evidence, that the Claimant would be allowed to cross the border. The Court also noted that the Immigration Act would not allow removal to a country that is not the Claimant's country of birth, nationality or former residence. See also *Dirshe, Safi Mohamud v. M.C.I.* (F.C.T.D., no. IMM-2124-96), Cullen, July 2, 1997, where the Court noted that a real possibility of rape while trying to get to the IFA makes it an unreasonable option. In fact, *Hashmat*, the Court found there to be undue hardship in reaching the IFA because the Claimant's wife and child, who were not Claimants, would have to travel with him to reach the IFA and there was evidence of widespread rape of women and children making that journey. In *Tahlil, Mohamed Sugule v. M.C.I.* (F.C., no. IMM-5920-10), Zinn, July 5, 2011; 2011 FC 817, the Court directed that if the applicant was removed from Canada to Somalia, he be returned directly to Bosaso and was not to travel into or through other areas of Somalia. In *Ajelal, Mustafa v. M.C.I.* (F.C., no. IMM-4522-13), Diner, November 19, 2014; 2014 FC 1093, the Court allowed the judicial review application noting that if the RPD wanted the Claimant to reach either of the two identified IFAs, it failed to state how he would avoid going through the Tripoli airport, or alternate routes to the places of supposed safe haven.
[260] *Syvyryn, Ganna v. M.C.I.* (F.C., no. IMM-1569-09), Snider, October 13, 2009; 2009 FC 1027; and *Kayumba, Bijou Kamwanga v. M.C.I.* (F.C., no. IMM-1920-09), Beaudry, February 10, 2010; 2010 FC 138. In *Agimelen Oriazouwani, Winifred v. M.C.I.* (F.C., no. IMM-6440-10), Shore, July 8, 2011; 2011 FC 827, the RPD's finding that an IFA existed did not take into account the specific evidence as to the unreasonableness of the IFA for the applicant and her two minor children especially in light of the Chairperson's Gender Guidelines. The RPD failed to consider the contradictory documentary evidence regarding female genital mutilation indicating that what is

i.   The Court has commented that the extent to
      which an applicant has settled in Canada is
      irrelevant to the question of whether it was
      reasonable for the applicant to relocate to an
      IFA.[261] As well, consideration of the presence of
      relatives in the country where asylum is sought is
      not relevant to the IFA test.[262]

Revocation of Jurisprudential Guide (Decision TB7-19851)

Although Nigeria is not the focus of this book,
IFA may be analyzed differently depending on
the nature of persecution and the political
construction of the country vis-à-vis the type of
agents of persecution. This is especially notable
for persons fleeing persecution from non-State
actors. Nigeria is one of the countries where IFA
is a relevant issue in most refugee claim cases.

In April 2020, IRB revoked the identification of
Decision TB7-19851 as a Jurisprudential Guide
(JG). IRB found that, "Developments in the
country of origin information related to the
Nigeria JG [had] diminished the value of the
decision as a JG."[263]

---

criminalized through legislation has not as yet become generalized in
practice in respect to tenable protection.
[261] *Utoh, supra.*
[262] *Smirnova, Svetlana v. M.C.I.* (FC., no. IMM-6641-12), Noël, April
12 2013; 2013 FC 347.
[263] IRB, "Notice of Revocation of a Jurisprudential Guide," <
https://irb-cisr.gc.ca/en/news/2020/Pages/notice-revocation-

In Nigeria, RPD required that a Claimant who feared persecution in one part of the country, say in Abuja, should exhaust all other cities where they could be free from persecution within Nigeria, say Port Harcourt, before seeking for refugee protection in Canada. That was the *ratio* in TB7-19851 rendered by RPD Member, Gamble, on May 17th, 2018. The decision found that, based on the documentary evidence available at the time, there were several large cities in Nigeria that might, depending on the facts of the case, serve as viable IFAs for persons fleeing non-State actors.

The IRB determined that, TB7-19851 is no longer binding but is still persuasive. In other words, it is identified as a RAD Reasons of Interest (RROI).

TB7-19851 will, therefore, be used as persuasive decision for determining the issue of IFA in Nigeria. Nigeria, unlike Iran where IFA is not available owing to the fact that the same State apparatus control the entire country, is a federation of different States. As such, there might be an IFA, "...in major cities in south and central Nigeria for Claimants fleeing non-State actors."[264]

---

jurisprudential-guide.aspx> (Retrieved: April 30th, 2020)
[264] *Ibid.*

141

CHARLES MWEWA

IRB further determined that, "Developments in the country of origin information, including those in relation to the ability of *single women* to relocate to the various internal flight alternatives proposed in the Nigeria jurisprudential guide, [had] diminished the value of the decision as a jurisprudential guide"[265] (emphasis added). Accordingly, as of April 6th, 2020 the identification of TB7-19851 as a JG was revoked. The decision, though, remains a persuasive RROI for future determinations.

An important note to the reader, this revocation does not preclude the RPD and the RAD from considering IFA in refugee claims for Nigerians. If raised at the hearing, either through intensive questioning or counsel's submissions, the Claimant is still required to fully answer and defend their claims with regards to IFA.

IFA for Nigerian Claimants is still persuasive and the adjudicator may consider the availability of IFA in the context of the case presented. Counsel and the Claimant should prepare for this aspect of the refugee determination and be ready to provide answer if asked.

---

[265] *Ibid.*

CHAPTER 9
RELIGIOUS AND CHRISTIAN
MINORITIES IN IRAN

The IRB publishes country-specific
information about different countries.
IRB adjudicators rely on this information
in the RDS. The National Documentation
Package (NDP), as the document is known,
assists the RPD in accessing the objective basis
of the Claimants' fear of persecution in their own
country of origin. The BOC narrative, which
highlights the subjective basis of fear of
persecution, must align with the NDP.

For the NDP to be efficacious, it must be the
latest one published at the IRB website.
Information change, and the IRB updates
country-specific information from time to time.
Counsel should ensure that she is relying on the
recommended NDP for that particular period,
which must be disclosed to the Claimant by the
RPD before the hearing.

The NDP is created to provide additional
assessment criteria in determining refugee or
other asylum-based claims. It documents *Country
of Origin Information* (COI) and policy guidance to
RPD adjudicators on handling refugee claims.
The information contained in the NDP is

necessary to justify the finding that the Claimant has founded fear of persecution in their country of citizenship or former habitual residence. Conversely, the NDP provides the certification of claims which may be "Clearly Unfounded" pursuant to s. 94 of the *Nationality, Immigration and Asylum Act* 2002.

Decision-makers must consider claims on an individual basis, taking into account the case specific facts and all relevant evidence, including: The policy guidance; the available COI; any applicable caselaw; and the Home Office casework guidance in relation to relevant policies.[266]

In this chapter, the following topics will be covered, adopted in part or in whole, from CPIN:[267] Iran's general religious demography;, including: Numbers of Christians in Iran; estimated number of "born" Christians in Iran; number of Iranian Christian converts – both from within and outside of Iran; house churches in Iran; legal framework on religious minorities; treatment of Christians in Iran (including arrest, detention and prosecution of Christians); and treatment of returning Christians to Iran; and etc.

---

[266] CPIN, "Iran: Christians and Christian converts," March 2018, p. 2
[267] CPIN, "Country Policy and Information Note. Iran: Christians and Christian converts," March 2020

In addition to the above, information on religious minority predating 2015 will be highlighted. The rationale is to give the prospective Claimant the necessary background and context under which persecution of Iranian religious minorities happens. It is important to note, however, that the RPD will only consider current information on Iran in its determination of a refugee claim.

The NDP for Iran vis-à-vis religious persecution based on the document produced by CPIN dubbed, "Country Policy and Information Note. Iran: Christians and Christian converts,"[268] is reproduced below, with minor modifications and emphases. The reader can find more useful information on religion in Iran at the IRB website[269] as well as under the *Useful Sources* section of this book.[270]

Christianity in Iran

The Central Intelligence Agency (CIA) World Factbook, noted that Iran has an estimated population of 83,024,745 million (July 2018 est.). A 2011 estimate by the same source states that

---

[268] CPIN, *ibid.*

[269] See specifically: < https://irb-cisr.gc.ca/en/country-information/ndp/Pages/index.aspx?pid=10448> (Retrieved: April 30th, 2020)

[270] See page 352 of this book.

99.4 percent of the population are Muslim (Shia 90-95 percent, Sunni 5-10 percent), 0.3 percent are 'other' religions (including Zoroastrian, Jewish and Christian) and 0.4 percent of the population are an 'unspecified religion.'[271] UN data from 2016 suggested that there are 79,598,054 Muslims in Iran, 9,826 Jews and 23,109 Zoroastrians.[272]

A 2013 International Campaign for Human Rights in Iran (ICHRI) report cited the World Christian Database (WCD) in 2010 as having reported approximately 66,700 Protestant Christians in Iran, which represent[ed] about 25 percent of the Iranian Christian community.'[273]

UN data from 2011 suggested that the number of Christians in Iran was 117,704.[274] The same source put the 2016 figure at 130,158.[275] Open Doors, interviewed by the UK Home Office on 8 August 2017, stated that many converts do not publicly report their faith due to persecution, so it is difficult to record the exact numbers of Iranian Christian converts. Open Doors believes the number to be 800,000, although this is a conservative estimate. Other estimates put the

---

[271] CIA World Factbook, "Iran –people and society," last updated April 3rd, 2019
[272] UN Statistics Division
[273] ICHRI, 'The Cost of Faith ...',16 January 2013
[274] UN Statistics Division
[275] *Ibid.*

number between 400,000-500,000 right up to 3 million.[276]

The US State Department's Religious Freedom Report for 2018, covering events in 2017 ('the USSD IRF report for 2017') noted the differing estimates of Christians in Iran. They cite different sources as quoting figures ranging from 117,700 to 300-350,000 or up to as many as one million.[277] An October 2018 *Christian Post* article,[278] also cited the Open Doors estimate[279] of nearly 800,000 Christians in Iran. A March 2019 US Congressional Research Service report on Iran put the figure at 'about 300,000.'[280]

The USSD IRF report for events in 2017 stated that: 'The constitution defines the country as an Islamic Republic, and Ja'afari Shia Islam to be the official State religion." The constitution stipulates all laws and regulations must be based on "Islamic criteria" and official interpretation of sharia. The constitution states citizens shall enjoy all human, political, economic, social, and

---

[276] Open Doors, "Interview with CPIT, UK Home Office," August 8th, 2017
[277] USSD, "International Religious Freedom Report for 2017," May 29th, 2018
[278] *Christian Post*, "Iran is witnessing 'One of fastest growing church movements," October 16th, 2018
[279] Open Doors, "World Watch List," u/d
[280] US CRS, "Iran: Internal Politics and U.S. Policy and Options," March 6th, 2019

cultural rights, "in conformity with Islamic criteria."

The constitution states the investigation of an individual's ideas is forbidden, and no one may be "subjected to questioning and aggression for merely holding an opinion." The law prohibits Muslim citizens from changing or renouncing their religious beliefs. The only recognized conversions are from another religion to Islam. Apostasy from Islam is a crime punishable by death. Under the law, a child born to a Muslim father is considered to be Muslim.

By law, non-Muslims may not engage in public persuasion or attempted conversion of Muslims. These activities are considered proselytizing and punishable by death. In addition, citizens who are not recognized as Christians, Zoroastrians, or Jews may not engage in public religious expression, such as worshiping in a church, or wearing religious symbols such as a cross. Some exceptions are made for foreigners belonging to unrecognized religious groups.

'The *Penal Code* specifies the death sentence for *moharebeh* (enmity against God), fisad fil-arz ("corruption on earth," which includes apostasy or heresy), and sabb al-nabi ("insulting the prophets" or "insulting the sanctities"). According to the *Penal Code*, the application of the death penalty varies depending on the religion of both the perpetrator and the victim.'[281]

For a review commissioned by the Independent Advisory Group on Country Information (IAGCI), Dr. Rebwar Fatah of Middle East Consultancy Services stated in November 2019 that while Articles 186, 187, 189 and 190 of the *Penal Code* define the profile of a person who qualifies as "moharebeh," a tangible description of what acts are encompassed by the term is not given. This has resulted in various confusions as to what should be considered a crime of moharebeh. This has led to an emphasis on interpretation so that adjustments can be made on an ad hoc basis. As such, Judges and those in authority are given more power to discriminate with impunity.[282]

Religious Minorities

The USSD IRF report for 2017 explained that Citizens who are members of one of the recognized religious minorities [Zoroastrians, Jews, and Christians] must register with the

---

[281] USSD, "International Religious Freedom Report for 2017," May 29th, 2018
[282] Dr. Rebwar Fatah, Middle East Consultancy Services, November 2019. Available on request

authorities. Registration conveys certain rights, including the use of alcohol for religious purposes. Failure of churchgoers to register and attendance at churches by unregistered individuals may subject a church to closure and arrest of its leaders by the authorities.[283] Furthermore, the report states that any citizen who is not a registered member of one of these three groups, or who cannot prove that his or her family was Christian prior to 1979, is considered Muslim.[284]

Christian Converts

The USSD IRF for 2017 further stated:

> Since the law prohibits citizens from converting from Islam to another religion, the government only recognizes the Christianity of citizens who are Armenian or Assyrian Christians, since the presence of these groups in the country predates Islam, or of citizens who can prove they or their families were Christian prior to the 1979 revolution. The government also recognizes Sabean-Mandaeans as Christian, even though the Sabean-Mandaeans do not consider themselves as such [...] The government does not recognize evangelical Protestants as Christian. '[...] Individuals who convert to Christianity are not recognized as Christians under the law. They may not register and are not entitled to the same

---

[283] USSD, "International Religious Freedom Report for 2017," May 29th, 2018
[284] *Ibid.*

rights as recognized members of Christian communities.[285]

Conversions in Europe

A fact-finding mission (FFM) report published in February 2013 by the Danish Immigration Service (DIS), Danish Refugee Council (DRC) and Norwegian Landinfo service interviewed several sources about Christians. The report stated that a number of Iranians had travelled to Turkey, Armenia and Azerbaijan in order to be baptized.[286]

The same report further noted:

> However, the source [an elder from the International Protestant Church of Ankara] stated that there are also many Iranians who come to Turkey in order to get baptized. He mentioned an event in Konya about two years ago when 50 people had been baptized over a weekend by an American pastor who flew in from Las Vegas. The source said that this pastor had issued certificates of baptism to people he did not know. According to an elder from the International Protestant Church of Ankara, such baptism events that include large numbers of people take place "all the time" in Turkey. There are a lot of conferences in Istanbul where people, including many Iranians, get baptized after attending for 1-2 days. 'An elder from the

---

[285] *Ibid.*
[286] DIS, DRC and Landinfo, FFM Report, February 2013

International Protestant Church of Ankara
further informed the delegation that in his
church (in Ankara), it would take a 22-week
course of introduction to the Christian faith
prior to being baptized. According to the source,
his church is running 2-3 courses per year with
20 persons in each class. He added that
approximately half of the individuals signing up
complete the course, and mentioned that in the
latest class, only five out of 20 finished.
Concerning those who are baptized, a small
amount has returned to Iran, most have gone to
another country and the rest have stayed in
Turkey.'[287] An August 2017 article by Kurdish
media company, Rudaw, reported on some 500
Christian converts who had sought asylum in
Turkey. The article explained 'Of those Rudaw
talked to in Turkey's Van, close to the Iranian
border —all Kurds —none revealed their name
and some chose not to appear on camera for fear
of reprisals.[...]He said that hundreds of Kurdish
youth in Iran have abandoned Islam and
embraced Christianity.[288]

The same Rudaw article added that there are
about 1,500 Kurdish asylum seekers in Van,
some of whom cite political, ethnic, or cultural
reasons as their impetus to leave Iran. But nearly
500 of them have converted to Christianity.

The majority of the people Rudaw talked to want
to go to the United States or Canada, while
others are hoping to go to Europe.'[289] A

---

[287] *Ibid.*
[288] Rudaw, "Christian converts leave Iran for Turkey, claiming
persecution," August 14th, 2017
[289] *Ibid.*

December 2018 article by National Public Radio (NPR) reported on a rise in the number of Iranians converting to evangelical Christianity in Turkey, with one reason for converting being due to the way Iran's interpretation of Islam treats women.[290] The author of a January 2019 article in the Journal of Eurasian Studies stated 'After more than 10 years of interval, I revisited the churches and the community in Istanbul again in 2016. It seems that within the years, the number of people especially in the Pentecostal Church in Istanbul increased tremendously. A former Iranian refugee resettled in the United States from Turkey returned to Istanbul with his family and is now leading the community. On a typical Sunday afternoon mass, there are now more than 70–80 people compared with an average of 25–30 people earlier.[291] And that in Turkey, there are no reliable statistics for converted cases. Iranian converts usually get together at different churches for Sunday sermons and community-building. These are Pentecostal Church of the Iranians, the Union Church, the Anglican Church in Istanbul, the Protestant Church in Ankara, and a house-church in Van and Denizli.[292] An October 2018

---

[290] NPR, "Iranians are converting to Evangelical Christianity in Turkey," December 14th, 2018
[291] S.K Akcapar, "Religious conversions in forced migration," January 10th, 2019
[292] *Ibid.*

article by Advancing Native Missions (ANM) reported on a number of Iranians converting to Christianity while in Serbia.[293]

World Watch Monitor noted in July 2017 that thousands of Iranian asylum-seekers across Europe are turning to Christianity, though observers are not convinced that all claims of conversion are genuine. A BBC documentary, 'Praying for Asylum', tells the story of a number of Iranian asylum-seekers in the Netherlands who say they have become Christians and would be exposed to persecution if they were deported. 'Iranian-born church leader Masoud Mohammad Amin, who founded Cyrus Church, one of largest Iranian churches in Europe, said he had baptized thousands of Iranians, from the streets of Paris to Turkey. [...] He said the church, in the Dutch city of Harderwijk, has been so successful that "8,000 people in the Netherlands and 8,000 people outside the country have been baptized." However, a Dutch pastor interviewed, Gijs van den Brink, who baptizes around 25 people a year, said he had been approached by some people whose motives he doubted. He said that if someone asks to be baptized on his first visit to his church, which is east of Utrecht, "then I know enough; I know that he has a case and that he is searching for baptism ...and I explain [to] him that it will not help him ... because our

---

[293] ANM, "Iranians become Christian in Serbia," October 18th, 2018

government is not mad: they can easily come to
know if you are a real believer or not...We're not
a group who is helping refugees to get asylum
here.'[294] *Fox News* reported in March 2017 that
Christianity is making a comeback in Europe –
and it's mostly thanks to Muslims, say experts in
Islam and faith leaders. A soaring number of
Muslims, many of them refugees from Syria, Iraq
and Afghanistan, are converting to Christianity,
breathing new life into Europe's once
floundering Christian churches. The Muslims are
flocking to various Christian denominations,
experts said, including becoming Protestants,
evangelical or Catholic. As many parts of Europe
are becoming more secular and houses of
worship are seeing congregants leave in droves, it
is Muslim converts who are reviving struggling
Christian churches.[295]

The Independent reported in December 2016 that
more and more refugees are converting from
Islam to Christianity as they settle in Germany,
churches have said. [...] Some of the new
converts were first introduced to Christianity in
Germany or en route to Europe, while others
had previously attempted to follow the religion

---

[294] *World Watch Monitor*, "Thousands' of Iranians claiming asylum in
Europe," July 19th, 2017
[295] *Fox News*, "Muslim converts breathe new life into Europe's
Christian churches', March 21st, 2017

in countries like Iran, where the faith is restricted or persecuted. 'There is concern that some conversions could be motivated by the belief that it will increase the chance of being granted asylum in Germany, where Christianity is the dominant religion.[296]

House Churches

Rise of the House Church

In February 2018, the Danish Immigration Service and the Danish Refugee Council (DRC) released a joint report ('the February 2018 joint DIS-DRC report') based on interviews conducted in September and October 2017 in Iran, Turkey and the United Kingdom. Within that report they explained how 'One source noted that house churches are quite common in Iran and their numbers are growing.'[297] An October 2018 *Christian Post* article noted that, "Iranian Christians are witnessing one of the 'fastest growing underground church movements.'"[298]

The February 2018 joint DIS-DRC report also reported that, "According to the source, the increasing number of house churches show that

---

[296] *The Independent*, "Muslim refugees are converting to Christianity in Germany," December 2016
[297] DIS-DRC, "Joint Report," February 2018
[298] *Christian Post*, October 16th, 2018

they have space to operate, even though they are illegal."[299]

The ACCORD query response on 'Iran: House churches; situation of practicing Christians; treatment by authorities of Christian converts family members' dated March 2017 quoted an email response from a representative of Elam Ministries and provided the following comments on the structure of house churches in Iran:

> [D]ue to the underground nature of these house churches, the structure is not uniform across the country. Some house churches are very informal and are simply a gathering of close family and friends on a regular or semi-regular basis for prayer, worship and bible reading. These may be very small groups (a couple of people, for example) or larger (a couple of dozen or more perhaps). Often house churches grow organically as new Christians share their new faith with family and friends. Many house churches will have no formal links with any other Christian groups. However, some house churches are part of house church 'networks' within a particular city or area, or some networks even span across a number of cities.

Some house churches have leaders who have been able to receive training and teaching from Christian ministries (either online or in person through residential courses provided outside of

---

[299] DIS-DRC, *supra.*

Iran), whilst other house church leaders may
have had no opportunity to receive training at all.
An increasing number of house churches have
"Internet pastors." where the pastor has had to
flee the country due to persecution, they may
continue to lead the church remotely via the
Internet. 'However, the pressure and persecution
on house churches in Iran means there are an
increasing number of isolated Christians in Iran.

[There are also] Christians who do not have
regular contact with other Christians. In most
cases, these isolated Christians mostly receive
their teaching via Christian TV programs, which
they can access by satellite. They may also receive
teaching and encouragement and a form of
fellowship via the Internet.[300]

Response to the Rise of House Churches

Landinfo, in their November 2017 report,
considered that:

> The reason why Iranian authorities define the
> organized house church movement to be a threat
> against national security, is that they relate the
> movement's activities to political opposition
> activities. House church meetings are conducted
> in secret, which means that the government can
> neither control who participates nor what

---

[300] ACCORD, "Iran: Query Response," June 14th, 2017

happens in the meetings. The government
therefore consider the meetings to be a potential
source of opposition activity that can threaten
the regime. Furthermore, there is contact
between many house churches and foreign
communities. This kind of Western connection is
perceived by the authorities as suspect, and as a
threat to the regime.[301]

The February 2018 joint DIS-DRC report reported that, "The authorities fear the expansion of the house churches phenomenon in Iran."[302]

The June 2018 DFAT Country Information Report on Iran also recorded "Authorities have interpreted the growth in house churches as a threat to national security. Official reports and the media have characterized house churches as "illegal networks" and "Zionist propaganda institutions."[303]

Monitoring of House Churches

The February 2018 joint DIS-DRC report also reported that:

[301] Landinfo, "Iran: Christian converts and house churches (1),"
November 27th, 2017
[302] DIS-DRC, *supra.*
[303] DFAT, "Country Information Report on Iran," June 7th, 2018

The authorities use informers to infiltrate the house churches. The infiltrators are identified and selected by the authorities. To prevent infiltration and intervention, house churches organize themselves as a mobile group consisting of a small number of people. A source mentioned that the prevention of external infiltration is difficult, as the authorities use informers who pretend to be converts. One source explained that it would be a strategy for the authorities to either monitor or arrest and release members of a house church to make an informant out of them. The authorities could use information on the person's background to put pressure on them. House churches are monitored by the authorities. If the authorities receive a report about a specific house church, a monitoring process will be initiated, one source noted. However, the authorities will not act immediately, as the authorities want to collect information about both the members and who is doing what in the community. Flourishing house churches are more in danger, as the authorities see these churches as a bigger threat. Whether the authorities will intervene depends on the activities of the house church and the size of the group. A source said that the house churches are systematically raided.[304]

And also:

One source pointed out that there has been a change in the authorities monitoring of social media and online activities. Another source added that there is a widespread monitoring of telecommunication and electronic communication if a Christian has caught the

---

[304] DIS-DRC, *supra.*

interest of the authorities. Certain keywords
serve as base for the electronic surveillance e.g.
"church", "Jesus," "Christian" and "baptism."
As it is well-known that the authorities are
tapping phones, the house members are cautious
and turn off their phones long before they reach
their meeting place."[305]

A March 2019 US Congressional Research
Service report on Iran stated, "The IRGC
[The Islamic Revolutionary Guard Corps]
scrutinizes churches and Christian religious
practice."[306]

Application of the Law in Practice

Practicing Christianity

The DFAT Country Information Report on Iran
dated June 7th, 2018, states:

> 'None of the three recognized minority religions
> proselytizes or accepts converts as members.
> Strict instructions not to minister to Iranians
> apply to the small number of Latin Catholic and
> Protestant churches in Tehran and elsewhere
> that cater to expatriates. The prohibition is
> enforced through bans on the use of Farsi in
> services; bans on Iranians attending non-Muslim
> religious facilities, including for non-religious

---

[305] *Ibid.*
[306] US CRS, "Iran: Internal Politics and U.S. Policy and Options,"
March 6th, 2019

events such as musical performances; and the regular contacting of churches by telephone by false potential converts in order to test the reactions of church officials to receiving such enquiries.

Security officials reportedly monitor registered congregation centres to verify that services are not conducted in Farsi, and perform identity checks on worshippers to confirm that non-Christians or converts do not participate in services. Authorities have closed several churches in recent years for failing to comply with these restrictions, including churches that had existed prior to 1979.[307]

The ban on holding church services in Farsi was corroborated by Open Doors' Iran profile as part of their 2020 world watch list.[308] The US State Department's Religious Freedom Report for 2018, covering events in 2017[309] noted that: "The government [...] regulated Christian religious practices closely to enforce a prohibition on proselytizing and conversion."[310] The United States Commission on International Religious Freedom (USCIRF) annual report on Iran for 2017 stated that even constitutionally recognized non-Muslim minorities, for example Armenian and Assyrian Christians, "face official harassment, intimidation, discrimination, arrests,

---

[307] DFAT, *supra.*
[308] Open Doors, "Iran," undated
[309] The 2017 USSD IRF Report
[310] USSD, "International Religious Freedom Report for 2017," May 29th, 2018

and imprisonment."[311] The Australian Institute of International Affairs published an Iran Study Tour Report in April 2018 which stated:

> Under the current Islamic regime, citizens are, at least in theory, free to practice the religion of their choice. Each religious minority is guaranteed a seat in parliament, as stipulated in Iran's constitution. However, whilst conversion to Islam is accepted and encouraged, it is illegal to convert to a different religion once one has identified as Muslim. This is considered apostasy and harsh penalties can apply. Apostasy is punishable by death in certain cases; however, the crime has never been codified in law.[312]

A March 2019 US Congressional Research Service report on Iran stated that, "Christians— along with the other two protected minorities, Zoroastrians and Jews—cannot publicly practice or advocate for their religion."[313]

Arrest and Detention of Christians

An October 2018 *Christian Post* article claimed that Christians were "under intense persecution" and cited Christian Solidarity Worldwide[314] to

---

[311] USCIRF, "Iran 2017 Annual Report," 2017
[312] AIIA, "Study Tour Report," April 2018
[313] US CRS, 'Iran: Internal Politics and U.S. Policy and Options', *supra.*
[314] CSW, October 2nd, 2018

point to three examples of prison sentences being issued to Christians.[315]

Freedom House stated in their report entitled, "Freedom in the World 2019," that, "[T]here is an ongoing crackdown on Christian converts; in the past several years, a number of informal house churches have been raided and their pastors or congregants detained."[316]

A December 2018 article written by *The Telegraph* stated the following:

> Iran has arrested more than 100 Christians in the last week, charities report, amid a growing crackdown by the Islamic Republic. 'Many of the 114 detained were converts to Christianity from a Muslim background, accused of "proselytizing." 'They had to report the history of their Christian activities and were told to cut contact with any Christian groups, according to Open Doors UK, a charity which speaks out on persecution against Christians.[317]

The joint report by Article 18, Middle East Concern, CSW and Open Doors International[318] quoted a figure from *Mohabat News* saying that 114 Christians were arrested in a single week in

---

[315] *Christian Post*, October 16th, 2018
[316] Freedom House, "Freedom in the World 2019," February 4th, 2019
[317] *The Telegraph*, "Iran Arrests more than 100 Christians', December 10th, 2018
[318] Published in January 2019

December.[319] However, the first mention of the figure of 114 appears to be a *World Watch Monitor* news story dated December 5th, 2018 which suggests the source of the figure is Article 18.[320] Assuming the figure is accurate, CPIT could find no further specific details about those who were arrested. Furthermore, CPIT could find no evidence to suggest that a similar number of Christians were arrested during any other month in 2018. The Article 18, Middle East Concern, CSW and Open Doors International joint report quotes the figure, but itself only mentions 15 specific arrests in December.[321] The *World Watch Monitor* news story stated they had been accused of proselytizing but the report also states that most were allowed to go home after a few hours.[322] In addition, an article published by *Mohabat News* on December 13th, 2018 entitled, "Over 100 Iranian Christians arrested by intelligence officials," stated that Mr. Borji [the advocacy director of religious freedom charity Article 18] said most of those arrested were allowed to go home after a few hours or days "as they had arrested so many of them and didn't know what to do with them all" but that those

---

[319] Article 18/MEC/CSW/Open Doors, "Joint Report," (p. 3-4), Jan 2019
[320] *World Watch Monitor*, "Staggering Number of Christians Arrested – 114 in a Week', December 5th, 2018
[321] *Ibid.*
[322] *Ibid.*

suspected to be leaders remain in detention.[323] The December 2018 *Telegraph* article continued, "It has become increasingly common for authorities to arrest worshippers, raid house churches, and confiscate Bibles."[324] The *Daily Telegraph*'s December 2018 article also quoted Zoe Smith, head of advocacy at Open Doors, as having said that:

> ... as the number of converts to Christianity increase, so the authorities place greater restrictions on churches. The restrictions are worse for churches seen to be attended by Christians who have converted from Islam. Not only that, but the government is asking unreasonably high bail amounts and seeing longer prison terms for Christians. [...] Church leaders are put under pressure to leave the country or face an arrest."[325]

The February 2018 joint DIS-DRC report stated:

> The authorities are primarily targeting the house church leaders and secondary the members and converts. Two other sources stated that the authorities target both the leaders of the house churches and the members. The typical pattern of targeting is by arresting and releasing the house church leaders, as the authorities want to weaken the house church. Ordinary members of house churches also risk arrest in a house church.

---

[323] *Mohabat News*, "Over 100 Iranian Christians Arrested by Intelligence Officials," December 13th, 2018
[324] *The Telegraph, supra.*
[325] *Ibid.*

However, they will be released again on the
condition that they stay away from proselytizing.

If they stop proselytizing, the authorities will
stop gathering information about them, a source
added. One source mentioned that it would be
possible for an arrested convert to pay his/her
way out of an arrest. The source added that even
if it is known that the person is a converted
Muslim, it would be a question of the amount of
money paid to be released. Whether a house
church member is targeted also depends on
his/her conducted activities and if he/she is
known abroad, the same source noted. Ordinary
house church members risk being called in for
interrogation on a regular basis as the authorities
want to harass and intimidate them, a source
explained. 'If a house church member is arrested
for the first time, he/she will normally be
released within 24 hours. If he/she has been
detained in prison, he/she will receive his charge
within 24 hours and come to court within ten
days, a source mentioned.[326]

Open Doors USA claimed that, "Leaders of
groups of Christian converts have been arrested,
prosecuted and have received long prison
sentences for 'crimes against the national
security.'" And the same report gave no specific
information on numbers, but said that "many"
Christians had been prosecuted and either
sentenced to imprisonment or were awaiting
trial.[327] In their November 2017 report, Landinfo

---

[326] DIS-DRC, "Joint Report," February 2018
[327] Open Doors USA, World Watch List, u/d

(the Norwegian COI Unit) cited Human Rights Without Frontiers (HRWF 2017) as having '...published the "Freedom of Religion or Belief & Blasphemy Prisoners Database," which lists people imprisoned for their faith in a number of countries. Under the Iran chapter, which was updated September 18th, 2017, 16 Christian prisoners are listed, of which 12 are Iranian citizens.[328] As of December 6th, 2018, HRWF's database listed 22 Christian prisoners, of which 19 are Iranian citizens.[329] The USSD IRF report for 2017 stated that:

> Christians, particularly evangelicals and converts from Islam, continued to experience disproportionate levels of arrests and detention, and high levels of harassment and surveillance, according to Christian NGO reports. Numerous Christians remained imprisoned at year's end on charges related to their religious beliefs. Prison authorities reportedly continued to withhold medical care from prisoners, including some Christians, according to human rights groups. According to human rights NGOs, the government also continued to enforce the prohibition on proselytizing.[330]

The same report also went on to state:

> *Christian World Watch Monitor* reported on the arrest or imprisonment of at least 193 Christians for their religious affiliation or activities in 2016.

---

[328] Landinfo, *supra*.
[329] HRWF, "Database," updated December 6th, 2018
[330] USSD, "International Religious Freedom Report for 2017," *supra*.

Authorities continued to arrest members of
unrecognized churches for operating illegally in
private homes or on charges of supporting and
accepting assistance from "enemy" countries.
Many arrests reportedly took place during police
raids on religious gatherings and included
confiscations of religious property. *News* reports
stated that Christians who were arrested were
subject to severe physical and psychological
mistreatment by authorities, which at times
included beatings and solitary confinement.[331]

In February 2018, Radio Farda reported that an
Iranian Christian convert who was arrested in
December 2017 was still in custody in the
northwestern city of Tabriz.[332] The DFAT
Country Information Report on Iran dated June
7th, 2018, stated:

> The judiciary has handed down long sentences in
> relation to house church activities: in July 2017,
> the Revolutionary Court convicted eight
> Christians of 'acting against national security
> through the establishment of a house church'
> and 'insulting Islamic sanctities' and sentenced
> the group to between ten- and 15-years'
> imprisonment. According to international
> observers, as of December 2016 approximately
> 90 Christians were in detention or awaiting trial
> because of their religious beliefs and activities.[333]

---

[331] *Ibid.*
[332] Radio Farda, "Christian Convert Arrested in Tabriz Still in jail,"
February 14th, 2018
[333] DFAT, *supra.*

A joint report by Article 18; Middle East Concern; CSW and Open Doors International, released in January 2019 (covering events in 2018) contained a table which they claim "includes cases which have appeared in public records, and does not constitute a comprehensive record of every Christian currently detained in Iran"[334] of 22 persons detained (plus 7 others whose names have not been publicized),[335] the first of which was in 2013; the most recent in December 2018. Of the 22 listed, 10 had been sentenced to a period of imprisonment, one of which had been released and another released on bail; a further 6 had been released (4 of which on bail).[336] A March 2019 US Congressional Research Service report on Iran stated that, "numerous Christians remain incarcerated for actions related to religious practice, including using wine in certain services."[337]

Prosecution of Christians

A Report of the Special Rapporteur on the situation of human rights in the Islamic Republic of Iran dated March 17th, 2017, reported they were:

---

[334] Article 18/MEC/CSW/Open Doors, Joint Report, *supra.*
[335] *Ibid.*
[336] *Ibid.*
[337] US CRS, 'Iran: Internal Politics and U.S. Policy and Options', *supra.*

...concerned about the targeting and harsh treatment of Christians from Muslim backgrounds and members of various Sufi groups, including the Nematollahi Gonabadi order and the Yarsan (also known Ahl-e Haqq), which are considered 'deviant faiths' by the authorities and some members of the clerical establishment. These groups continue to face arbitrary arrest, harassment and detention, and are often accused of national security crimes such as 'acting against national security' or 'propaganda against the State.' Under Iranian law, individuals, including Christians of Muslim backgrounds, can be prosecuted for apostasy, although it is not specifically codified as a crime in the Islamic *Penal Code*."[338]

The annual report produced by the United States Commission on International Religious Freedom (USCIRF) in April 2018 stated:

Evangelical Christians and Christian converts, however, are particularly targeted for repression because many conduct services in Persian and proselytize to those outside their community. Pastors of house churches are commonly charged with unfounded national security-related crimes, as well as apostasy and illegal house-church activities. While Iranian authorities have for decades raided house church services and arrested hundreds of worshipers and church leaders, the severity of sentencing has increased in recent years. In May 2017, four evangelical Christians, three of them Azerbaijani citizens,

---

[338] Special Rapporteur on [...] human rights in the Islamic Republic of Iran, "Report," March 17th, 2017

were sentenced to 10 years in prison each for
house church activities and evangelism. The
following month, Pastor Youcef Nadarkhani,
who previously served a prison sentence for
apostasy and is among those highlighted by
USCIRF's Religious Prisoners of Conscience
Project, faced trial along with three co-
defendants because of their house church
activities. Each of the four Christians was
sentenced to 10 years in prison, with Nadarkhani
receiving an additional two years in exile.[339]

Article 18, in an interview with the UK Home
Office in July 2017, stated that apostasy charges
are rarely stated on court documents although
individuals are verbally charged, questioned,
intimidated and threatened with apostasy.[340]

Open Doors, interviewed by the UK Home
Office on August 8th, 2017 stated that almost all
those who are arrested are arrested for actions
against "national security," which is very broad.
These arrests are unlawful. "National security" is
the reason given for arrests; people are not
arrested for apostasy. Although apostasy is
punishable by death in Iran, the Islamic Republic
has never codified the crime of apostasy. Instead,
relying on the *Iranian Constitution*, the *Islamic Penal
Code* authorizes the enforcement of certain
Islamic laws known as *hodud* crimes even when

---

[339] USCIRF, "2018 Annual Report," April 2018
[340] UK Home Office, "Interview with Article 18, July 12th, 2017.
Copy available on request

the crime is not specifically mentioned in the *Criminal Code*.[341]

In their November 2017 report, Landinfo (the Norwegian COI Unit) – based on a range of sources – concluded: "Although it is not uncommon for arrested converts to be threatened with possible apostasy charges,"[342] it is very rare that it has actually happened. This is shown by the practice of Iranian prosecuting authorities and courts. In the history of Islamic Republic (from 1979 up to today), only on very rare occasions have Christian converts been charged with apostasy.[343] It is also rare that converts have been convicted of blasphemy.[344] Organized Christian activity and contact with Christian organizations abroad is instead defined as political activity and as a threat against the country's Islamic identity and national security.[345] Consequently, it is the *intelligence services*[346] that monitor, arrest and interrogate converts, and prosecutions are held before the Revolutionary Court.[347] The Australian Government's

---

[341] UK Home Office, "Interview with Open Doors," August 8th, 2017. Copy available on request

[342] Landinfo 2017, p. 11

[343] IHRDC 2014b, p. 15, 29-35; ICHRI 2013a, pp. 31-32

[344] ICHRI 2013a, p. 10; more about this in Landinfo 2017, p. 12

[345] Open Doors USA 2017b; World Watch Monitor 2016

[346] The intelligence services in Iran are the agents of persecution against most religious minority groups.

[347] Landinfo, *supra.*; also see ICHRI 2013a, p. 49

Department of Foreign Affairs and Trade (DFAT) Country Information Report on Iran dated June 7th, 2018, which is based on a range of sources, information from their Embassies in country and visits to the country concerned, reported:

> While apostasy and blasphemy cases are no longer an everyday occurrence in Iran, authorities continue to use religiously-based charges (such as 'insulting Islam') against a diverse group of individuals. In recent years, the group has included Shi'a members of the reform movement, Muslim-born converts to Christianity, Baha'i, Muslims who challenge the prevailing interpretation of Islam (particularly Sufis), and others who espouse unconventional religious beliefs (including members of recognized religious groups). Some religiously-based cases have clear political overtones, while other cases do seem to be primarily of a religious nature, particularly when connected to proselytization.[348]

Landinfo, in their November 2017 report, explained the underlying rationale: "In general, the government regards religious pluralism beyond their control as a security risk."[349] Iran does not have freedom of association, and all organized activity, whether political, religious or cultural, must be applied for and authorized by the Ministry of the Interior and the Ministry of

---

[348] DFAT, *supra.*
[349] Khalaji, 2013

Culture and Islamic Guidance.[350] Activities that are considered to undermine or threaten the legitimacy and stability of the Islamic regime are not allowed and may have criminal consequences. The regime bases its legitimacy on Islam being the religion of the people, and that the government exercises the will of the people through an Islamic regime. Any religious movement that differs from or provides an alternative to orthodox *Shiite Islam*[351] is interpreted as a threat to the State itself. Religious activists are, therefore, viewed with suspicion and risk being prosecuted.[352]

The February 2018 joint DIS-DRC report explained how "Christian converts are typically

---

[350] Elam Ministries, email 2017; ICHRI 2013b, p. 32
[351] A schism emerged after the death of the Prophet Muhammad in 632, and disputes arose over who should shepherd the new and rapidly growing faith. Some believed that a new leader should be chosen by consensus; others thought that only the prophet's descendants should become caliph. The title passed to a trusted aide, Abu Bakr, though some thought it should have gone to Ali, the prophet's cousin and son-in-law. Ali eventually did become caliph after Abu Bakr's two successors were assassinated. After Ali also was assassinated, with a poison-laced sword at the mosque in Kufa, in what is now Iraq, his sons Hasan and then Hussein claimed the title. But Hussein and many of his relatives were massacred in Karbala, Iraq, in 680. His martyrdom became a central tenet to those who believed that Ali should have succeeded the prophet. (It is mourned every year during the month of Muharram.) The followers became known as Shiites, a contraction of the phrase Shiat Ali, or followers of Ali (John Harney, *The New York Times*, "How Do Sunni and Shia Islam Differ?" January 3rd, 2016)
[352] Landinfo, *supra*.

not charged with apostasy; convert cases are usually considered as national security matters which are handled by the Revolutionary Court. A source added that the authorities perceive activities related to conversion as political activities."[353]

In August 2018, Assist News Service reported that 12 members of a house church in Bushedr, south western Iran, were arrested and sentenced to one year in prison on charges of "propaganda activities against the system and in favour of Zionist Christianity through holding house meetings, evangelism, and invitation to Christianity and inclination to the land of Christianity."[354] In October 2018 *World Watch Monitor* reported on two Iranian Christians who were given prison sentences for "spreading propaganda against the regime." The article stated that,

> Saheb Fadaei and Fatimeh Bakhteri, who belong to the non-Trinitarian 'Church of Iran,' were sentenced to 18 and 12 months, respectively, and that the court found that, 'for Christians to claim that Jesus is Lord and that the Bible is their final authority can be perceived as an attack against Islam.' The article further stated that Sahed Fadaei was already servicing a 10-year sentence for propagating 'house churches' and promoting

---

[353] DIS-DRC, *supra.*
[354] *Assist News*, "House Church Members in Iran Sentenced to Year in Prison," August 18th, 2018

'Zionist Christianity,' alongside his pastor,
Youcef Nadarkhani and two others.[355]

A March 2019 US Congressional Research
Service report on Iran stated that there have
been "prosecutions of Christians for converting
from Islam" but give no detail on numbers or
reasons behind these.[356] In October 2019 Open
Doors reported that nine members of a house
church, including a pastor, were arrested. Five
were transferred to Evin Prison after the judge
rejected the lawyer representing them and the
remaining four were given five-year sentences for
"acting against national security."[357]

Other Incidents

The US State Department's Religious Freedom
Report for 2018, covering events in 2017 ("the
2017 USSD IRF report") noted that, "The
government continued to harass, interrogate [...]
Christians (particularly converts)."[358] The same
report also went on to state:

> According to human rights organizations,
> Christian advocacy groups, and NGOs, the

---

[355] *World Watch Monitor*, "Iranian Christians Sentenced," October 2nd,
2018
[356] US CRS, *supra.*
[357] Open Doors, 'Police Raid Church in Iran, 9 Christians Sentenced
to Five Years," October 23rd, 2019
[358] USSD, *supra.*

government continued to regulate Christian
religious practices. Official reports and the media
continued to characterize Christian house
churches as "illegal networks" and "Zionist
propaganda institutions." Christian community
leaders stated that if the authorities found
Armenian or Assyrian churches were baptizing
new converts or preaching in Farsi, they closed
the churches. Authorities also reportedly barred
unregistered or unrecognized Christians from
entering church premises, closed churches that
allowed them to enter, and arrested Christian
converts. Christian advocacy groups stated the
government, through pressure and church
closures, had eliminated all but a handful of
Farsi-language church services, thus restricting
services almost entirely to the Armenian and
Assyrian languages. Security officials monitored
registered congregation centers to perform
identity checks on worshippers to confirm non-
Christians or converts did not participate in
services. In response, many citizens who had
converted to Protestantism or other Christian
faiths reportedly practiced their religion in secret.

Other unrecognized religious minorities such as
Bahais and Yarsanis were also forced to gather in
private homes to practice their faith in secret.[359]

A report published by Deutsche Welle (DW) in
January 2016 described what happened to one
particular Iranian Christian convert. The article
stated:

In Tehran, the man "was yanked from the street
into a taxi" and told, "You will give up your
faith, you will return to Islam, or you will die." A

---

[359] *Ibid.*

gun was pointed to his head and the trigger was pulled. However, it wasn't loaded. After the "feigned public execution," the man was thrown into a prison in Tehran where his keepers extinguished their cigarettes on his bare skin. Relatives of the man were able to buy his freedom. Today, he lives in Germany, but still fears the Iranian secret service [...].[360]

A March 2019 US Congressional Research Service report on Iran stated that, "At times, there have been unexplained assassinations of pastors in Iran."[361] In May 2019 Radio Farda reported on an Assyrian Christian church being shut down by Iranian authorities. The article stated:

> The Assyrian Christian community in the northwestern Iranian city of Tabriz has been left in a state of shock after intelligence agents forced a Presbyterian church to close earlier this month, Assyrian International News Agency (*Aina*) reports. "Religious freedom charity Article18 said: 'Intelligence agents stormed the 100-year-old church, officially recognized as a national heritage site in Iran, on Thursday, May 9, changed all the locks, tore down the cross from the church tower, and ordered the churchwarden to leave.'" "They made it clear that the Assyrian people are no longer allowed to hold any worship service there," Article18 reported. "The source also said church members had been fearful since just a few days after Christmas when

---

[360] DW, "What it's like to be a Christian in Iran," January 25th, 2016
[361] US CRS, *supra.*

agents from the intelligence ministry prevented pastors from other churches to visit the Tabriz church for a joint-worship service with other Assyrian and Armenian Christians. Quoting a source, Aina reported on May 9, 'a large number' of agents from the ministry of intelligence and a state agency called Eiko entered the 'church compound and changed all the locks on the doors, removed the cross from the tower, installed some monitoring instruments and started to threaten and force our custodian to leave his place inside the compound immediately."'[362]

Activities Which Could Attract Attention from the Authorities

Landinfo's November 2017 report, referring to Elam Ministries' conversation with the Danish Immigration Service, noted:

> Elam Ministries has also pointed out that the authorities' priorities appear to be a matter of resources. The authorities apparently do not use their resources on new believers, because their priority is stopping the establishment of new house churches. Therefore, they are most interested in striking at the leaders of house churches and networks, according to Elam (as quoted in DIS 2014, p. 27).'[363]

Article 18, interviewed by the UK Home Office on July 12th, 2017, stated that people in Turkey

---

[362] Radio Farda, "Iranian Intelligence Shuts down Church, Removes Cross," May 26th, 2019
[363] Landinfo, *supra.*

have said that they have been told by Iranian interrogators that they do not have a problem if a person confines their beliefs to themselves and pray privately. But the moment they appear to be speaking to others about Christianity, or express their beliefs in the form of worship with others [publicly, like in a house church] "then we have a problem."[364] In August 2017, when asked by the UK Home Office what attracts the authorities to new converts and what kind of activities could, therefore, lead to ill-treatment, Open Doors and Article 18 suggested the following would, although these can depend on the city:

- Any kind of gathering
- Sharing the gospel
- Being in possession of more than one Bible (usually one Bible will be tolerated by the authorities, but not always)
- Possession of a library of Christian literature
- Holding discipleship classes
- Studying theology
- Contact with Christian organizations
- Attending Christian conferences and seminars inside the country or abroad where teaching takes place
- Hosting or, in some cases, even attending house churches[365],[366]

---

[364] Article 18, "Interview with CPIT, UK Home Office," July 12th, 2017. Copy available on request
[365] Open Doors, "Interview with CPIT, UK Home Office," August 8th, 2017. Copy available on request
[366] Article 18, 'Interview with CPIT, UK Home Office', *supra*. Copy available on request

DFAT Country Information Report on Iran dated June 7th, 2018, which is based on a range of sources, stated:

> International observers advise that Iranians who convert to Christianity outside the country are unlikely to face adverse attention from authorities upon return to Iran, provided they have not previously come to the attention of authorities for political activities conducted in Iran, maintain a low profile and do not engage in proselytization or political activities within the country.[367]

DFAT also concluded that:

> ...small, self-contained house church congregations that maintain a low profile and do not seek to recruit new members are unlikely to attract adverse attention from authorities beyond monitoring and, possibly, low-level harassment. Members of larger congregations that do engage in proselytization and have connections to broader house church networks are more likely to face official repercussions, which may include arrest and prosecution. The leaders of such congregations are at particular risk in this regard.[368]

The February 2018 joint DIS-DRC report, based on interviews conducted in Iran, Turkey and the United Kingdom between September and October 2017, stated that:

---

[367] DFAT, *supra.*
[368] *Ibid.*

If a converted person uses the religion politically to, for instance, compare disadvantages of Islam with advantages of Christianity or another religion on social media, it could be a problem for him, a source mentioned. Most Iranians are not very religious, but they might see conversion as a way to come closer to Western values, and as a protest against the system, another source mentioned. However, it was underlined that it would apply to a person who has made his/her own analysis of the two religions and not someone who has used "copy paste" phrases.[369]

The Australian Institute of International Affairs published an Iran Study Tour Report in April 2018 which stated:

It appears that there is a high (unofficial) rate of conversion to Christianity, placing it amongst the highest conversion rates in the world. Whilst those who promote Christianity in public are persecuted, those who practice Christianity privately are largely left to their own devices.[370]

Impact on Others

Treatment of family members. The ACCORD query response dated March 2017 quoted an email response from a representative of Elam Ministries and provided the following comments

---

[369] DIS-DRC, *supra.*
[370] AIIA, "Study Tour Report," April 2018

with regard to the treatment of family members of Christian converts by state authorities:

> We can certainly confirm that family members of Christians (especially Christian converts) are not spared suffering. For example, in one case of a house raid and arrest of a Christian couple perpetrated by Iran's Ministry of Intelligence (MOI) in July 2014, the 12-year old son of the couple was at home during the house raid. He was hit by the officers while being questioned about his own faith. He was also arrested along with his parents. Further, we have heard examples of elderly parents being harassed regarding their child's conversion to Christianity.[371]

The March 2017 email response by Elam Ministries with ACCORD notes that family members of imprisoned Christians are also affected in ways other than direct actions by state actors:

> Of course, the family members of those in prison for their faith suffer deeply through loss of their loved one. For example, Pastor Farshid Fathi was in prison for 5 years between 2010 and 2015. His son was about 1 years old when his father was imprisoned for his faith. He was without his father for over 5 years and had no memory of his father when he was finally released. Many families also suffer financially when the primary breadwinner is imprisoned. For example, Ebrahim Firouzi is currently imprisoned for his faith in Rajai Shahr prison (Karaj) and his sister and mother are struggling

---

[371] ACCORD, "Iran: Query Response," June 14th, 2017

financially because he was the primary breadwinner for the family. Families suffer severely financially in other ways. Extortionate bail sums are demanded for the temporary release of Christian detainees. Often family house deeds or family business permits are submitted to cover this bail demand. If the Christian flees the country before their court hearing, the bail is lost to the family. Moreover, inheritance laws in Iran mean that Christian family members cannot inherit money from relatives. Muslim family members are always preferred to receive the inheritance. There are many other ways that family members suffer because of the conversion of an individual." (Elam Ministries, 28 March 2017).[372]

Open Doors, interviewed by the UK Home Office on 8 August 2017, stated that it's often reported by the Christians who have fled the country that their families are targets of harassment to force them to cut their continuing connection with house church members and active Christians inside Iran.[373]

Treatment of Returning Christians to Iran

Profile, Activities and Social Media

---

[372] *Ibid.*
[373] Open Doors, "Interview with CPIT, UK Home Office," *supra.*

February 2018 joint DIS-DRC report, based on interviews conducted in Iran, Turkey and the United Kingdom between September and October 2017, stated that:

> Several sources addressed the issue regarding Iranian converts returning from Europe. According to two sources, converted returnees who do not carry out activities related to Christianity upon return will not be of interest to the authorities. Middle East Concern made the distinction whether the converted person was known before leaving Iran or not; returning will cause problems if the convert has been known by the authorities before leaving.
>
> If the opposite is the case, going back to Iran would not be problematic. Converts who announce their conversion in public may face serious problems. 'If the returned convert has been very outspoken about his/her conversion on social media, including Facebook, the authorities might become aware of it and arrest and interrogate the convert upon return.
>
> A Western embassy said that the subsequent process would depend on what the returnees inform the authorities about. The embassy did not consider that the converts would receive harsh punishment if they are not high-profiled and are not involved in propagating Christianity or activities perceived as a threat to national security. 'Declaring conversion on Facebook in itself does not lead to persecution but likely to monitoring. One source explained that a photo indicating a conversion posted on the Internet would be evaluated by the authorities along with the profile and activities of the converted person. If the person did not have any previous

affiliation with Christianity before leaving the country, he/she will not be persecuted.[374]

A Danish Immigration Service update on the situation for Christian converts in Iran, June 2014, citing various sources stated that:

> With regard to the situation of converts who return to Iran after being baptized abroad, be it in Turkey, Armenia, UAE or another country, the source found that they may return to Iran quietly and not encounter any problems. If the person is already monitored by the authorities, he or she could risk consequences upon return to Iran. 'According to AIIS [Amnesty International's International Secretariat] it is difficult to obtain information on potential risks an individual may face upon returning to Iran after conversion abroad. If Iranian informants have gathered information regarding an individual who has returned to Iran, the authorities may arrest them for questioning. It is possible that charging and conviction will ensue the arrest and questioning.

> A wide group of people could be in that position: students, political activists, family members of political persons might even be questioned as well as Christian converts. 'Regarding whether baptism abroad would put a person at risk from the authorities in Iran, AIIS considered that the importance of baptism should be balanced against how the Iranian authorities perceive a convert.

---

[374] DIS-DRC, *supra.*

A person who has attended trainings and sessions abroad may be considered a convert, although he or she may not have officially been baptized. 'Asked about the situation for a convert who returns to Iran after having converted abroad, i.e. in Europe or a Western country, Mansour Borji [Advocacy Officer for Article 18] found that there would be no difference in the way the Iranian authorities would deal with the case. If the person is known to the authorities and they have shown an interest in him or her before he or she left the country, there could be a risk to him or her upon returning. If the person is unknown to the authorities, the source did not consider that there would be a huge threat towards him or her.

The source referred to a case of a family who went back to Iran and upon return, they were threatened and followed around/harassed. It was considered that perhaps relatives or others had reported them to the authorities causing the harassment. Ultimately, the family left Iran again. They had secretly begun to attend a house church. 'Concerning the consequences for an individual upon return to Iran after having converted abroad, CSW [Christian Solidarity Worldwide] said that any convert who wishes to practice his or her faith upon return, would face serious risk. 'When asked about the consequences of returning to Iran after having been baptized abroad, Elam Ministries said that many Iranians do go abroad and return to Iran after a while. If the authorities in Iran become aware of the fact that a person has been baptized abroad such an individual may risk interrogation and repercussions. The source considered that the authorities may find out that an individual has been baptized through informers and telephone/Internet tapping. 'It was considered that persons who return from Western countries after converting would have to be very careful about doing any evangelizing. When considering the situation of an individual who has converted in Europe who then returns to Iran, their situation would be much the same as that of Iranians who convert in Iran. Such individuals would have to lay low and not speak openly about their conversion. If their conversion is uncovered and the authorities are notified, there is a risk that such an individual will be suspected of links with foreign organizations much the same as a convert who has been living in Iran. 'The source added that those who are outside of Iran for extended periods of time may be more at risk in that the authorities may suspect them of spying. It was further added that this counts not only for Christian converts but also for other Iranians. 'Asked about the situation of Christian converts who return to Iran after coming to Turkey or another country, and meeting with other believers, the representatives of the Union Church informed the delegation that if the converts stay "quiet"; i.e., they do not associate with other believers, they may not be discovered and the visits to a foreign country will then not make a lot of a difference for them. 'According to the representatives of the Union Church, even if not known to authorities, converts can face shunning and even "honour killing" by their families. 'If a Christian convert is not affiliated with a house church, an international organization in Turkey said that the risk to him or her [upon return] would depend on how he or she lives his or her Christian life. If such an individual plainly prays at home and does not share his or her faith to others, there would be no risk to him or her. However, within the

evangelical groups that these converts may
follow, evangelizing is important and therefore if
he or she starts doing this, there could be a risk
of harm from the authorities. 'Elam Ministries
said that if such a person who returns from
abroad is not connected to a house church or
network, there would be no particular threat,
however as far as his or her Christian faith is
concerned all aspects of his or her life will be
affected because of their new faith and as a
result, he or she will run into the same issues that
other converts face for example with regards to
school, marriage, university, employment and
housing. They must be secret believers and are
unable to speak of their faith to anyone else and
to live an openly Christian lifestyle. 'According to
an international organization in Turkey there are
reportedly large numbers of Iranians in Turkey
who are involved in informal house church
movements with links to similar networks in
Iran. Available information to international
organizations monitoring the situation in Iran
suggests that persons who come to the notice of
the authorities on account of their conversion to
Christianity are interrogated in relation to
perceived threats to society and to the Iranian
regime, such as unqualified threats to public
order or insults to Islamic sanctities as
understood under Iranian law. 'When asked if an
international organization in Turkey considered it
would make a difference if a person had been
trained or baptized in Turkey or in a European
country, the source said that if it only concerns
conversion, there would probably be no
difference. If baptism is uncovered, it could pose
problems for the individual. The person's link to
a network abroad would also raise the profile.
However, there are no reports of persons who
have been detained and officially charged with

conversion-related offences after returning to
Iran from Turkey.[375]

Open Doors told the UK Home Office on
August 8th, 2017, that a person who converts to
Christianity inside Iran is thought to be less of a
threat than a person who converts outside of
Iran, who is likely to be thought of as an
evangelist. The regime is very suspicious of
contact with the outside world. The Iranian
regime would not explore the validity of a
person's conversion when they return to Iran. It
would be accepted at face value. A 'convert' who
returns to Iran (even if the conversion is not
recognized as genuine in the place of conversion
such as the UK) may be forced to sign a
commitment to return to Islam. This is likely to
involve detention and interrogation. Some
people leave the country again. Treatment varies
from city to city and may not always involve
detention.[376]

Elam Ministries interviewed by the UK Home
Office on September 6th, 2017, stated that it was
very rare for people to return to Iran. When
asked the reasons why some people return, they
stated that those who return have families,

---

[375] DIS, Update on the Situation for Christian Converts in Iran, June
2014
[376] UK Home Office, "Interview with Open Doors," *supra.*

property or businesses. Many of those who return go back as their families have had to put up large sums of money for their bail and if they do not go back their families will have to cover the bail money. Lots of people have to give house deeds to ensure the release of family members; the defendant does not want their family to lose property.[377]

A Finnish Immigration Service report on Christian converts in Iran, dated August 21st, 2015, citing various sources stated:

> No research data on the return of Christian converts to Iran is available, but the common perception is that they will get into trouble mainly if they try to proselytize or otherwise make their religious views public. The state's interest is focused more on the public practice of religion and proselytizing than on one's private convictions.[378]

CPIT could find no other sources that stated returnees would be forced to sign a commitment to return to Islam.

Religious Freedom in Iran

Sources indicate that Shia Muslims represent

---

[377] UK Home Office, "Interview with Elam Ministries," September 6th, 2017. Copy available on request
[378] Finnish Immigration Service, "Christian Converts in Iran," August 21st, 2015

(about) 90 percent[379] or 90 to 95 percent[380] of the country's population. Sources indicate the share of Sunni Muslims as about 9 percent,[381] 10 percent[382] or 5 to 10 percent[383] of the population. As noted by Minority Rights Group International (MRG), Iran's Shia Islam is "strongly dominated by the Twelver Ja'fari School (referred to as Ithna'ashari in Arabic)". Other Islamic groups besides Twelver Shia and Sunni Islam include Ismaili Islam and Ahl-e Haqq.[384]

MRG, a UK-based NGO campaigning for the rights of minority ethnic, religious and linguistic communities, states in its July 2014 World Directory of Minorities and Indigenous Peoples that: "'[M]ost Kurds, Turkmens, Baluch and some Arabs are Sunni' although these communities 'do not form a cohesive coherent whole as Sunnis' and 'tend to express their identity in ethnic terms.'"[385] Global Security, a US-based think tank that provides information and analysis on a variety of security-related issues, notes that there are also "small

---

[379] AA, March 2015a; USDOS, July 28th, 2014, section 1
[380] CIA, 1 September 2015, based on 2011 estimates
[381] USDOS, July 28th, 2014, section 1
[382] AA, March 2015a, MRG, July 2014
[383] CIA, September 1st, 2015
[384] MRG, July 2014
[385] *Ibid.*

communities" of ethnic Persians in southern Iran and Khorasan who are Sunnis.[386]

Furthermore, the July 2014 US Department of State (USDOS) International Religious Freedom Report (which covers the year 2013) notes that, "[T]here are no official statistics available on the size of the Sufi Muslim population" but that "some reports estimate [that] between two and five million people practice Sufism."[387]

According to the 2011 National Population and Housing Census 2011 presented by the Statistical Centre of Iran (AMAR), non-Muslims (referred to as Christian, Jewish and Zoroastrian) account for 0.3 per cent of the population, while other groups (labelled as "nonstated" groups) make up another 0.3 percent.[388] The USDOS, however, notes that groups including Bahais, Christians, Jews, Sabean-Mandaeans, and Zoroastrians represent one percent of the population, with Baha'is and Christians being the "two largest non-Muslim minorities."[389] Sources indicate the number of Baha'is as approximately 300,000[390] or 300-350,000.[391] The USDOS quotes United Nations (UN) figures as indicating that "300,000

---

[386] Global Security, September 7th, 2011
[387] USDOS, July 28th, 2014, section 1
[388] AMAR, August 2012, p. 26
[389] USDOS, *supra.*
[390] *Ibid.*
[391] MRG, *supra.*

Christians live in the country, although the Statistical Center of Iran (AMAR) reports the number of Christians as 117,700 while "some NGOs estimate [that] there may be as many as 370,000." The July 2014 USDOS report elaborates on the figures of Christians in Iran:

> The majority of Christians are ethnic Armenians concentrated in Tehran and Isfahan. Unofficial estimates of the Assyrian Christian population range between 10,000 and 20,000. There are also Protestant denominations, including evangelical groups. Christian groups outside the country estimate the size of the Protestant Christian community to be less than 10,000, although many Protestant Christians reportedly practice in secret.

According to the United States Commission on International Religious Freedom (USCIRF), the number of Zoroastrians is between 30,000 and 35,000.[392] The USDOS notes that AMAR, "estimated in 2011 that there were approximately 25,300 Zoroastrians, who are primarily ethnic Persians" whereas "Zoroastrian groups report 60,000 members."[393]

The United States Commission on International Religious Freedom (USCIRF) indicates that some 20,000 persons belong to the Jewish

---

[392] USCIRF, April 30th, 2015, p. 47
[393] USDOS, *supra.*

community.[394] As indicated by the USDOS, "[T]here are from 5,000 to 10,000 Sabean-Mandaeans."[395] Results of the 2011 National Population and Housing Census reported by AMAR indicate that the number of Muslims has increased from approx. 70 million in 2006 to about 74.68 million in 2011. AMAR also notes a rise in the Christian population from 109,415 in 2006 to some 117,704 in 2011. The number of Jews is indicated to have decreased from 9,252 in 2006 to 8,756 in 2011, while the number of Zoroastrians is reported to have risen from 19,823 in 2006 to 25,271 in 2011.[396]

In Iran, the government executed at least 20 individuals on charges of *moharebeh*, translatable as "enmity towards god," among them a number of Sunni Kurds. A number of other prisoners, including several Sunni preachers, remained in custody awaiting a government decision to implement their death sentences. According to the Iran Human Rights Documentation Center database of prisoners, at least 380 religious practitioners remained imprisoned at the end of the year for their membership in, or activities on behalf of, a minority religious group, including approximately 250 Sunnis, 82 Baha'is, 26 Christian converts, 16 non-Sunni Sufis, 10 Yarsanis, three Sunni converts, and two

---

[394] USCIRF, *supra.*
[395] USDOS, *supra.*
[396] AMAR, *supra.*

Zoroastrians. According to representatives of the Baha'i community, the government continued to prohibit the Baha'is from officially assembling or maintaining administrative institutions, actively closed such institutions, harassed Baha'is, and disregarded their property rights. Christians, particularly evangelicals and converts, continued to experience disproportionate levels of arrests and high levels of harassment and surveillance, according to reports from exiled Christians.[397]

In the past year, religious freedom in Iran continued to deteriorate for both recognized and unrecognized religious groups, with the government targeting Baha'is and Christian converts in particular. While several high-profile Baha'i prisoners were released during the reporting period following completion of their sentences, others were arbitrarily detained based on their religion, and long-term trends of economic and educational persecution of the community continue. Christian converts and house church leaders faced increasingly harsh sentencing: many were sentenced to at least 10 years in prison for their religious activities. Religious reformers and dissenters faced prolonged detention and possible execution,

---

[397] https://2009-2017.state.gov/j/drl/rls/irf/religiousfreedom/#wrapper (Retrieved: September 8th, 2019)

while the government's growing ability to enforce official interpretations of religion online posed new threats to the freedom and safety of Internet users.

In a new, troubling development, the suspension of a Zoroastrian elected to the local council of Yazd sparked national debate about limiting the political rights of religious minorities. While the Rouhani Administration signaled its intent to address some religious freedom violations, these promises have yet to be implemented and the number of individuals imprisoned for their beliefs continues to climb. Based on these particularly severe religious freedom violations, USCIRF again recommends in 2018 that Iran be designated as a "country of particular concern," or CPC. Since 1999, the United States Department of State has designated Iran as a CPC under the International Religious Freedom Act (IRFA), most recently in December 2017.[398]

Pre-2015, Christianity Reports in Iran[399]

---

[398] Annual Report of the U.S. Commission on International Religious Freedom, "Iran," April 2018, p. 44, https://www.uscirf.gov/sites/default/files/2018USCIRFAR.pdf (Retrieved: September 8th, 2019)
[399] Research Directorate, Immigration and Refugee Board of Canada, Ottawa, "Iran: Teachings, interpretations and knowledge of Christianity among non-ethnic Christians," March 18th, 2014 (https://irb-cisr.gc.ca/en/country-information/rir/Pages/index.aspx?doc=455192&pls=1)

Background

According to a publication about Protestants and
Christian converts in Iran, written by the
International Campaign for Human Rights in
Iran (ICHRI), an independent New York-based
non-profit organization that aims to promote
human rights in Iran through research and
international media advocacy, the majority of
Christians in Iran are "ethnic Christians, which
refers to Armenians and the Assyrians (or
Chaldeans) who possess their own linguistic and
cultural traditions."[400] ICHRI states that "most
ethnic Christians are members of their
community's Orthodox church,"[401] "but some
are also Catholics or Protestants."[402] According
to ICHRI, "[n]on-ethnic Christians are for the
most part members of Protestant churches."[403]
Sources similarly indicate that non-ethnic
Christians are mostly "Protestants and
Evangelicals."[404] The International Federation
for Human Rights (FIDH) states that "many
[non-ethnic Christians] are converts from
Islam."[405] ICHRI also says that "most, though
not all [non-ethnic Christians], are converts who

---

[400] ICHRI 2013, 6
[401] *Ibid.*
[402] *Ibid.*, 17
[403] *Ibid.*, 6
[404] Minority Rights Group International n.d.; FIDH July 25th, 2010
[405] *Ibid.*

came from Muslim backgrounds."[406]

In a telephone interview with the Research Directorate, a senior researcher in the Human Rights in Iran Unit at Brooklyn College, City University of New York, indicated that the experiences of ethnic and non-ethnic Christians in Iran are "entirely different."[407] The ICHRI states that "authorities have granted ethnic Christians some rights to religious practice, such as holding their church services, running religious schools, and celebrating their major religious holidays," though they are not permitted to hold Persian language services.[408] According to the UN Report of the Special Rapporteur on the Situation of Human Rights in the Islamic Republic of Iran, "[i]n general, Christian religious practice is monitored and heavily regulated. For example, Muslim converts to Christianity cannot enter Armenian or Assyrian Churches, as all churchgoers must register with the Government. Authorities often place cameras in churches..."[409]

ICHRI indicates that Protestants face "far more aggressive government restrictions and human rights abuses than ethnic Christian groups."[410]

---

[406] ICHRI 2013, 6
[407] Feb. 21, 2014
[408] ICHRI 2013, 6
[409] UN Mar. 13th, 2014, 80
[410] *Ibid.*

ICHRI states that this is "largely" due to the use
of the Persian language for church services and
literature, "their commitment to proselytizing,"
which may "facilitate conversion," as well as
potential affiliations with church networks
located abroad (ibid.). The BBC reports that
"[e]vangelical Christians are not recognized and
face heavy discrimination."[411] According to the
report by the UN Special Rapporteur, "The
Christians most commonly prosecuted appear to
be converts from Muslim backgrounds or those
that proselytize or minister to Iranian Muslims.
Iranian authorities at the highest levels have
designated house churches and evangelical
Christians as threats to national security."[412] The
UN Special Rapporteur adds that [i]n recent
years, Christians, many of whom are converts
from Muslim backgrounds, have faced a similar
pattern of persecution. At least 49 Christians
were reportedly being detained in the Islamic
Republic of Iran as at January 2014. In 2013
alone, the authorities reportedly arrested at least
42 Christians, of whom 35 were convicted for
participation in informal "house churches",
association with churches outside the Islamic
Republic of Iran, perceived or real evangelical
activity, and other standard Christian activities.
Sentences range from one to 10 years of

---

[411] October 11th, 2011
[412] UN Mar. 13th, 2014, 11

imprisonment.

Denominations

Sources indicate that some non-ethnic Christians in Iran identify with denominations, and some do not.[413] The Pastor indicated that some non-ethnic Christians may or may not know about the existence of different denominations.[414] The Pastor also said that whether or not a non-ethnic Iranian Christian knows their denomination depends on the person mentoring them.[415] In a telephone interview with the Research Directorate, the President of Iranian Christians International (ICI), a non-profit Colorado-based evangelical Christian group that "ministers to the approximately 8 million Iranians and Afghans living outside their countries today,"[416] indicated that "most house churches" do not focus on the issue of denomination; they teach their own theology and doctrine, but will not necessarily specify which denomination they belong to.[417]

The senior researcher indicated that there are many ways that non-ethnic Iranian Christians identify or describe themselves, for example, some may identify as Protestant, Pentecostal or

---

[413] Senior Researcher Feb. 21, 2014; Pastor Feb. 24, 2014
[414] *Ibid.*
[415] *Ibid.*
[416] ICI n.d.
[417] *Ibid.*, Feb. 26, 2014

another denomination, while others may identify as Evangelical or belonging to the Evangelical movement, Proselytizing, or belonging to the Assembly of God, an Evangelical Iranian group, an International Christian movement, the International set of churches (an international church network), or a Bible Church. The senior researcher added that many of these terms are not commonly used in Persian and may be challenging to translate to English. Sources also indicated that some non-ethnic Christians identify themselves as being a follower of a particular Christian television channel, television personality or televangelist.[418]

According to the senior researcher, although some Iranian converts take a theological meaning of Christianity, some others take a social meaning from the religion. The senior researcher said that sometimes Christianity is defined as a way of moving away from social norms that people find to be restrictive in Iran, and moving towards a form of social liberation. The Danish and Norwegian fact-finding mission indicated that, according to an international organization in Ankara, in some cases "the appeal lies less in Christianity as such and more in being part of a community which is warm and welcoming."[419]

---

[418] Senior Researcher Feb. 21, 2014; Pastor Feb. 24, 2014
[419] Feb. 17, 2014

Sources indicated that some non-ethnic Christians define Christianity in relation to Islam.[420] The Pastor indicated that some Iranians convert to Christianity because of their "hatred of Islam rather than for their love of Jesus."[421] The President of ICI similarly stated that some people convert to Christianity and other religions as a rebellion. The Danish and Norwegian fact-finding mission indicated that, according to a source, "a large number of people in Iran are fed up with the way political Islam is practiced by the regime and are looking for alternatives."[422]

Two sources note the active presence of Jehovah's Witnesses and Mormons in Iran,[423] as well as other "non-conventional forms of Christianity."[424]

Teachings and Interpretations
of Christianity

Sources indicate that there is great variance in the way Christianity is interpreted by non-ethnic protestant and converted Christians in Iran.[425] In a telephone interview with the Research

---

[420] Senior Researcher Feb. 21, 2014; Pastor Feb. 24, 2014; ICI Feb. 26, 2014

[421] *Ibid.*

[422] Feb. 16, 2014

[423] ICI Feb. 26, 2014; Pastor Feb. 24, 2014

[424] *Ibid.*

[425] Senior Researcher, Feb. 21st, 2014; Pastor, Feb. 24th, 2014

Directorate, the Pastor of the Iranian Church of Richmond Hill in Toronto, who received his ministry credentials with the Evangelical Free Church of Canada, said that interpretations of Christianity are based on a person's denomination and how he or she learns about Christianity.[426] According to the senior researcher, for non-ethnic Christians, there are many differences in the practices, teachings and knowledge of Christianity, and a person's identification with the religion.[427]

Several sources indicate that there can be a range of knowledge about Christianity among non-ethnic Christians in Iran.[428] The Pastor indicated that a person's knowledge of Christianity is dependent on the type of exposure they have had to Christianity.[429] The senior researcher said that Iranian non-ethnic Christians do not grow up in a Christian-centred society.[430] The President of ICI indicated that sometimes the information that converts have received about Christianity comes from teachings in Islam, which are not the same as Christian teachings.[431] The senior researcher indicated that some non-ethnic

---

[426] *Ibid.*, Mar. 21st, 2014
[427] Feb. 21st, 2014
[428] ICI, Feb. 26th, 2014; Senior Researcher, *supra.*; Pastor, *supra.*
[429] Feb. 24th, 2014, *supra.*
[430] Feb. 21st, 2014
[431] Feb. 26th, 2014

Christians are ordained outside of Iran or have otherwise acquired a high level of Christian education, while others know very little about Christianity.[432] A fact-finding mission conducted by the Danish Refugee Council, Landinfo, and the Danish Immigration Service indicates that, according to an international organization in Ankara, "converts may not be very knowledgeable about Christianity."[433] A senior legal advisor at the Swedish Migration Board interviewed by the Christian Broadcasting Network (CBN), and evangelical news outlet, said that "not all converts have a deeper knowledge or details about the religion."[434]

Sources indicate that some non-ethnic Iranian Christians do not believe in the Trinity.[435] According to the President of ICI, there are some groups who present Christianity through an Islamic lens, such as the "Jesus-only group," who does not believe in the Trinity.[436] The Danish and Norwegian fact-finding mission similarly states that "many of the house churches in Iran are non-Trinitarian which means that they believe in 'Jesus only' "making them "quite different from established Protestantism."[437]

---

[432] Feb. 21st, 2014, *supra*.
[433] Denmark and Norway, Feb. 17th, 2013
[434] CBN, June 14th, 2013
[435] Senior Researcher Feb.21st, 2014; Denmark and Norway Feb. 18th, 2013
[436] Feb. 26th, 2014
[437] Feb. 15th and 18th, 2013

Practices – House Churches

Sources report that some non-ethnic Iranian Christians attend house churches.[438] The Danish and Norwegian fact-finding mission to Iran reports that, according to a Western embassy, "established churches effectively do not accept converts and consequently, converts are pushed to the underground house churches."[439] The President of ICI also indicated that some converts attend house churches.[440]

The President of ICI indicated that pastors of house churches are "usually not well trained."[441] The senior researcher noted that some house churches have Bible classes, some of which are taught by new Christians themselves, and some house churches are "non-traditional," and may be led by clergy without a theological understanding.[442] The President of ICI indicated that the knowledge of Christianity gained in house churches varies, and depends on which house church a person has attended.[443] He added that there may be many gaps in knowledge among Christians who attend house churches, as

---

[438] Senior Researcher, *supra*; Pastor, *supra*.
[439] Feb. 17th, 2013
[440] Feb. 26th, 2014
[441] *Ibid.*
[442] Feb. 21st, 2014
[443] Feb. 26th, 2014

their teachings may be, in his view, "incomplete and insufficient."[444]

Several sources indicate that some Iranian house church leaders are trained abroad.[445] The Pastor indicated that sometimes leaders of churches are trained in Turkey or Armenia.[446] The senior researcher also stated that sometimes people who teach in house churches attend seminars in Turkey, Armenia or elsewhere and learn about Christian teachings and how to promote conversions.[447] The Danish and Norwegian fact-finding mission adds that, according to an Iranian leader of a home church network, training of leaders of house churches can also occur through television satellite channels.[448] According to the same source, leaders also "rely on informal modes of learning through personal mentoring, a sort of apprenticeship that also involves the reading of theological books and learning from more knowledgeable and experienced leaders."[449]

According to the Pastor, there is a limited number of people preaching and providing Christian teachings in Iran, which has led to, in

---

[444] *Ibid.*
[445] Senior Researcher, *supra.*; Denmark and Norway Feb. 20th, 2013; Pastor, *supra.*
[446] Feb. 24th, 2014
[447] Feb. 21st, 2014
[448] Feb. 20th, 2013
[449] *Ibid.*

his opinion, some "bad teachings" and misunderstandings about Christianity.[450] Corroborating information could not be found among the sources consulted by the Research Directorate within the time constraints of this Response.

Television Satellite Stations

Several sources report that there are Christian television satellite stations that broadcast in Iran.[451] The Pastor explained that this is because of the lack of freedom to teach Christianity to non-ethnic Christians.[452] The senior researcher indicates that some people's concept of conversion is just following a Christian television show because some non-ethnic Iranian Christians may not have access to other Christians, and may therefore acquire their "entire understanding" of Christianity from a Christian television show.[453] Corroborating information could not be found among the sources consulted by the Research Directorate within the time constraints of this Response.

---

[450] Feb. 24th, 2014

[451] Senior Researcher Feb. 21st, 2014; Pastor Feb. 24th, 2014; ICI, Feb. 26th, 2014)

[452] Feb. 24th, 2014, *supra.*

[453] Feb. 21st, 2014, *supra.*

Christian Materials

Sources indicate that Christian Bibles are confiscated in Iran.[454] The Senior Researcher indicated that Persian-language bibles are confiscated, mostly from house churches.[455] The Senior Researcher added that, although the government allows one translation of the Persian language bible with an Islamic interpretation, Persian-speaking Protestants generally do not use this version.[456] The Pastor indicated that if someone has a Bible, they can get into "big trouble" and that Bibles are "not readily available."[457] However, in contrast, the senior researcher indicated that most non-ethnic Christians have Bibles.[458]

According to the senior researcher, the Persian translation of the Bible is not printed in Iran.[459] The President of ICI said that some churches print small quantities of Bibles, but this can be dangerous.[460] The President of ICI said that, although Bibles were smuggled in before, "in recent years" there is less smuggling because it is expensive and sometimes shipments are

---

[454] US May 20th, 2013, p. 4; Senior Researcher Feb. 21st, 2014, *supra*.
[455] *Ibid.* Mar. 26th, 2014
[456] *Ibid.*
[457] *Ibid.*, Feb. 24th, 2014
[458] Senior Researcher Feb. 21st, 2014, *supra*.
[459] *Ibid.*
[460] *Ibid.*, Feb. 26th, 2014

confiscated.[461]

The President of ICI indicated that although hard copies of Bibles are not very accessible, Bibles can be accessed online.[462] He added that Internet speeds are intentionally slow, and it is difficult to download documents.[463] The Danish and Norwegian fact-finding mission to Iran reports that, according to Elam Ministries, a UK-based evangelist Christian organization that aims to "strengthen and expand" Christianity in Iran by accelerating church growth and training Iranian church leaders, access to materials is inhibited by the "filtering and blocking" of websites by the authorities. According to the ICHRI," Persian-language Christian websites are blocked, and the four Persian language Christian satellite stations are intermittently jammed. However, according to the President of ICI, Christians from non-ethnic backgrounds can do research about Christianity "on their own," as information about Christianity is available on the Internet. The senior researcher indicated some non-ethnic Christians have DVDs which contain Christian materials, such as songs and videos. The Senior Researcher said that some people convert "before ever touching a Bible," and then

---

[461] *Ibid.*
[462] *Ibid.*
[463] ICI, Feb.26th, 2014

later absorb Christian materials.

Corroborating information could not be found among the sources consulted by the Research Directorate within the time constraints of this Response.

Christian Holidays

The Pastor expressed the view that knowledge of Christian holidays may be limited for non-ethnic Iranian Christians, depending on their exposure to Western culture and events, which are "heavily influenced" by Christian traditions (24 Feb. 2014). The Danish and Norwegian fact-finding mission similarly indicates that most conversions are directly related to the reading of the Bible. Converts, as a result, are readily referring to the source, i.e. the Bible, and the stories that are encountered in it and perhaps not so much to the well-known religious holidays that Christians generally refer to. It was explained that there is no mention of an actual Christmas celebration in the Bible. The Christmas celebration is a tradition that emerged later on in history after Christianity had been embraced as state religion. It is thus a product of Christian culture more than of biblical faith. Also, according to the Bible, the Easter story of Jesus death and resurrection is commemorated consistently by Christians every Sunday, forming the central theme of sermons and through the sharing of communion (bread and wine). Easter of course was also observed by Jews in biblical times, being rooted in the Old Testament story of Israel's deliverance out of Egypt. Consequently, the theological meaning of why Jesus came and why he died and rose again is the very core of what Iranian converts believe and celebrate consistently. However, the significance lies in the meaning of these stories for their personal lives and relationship with God, rather than in the way these events may be celebrated at special occasions during the year. The Christian holidays tend to get more attention in societies that have a historical cultural heritage of Christianity and thus follow the Christian calendar.[464]

The Pastor indicated that some non-ethnic Christians in Iran practice on Friday, because it is a day off in Iran. Corroborating information could not be found among the sources consulted by the Research Directorate within the time constraints of this Response.

Baptisms

According to the senior researcher, not all non-ethnic Christians are baptized. The President of

---

[464] Denmark and Norway, Feb. 14th, 2013

ICI indicated that baptisms of non-ethnic Christians are "not done in Iran these days" because the government said that a person who performs baptisms will be subject to severe punishment. The Danish and Norwegian fact-finding mission found that, according to the Assembly of God [reportedly "a recognized church that operates in Persian" in Iran[465] they stopped baptizing Muslims some years ago.[466] Reference was made to a pastor that had been locked up for baptizing prior to this, and it was added that baptism is not a requirement in order to become a member of the Assembly of God Church.[467] The senior researcher similarly indicated that ethnic churches "more or less" stopped baptizing non-ethnic Christians, however this "doesn't mean that it does not happen secretly." The senior researcher added that conducting baptisms is perceived to be dangerous and individuals in the church fear reprisals. The Danish and Norwegian fact-finding mission to Iran found that, according to an international organization in Ankara "many of the house church members are not baptized as baptism is the proof of conversion" and the consequences someone could face are "serious, according to the law." The President of the ICI indicated punishment may include the death penalty. Similarly, the ICHRI reports that Iranian

---

[465] ICHRI 2013, p. 66
[466] Denmark and Norway, 2013, p. 13
[467] *Ibid.*

authorities perceive apostasy as a crime "punishable by death."

The Pastor indicated although Iranian pastors living in Iran normally do not baptize Muslims because of the dangers, some non-ethnic Christians may "still be baptized" in Iran.[468] The Danish and Norwegian fact-finding mission states that, according to an elder from the International Protestant Church of Ankara, sometimes house churches may baptize someone. The senior researcher also said that some people are baptized in house churches "depending on the house church," and added that the decision of whether to baptize someone lies with the *defacto* leader of the house church.[469] He added that some non-ethnic Christians who have been baptized consider themselves to have converted to Christianity before they were baptized.[470]

Several sources indicate that some non-ethnic Christians are baptized outside of Iran, such as in Turkey,[471] or Armenia and Azerbaijan.[472] The President of ICI indicated that, in his view, this process "may take some time" as the Pastor

---

[468] Pastor Mar. 21st, 2014
[469] Senior Researcher, Feb. 21st, 2014
[470] *Ibid.*
[471] *Ibid.*; also see Pastor Feb. 24th, 2014; ICI, Feb. 26th, 2014
[472] Denmark and Norway 2013, p. 13, *supra.*

would build a relationship with the person to ensure that their request for baptism is "genuine."[473]

The Pastor indicated that many non-ethnic Christians, even if they were baptized, will not have baptismal records.[474] He said that, if a baptismal record is given to authorities, the record would incriminate the person who was baptized, and the person who performed the baptism and signed the record would "face problems with the regime."[475] The Pastor added that some non-ethnic Christians who have been baptized might receive their baptismal records late, such as when they are leaving Iran or when they have left Iran.[476] He also said that letters of baptism "may come from a third party," such as American Christian organizations which are connected with underground churches and baptize Iranians in secret.[477] According to the Danish and Norwegian fact-finding mission to Iran, referring to a source from the Assembly of God:

> [R]egarding documentation of baptism, the source considered it very unlikely that established churches would issue such documents. Whether house churches would

---

[473] See Pastor Feb. 24th, 2014; ICI, Feb. 26th, 2014, *supra.*
[474] Pastor, Feb. 24th, 2014
[475] *Ibid.*
[476] *Ibid.*
[477] *Ibid.*

issue such documents, the source considered
that they might baptize each other within the
movement but that they have no formal
theological education and they are very much
on their own. Finally, the source stated that
the source could not imagine that any official
church leader would baptize Muslims
formally and officially.[478]

Pre-2015, Religious Crimes in Iran[479]

An August 2014 note of the UN Secretary-
General to the UN General Assembly states that
the *Islamic Penal Code* (IPC) that came into force
in 2013 "omits references to apostasy, witchcraft
and heresy."[480] However, as indicated by the Iran
Human Rights Documentation Center (IHRDC),
the IPC includes criminal provisions for swearing
at the Prophet.[481]

Apostasy

Converting to another religion typically defines
apostasy:

---

[478] Denmark and Norway, *supra.*, Feb. 13th, 2013
[479] ACCORD, *supra.* Also see Iran Human Rights Documentation
Center, "Apostasy in the Islamic Republic of Iran," July 30th, 2014
(https://iranhrdc.org/apostasy-in-the-islamic-republic-of-iran/ -
retrieved: January 12th, 2017)
[480] UN General Assembly, August 27th, 2014, p. 4
[481] IHRDC, July 30th, 2014, p. 1

Although apostasy is punishable by death in Iran, the Islamic Republic has never codified the crime of apostasy. Instead, relying on the Iranian Constitution, the Islamic Penal Code authorizes the enforcement of certain Islamic laws known as *hodud* crimes even when the crime is not specifically mentioned in the criminal code. The fact that apostasy is not explicitly proscribed by the Iranian legal framework, and the differences in interpretations of Islamic law regarding apostasy, contribute to a lack of legal certainty for those living under Iranian laws.[482] Iranian authorities would usually charge one of "…charged with apostasy, insulting Islam, membership in groups or organizations opposed to the Islamic Republic and engaging in propaganda on their behalf."[483] The penalty for apostasy is death, which UDHR says is contrary to internal law: "Therefore, imposing the death penalty for apostasy and swearing at the prophet is a clear violation of the right to life as recognized under the UDHR and the ICCPR."

As noted in the July 2014 US Department of State (USDOS) International Religious Freedom Report on the year 2013, the Iranian state "automatically considers a child born to a Muslim father to be a Muslim and deems conversion from Islam to be apostasy."[484] The June 2015 Country Report on Human Rights Practices of the USDOS, which covers events of

---

[482] Iran Human Rights Documentation Center, "Apostasy in the Islamic Republic of Iran," September 25, 2014 < https://iranhrdc.org/apostasy-in-the-islamic-republic-of-iran/> accessed on January 21st, 2023

[483] *Ibid.*

[484] USDOS, July 28th, 2014, section 2

2014, states:

> The law does not stipulate the death penalty for apostasy or heresy, but courts handed down capital punishments in prior years based on their interpretation of fatwas (legal opinions or decrees handed down by an Islamic religious leader).[485]

A May 2014 publication of the US Library of Congress (LoC) on laws criminalizing apostasy in the Middle East briefly outlines the legal situation with regard to apostasy in Iran:

"Iran's current Penal Code, which was approved by the country's Guardian Council on January 18, 2012, does not include provisions criminalizing apostasy. However, a draft form of the Code containing several provisions on apostasy had been approved by the Iranian Parliament in principal on September 9, 2008, but was not subsequently adopted.

While Iranian law does not provide for the death penalty for apostasy, the courts can hand down that punishment, and have done so in previous years, based on their interpretation of Shari'a law and fatwas (legal opinions or decrees issued by Islamic religious leaders)."[486]

---

[485] USDOS, June 25th, 2015, section 1a
[486] LoC, May 2014, p. 7

An October 2013 report of the International Federation for Human Rights (FIDH) notes that "[a]postasy, sorcery, witchcraft and other such issues have not been explicitly mentioned in the new IPC, although Apostasy has been specifically referred to in the Press Code (Article 26)". The source further states that "[u]nder the sharia, the punishment for apostasy is death, which a judge can impose by invoking Article 167 of the *Constitution*."[487]

The UK-based *Economist* newspaper states that judgment on apostasy "rests on *fatwas* by the country's dozen-odd grand ayatollahs, who are divided on the matter," mentioning that "*the supreme leader supports the death penalty for apostasy*."[488]

In July 2014, the Iran Human Rights Documentation Center (IHRDC) published a detailed report on judicial dealings with apostasy as well as swearing at the Prophet in Iran. The report states that "[u]nder Iranian law, a Muslim who leaves his or her faith or converts to another religion can be charged with apostasy" and that apostasy is a capital offence. Although apostasy "has not been explicitly mentioned as a crime" in the IPC, "provisions in the *Islamic Penal Code* and

---

[487] FIDH, October 2013, p. 6 [emphasis added].
[488] *Economist*, September 14th, 2012

the Iranian *Constitution* state that Shari'a, or Islamic religious law, applies to situations in which the law is silent, thus enabling the judiciary to "bring apostasy charges based on its interpretation of Shari'a law."[489]
The role of state law with regard to apostasy is detailed as follows:

> Despite the fact that Iranian courts have found many individuals guilty of apostasy, there is no provision in the IPC [Islamic *Penal Code*] criminalizing the act. There are, however, several legal provisions that give judges the discretion to find defendants guilty of **apostasy**. Article 167 of Iran's *Constitution* declares:
>
> > "The judge is bound to endeavour to judge each case on the basis of the codified law. In case of the absence of any such law, he has to deliver his judgment on the basis of authoritative Islamic sources and authentic *fatwa*. He, on the pretext of the silence of or deficiency of law in the matter, or its brevity or contradictory nature, cannot refrain from admitting and examining cases and delivering his judgment."
>
> Accordingly, Article 220 of the IPC states, Article 167 of the Constitution of the Islamic Republic of Iran applies regarding the *hudūd* not specified in this code. *Hudūd* is the plural for *hadd*. Article 15 of the IPC defines hadd as a punishment for which its cause, category, quantity and quality are determined by Shari'a

---

[489] IHRDC, July 30th, 2014, p. 1

> law. As such, Article 220 of the IPC effectively
> states that crimes punishable under Iranian law
> are not limited to the ones specified in the IPC.
> This provision leaves the door open for
> prosecutors and judges to bring charges and
> render convictions based on crimes not explicitly
> defined or even mentioned in any code. Article 8
> of the Establishing Law for the Public and
> Revolutionary Courts also states that judges
> should rely on existing laws as well as Article 167
> of the *Constitution* in resolving disputes. The
> principle that Shari'a law should be enforced
> when there is no codified law is also applicable in
> civil matters (emphasis added).[490]

The same report states that due to the lack of specific provisions on apostasy in the IPC, "there is no explicit provision describing the manner in which a charge of apostasy may be proven". The report outlines that Article 160 of the IPC deals with methods of proving criminal conduct in general: "Nevertheless, Article 160 of the IPC mentions the different methods by which the commission of a crime may be proven. According to this article, confessions, the testimony of two male witnesses or the 'knowledge of the judge' can each be the basis for a conviction."[491]

As regards Shi'a jurisprudence on apostasy, the IHRDC notes that a distinction is made whether an apostate is born to Muslim or non-Muslim

---

[490] IHRDC, *ibid.*, pp. 10-11
[491] IHRDC, *ibid.*, p. 13

parents. Furthermore, Shia jurists hold that female apostates should be exempted from execution:

> Shi'a jurisprudence makes a distinction between an apostate who is born to Muslim parents (murtad-i fitri) and an apostate who is born to non-Muslim parents (murtad-imilli). According to jurists such as Ayatollah Khomeini, the repentance of apostates born to Muslim parents cannot be accepted. Therefore, such apostates are to be killed. Even if only one of the parents is a Muslim at the time of conception, that person is considered to be a Muslim. An apostate who is not born to Muslim parents is considered to be a murtad-i milli. Such an apostate will be given a chance to repent, and he is only to be executed if he does not repent. Some jurists have held that a murtad-e milli should be given a three-day period to repent, and he should be killed if he refuses to repent after three days. [...]

> Based on a number of oral traditions attributed to Shi'a Imams, Shi'a jurists believe that female apostates are not to be killed. Ayatollah Khomeini states that a female apostate is to be imprisoned for life, beaten at times of prayer and afforded only a small amount of food. If she repents, she is to be set free.[492]

As regards judicial practice, the IHRDC notes that apostasy cases are "rare occurrences" in

---

[492] IHRDC, *ibid.*, pp. 8-9

Iran. Nonetheless, as the report goes on to say, a "diverse group of individuals" has been charged with apostasy and swearing at the Prophet, "Muslim-born converts to Christianity, Bahá'ís, Muslims who challenge the prevailing interpretation of Islam, and others who espouse unconventional religious beliefs have been targeted and prosecuted by the Iranian state." The report adds that "[i]n some instances, apostasy cases have clear political overtones, while others seem to be primarily of a religious nature."[493]

The June 2015 USDOS Country report on human rights practices during 2014 notes that if an alleged act of "libel, insult, or criticism involves Islam or national security, the responsible person may be charged with apostasy and crimes against national security, respectively."[494] A June 2014 report of DIS fact-finding mission report on the situation of Christian converts states with reference to information provided by an international organization in Turkey that "[t]he latest case where a convert has been charged with apostasy is that of Yousef Naderkhani, a Church of Iran pastor"[495] who was "charged with apostasy in 2010, but was later acquitted."[496] The

---

[493] IHRDC, *supra.*, p. 1
[494] USDOS, June 25th, 2015, section 2a
[495] DIS, June 23rd, 2014, p. 7
[496] DIS, *ibid.*, p. 13.

international organization in Turkey and
Amnesty International (AI) are referred to as
noting the following developments in charges
brought against Christian converts since 2009-
2010:

> In 2009-2010, when Naderkhani's case came up,
> courts were being pressured by the regime to
> make use of apostasy charges in cases regarding
> converts. However, the courts were reluctant as
> apostasy cases were reserved to special religious
> courts for clergy. Religious courts were legally the
> only courts that could try apostasy charges and
> therefore, only in the instance where a religious
> cleric had converted, would such a charge be
> applicable. Instead, in courts outside of the
> religious courts, the cases involving converts
> would then rather be on charges of disturbing the
> public order than apostasy.

> Since 2011, the only significant change in the way
> the authorities are treating the converts to
> Christianity is the crystallization that apostasy is
> not applicable to converts to Christianity. The
> Iranian authorities stated in 2009 to 2011 that
> house churches were linked to outside
> movements, for example Zionist movements,
> and organizations abroad, for example in the US.
> The regime sees the efforts of evangelical
> movements as a drive against the Iranian regime.
> As a result, evangelical churches and house
> churches are viewed in a national security frame.
> This view of the regime explains why some cases
> involving converts, specifically leaders of house
> churches, also involved charges of a more
> political nature. [...]

According to AIIS, the pattern of persecution of
religious minorities appears to have seen a shift
over time. In the early years following the 1979
Islamic Revolution into the 1980s and 1990's,
there appeared to be more cases regarding
religious minorities in which the accusations
against individuals explicitly mentioned the
religious belief or faith of an individual. […]

Now, the authorities are likely to charge converts
with vaguely worded and broadly defined charges
such as 'forming of illegal groups', 'acting against
national security through illegal gatherings' and
other similar charges that are imprecise and
potentially could capture a range of activities. It
was added that this trend was not specific to the
group of Christian converts but that these sorts
of charges are used to silence a large group of
people, including members of religious
minorities such as Baha'is, members of ethnic
minorities, and others who peacefully express
their rights.[497]

In a March 2014 report to the Human Rights
Council (HRC), the UN Special Rapporteur on
the situation of human rights in the Islamic
Republic of Iran quotes sources as reporting that
"although prosecutions for the capital offence of
apostasy are very rare, officials routinely threaten
to prosecute Christian converts for apostasy".
While apostasy is "not found in any Iranian
criminal law", this offense "has been prosecuted
based on an Islamic law interpretation."[498]

---

[497] DIS, June 23rd, 2014, pp. 7-8
[498] HRC, March 18th, 2014, p. 11

The June 2014 fact-finding mission report of
DIS quotes Mansour Borji, an advocacy officer
at Article 18, a London-based initiative of the
United Council of Iranian Churches, as saying
that there are "no recent cases in court where an
individual has been charged with apostasy".
However, the same report refers to
representatives of the Istanbul-based Union
Church, according to whom a "high number" of
people has been arrested and "accused of
apostasy."[499]

The same report goes on to quote Elam
Ministries, a UK-based Iranian Christian NGO,
as informing that "[w]hen a house church is
raided, the authorities will detain the whole of
the group and interrogate them often
intimidating and threatening them with charges
of apostasy but most often they are released
without charges."[500]

A May 2015 thematic report of the Netherlands
Ministry of Foreign Affairs (Ministerie van
Buitenlandse Zaken, BZ) indicates in its section
on apostasy that at present, prosecution takes
place through application of *Penal Code* articles
that relate to crimes against state security, with
moharebeh (enmity against God and thus against

---

[499] DIS, *supra.*, p. 11
[500] DIS, *ibid.*, p. 32

the state) and *mofsed-e-filarz* (spreading corruption against the social order) being the most frequently invoked offences. Both offences may be punished by death. The BZ states that during the reporting period (December 2013 to April 2015), the death penalty for "moharebeh" was imposed several times.[501]

Pre-2018, House Churches and Converts in Iran[502]

Control with the House Churches and Converts

It is difficult for the authorities to control house churches as they are dispersed, not structured and unknown. The closure of churches affiliated with the "Assembly of God" in 2013 has resulted in the spread of house churches, as people who were attending the church services began to go to house churches instead. One source noted that house churches are quite common in Iran and their numbers are growing.

---

[501] BZ, May 7th, 2015, p. 11
[502] Denmark. Danish Immigration Services, "Iran. House Churches and Converts," (https://www.nyidanmark.dk/-/media/Files/US/Landerapporter/Report---House-churches-and-Converts---220218.pdf?la=en-GB&hash=3A687E2BB8A90B45E253B94BE1AC49684E0A0375, retrieved: January 16th, 2019); also see ACCORD, "Query Response: Iran: House Churches; Situation of Practising Christians; Treatment by Authorities of Christian Converts' Family Members," June 14th, 2017 (https://www.refworld.org/docid/5943a44d4.html)

According to the source, the increasing number of house churches show that they have space to operate, even though they are illegal. The authorities fear the expansion of the house churches phenomenon in Iran.

The authorities use informers to infiltrate the house churches. The infiltrators are identified and selected by the authorities. To prevent infiltration and intervention, house churches organize themselves as a mobile group consisting of a small number of people. A source mentioned that the prevention of external infiltration is difficult, as the authorities use informers who pretend to be converts. One source explained that it would be a strategy for the authorities to either monitor or arrest and release members of a house church to make an informant out of them. The authorities could use information on the person's background to put pressure on them.

House churches are monitored by the authorities. If the authorities receive a report about a specific house church, a monitoring process will be initiated, one source noted. However, the authorities will not act immediately, as the authorities want to collect information about both the members and who is doing what in the community. Flourishing house

churches are more in danger, as the authorities
see these churches as a bigger threat. Whether
the authorities will intervene depends on the
activities of the house church and the size of the
group. A source said that the house churches are
systematically raided.

There have not been any significant changes in
the authorities' control with house churches
recently. One source pointed out that there has
been a change in the authorities monitoring of
social media and online activities. Another source
added that there is a widespread monitoring of
telecommunication and electronic
communication if a Christian has caught the
interest of the authorities. Certain keywords
serve as base for the electronic surveillance e.g.
"church," "Jesus," "Christian," and "baptism."
As it is well-known that the authorities are
tapping phones, the house members are cautious
and turn off their phones long before they reach
their meeting place. Furthermore, the authorities
are more alerted to activities threatening the
established system.

There has been a change in the way the Iranian
authorities look at Christians in general. The
change started after the green revolution in 2009,
as the Christians are perceived to bring ideas of
freedom. It is unknown to what extent the
Iranian authorities have the capacity to monitor

everybody. The authorities do not monitor everyone all the time; what the authorities want is to create a fear among people that they are being monitored all the time, a source highlighted.

Follow-up Activities of the Authorities in Cases Related to Members of House Churches and Converts

Neighbours, who have become aware of unusual activities around a house, can cause a house church to be revealed for the authorities. A foreigner interacting with Christians in Iran added that otherwise, the authorities do not have the possibility to know about the house church as members are discrete about it. It is unlikely that a family member will report to the authorities on a converted family member. However, it occurs in cases where the family member is a government employee or whose professional and/or social status is affected by the Christian family member. One source added that many families are loyal to the regime and have a *Basij* member within the family. If there are children in the family, they could also inform their teachers about activities in their homes, at school.

The authorities are primarily targeting the house church leaders and secondary the members and converts. Two other sources stated that the authorities target both the leaders of the house churches and the members.

The typical pattern of targeting is by arresting and releasing the house church leaders, as the authorities want to weaken the house church. Ordinary members of house churches also risk arrest in a house church. However, they will be released again on the condition that they stay away from proselytizing. If they stop proselytizing, the authorities will stop gathering information about them, a source added. One source mentioned that it would be possible for an arrested convert to pay his/her way out of an arrest. The source added that even if it is known that the person is a converted Muslim, it would be a question of the amount of money paid to be released. Whether a house church member is targeted also depends on his/her conducted activities and if he/she is known abroad, the same source noted. Ordinary house church members risk being called in for interrogation on a regular basis as the authorities want to harass and intimidate them, a source explained.

If a house church member is arrested for the first time, he/she will normally be released within 24 hours. If he/she has been detained in prison, he/she will receive his charge within 24 hours and come to court within ten days, a source mentioned.

A conversion and an anonymous life as a converted Christian in itself do not lead to an arrest, but if the conversion is followed up by other activities as for instance proselytizing and training others, the case differs; the same applies if family members report the convert to the authorities. One source highlighted that if a convert does not proselytize or promote a house church, the authorities will not know about him/her. Middle East Concern, however, did not consider a life as an anonymous Christian as sustainable, as converts, in this case, have to lie about their faith and act against their religion. Amnesty International added that a conversion might be revealed to the surrounding community if the convert does not participate in Islamic events as many social norms and cultural activities are connected to Islam.

Converts who tell their family about their conversion risk getting into trouble; they risk exclusion and threats from the family who might think that the converted family members will create a problem for them. According to one source many converts do not tell their families about the conversion.

Several sources addressed the issue regarding

Iranian converts returning from Europe. According to two sources, converted returnees who do not carry out activities related to Christianity upon return will not be of interest to the authorities. Middle East Concern made the distinction whether the converted person was known before leaving Iran or not; returning will cause problems if the convert has been known by the authorities before leaving. If the opposite is the case, going back to Iran would not be problematic. Converts who announce their conversion in public may face serious problems.

If the returned convert has been very outspoken about his/her conversion on social media, including Facebook, the authorities might become aware of it and arrest and interrogate the convert upon return. A Western embassy said that the subsequent process would depend on what the returnees inform the authorities about. The embassy did not consider that the converts would receive harsh punishment if they are not high-profiled and are not involved in propagating Christianity or activities perceived as a threat to national security.

Declaring conversion on Facebook in itself does not lead to persecution but likely to monitoring. One source explained that a photo indicating a conversion posted on the Internet would be evaluated by the authorities along with the profile and activities of the converted person. If the person did not have any previous affiliation with Christianity before leaving the country, he/she will not be persecuted.

If a converted person uses the religion politically to for instance compare disadvantages of Islam with advantages of Christianity or another religion on social media, it could be a problem for him, a source mentioned. Most Iranians are not very religious, but they might see conversion as a way to come closer to Western values, and as a protest against the system, another source mentioned. However, it was underlined that it would apply to a person who has made his/her own analysis of the two religions and not someone who has used "copy paste" phrases.

A baptism in itself will not have significance, according to two sources. A foreigner interacting with Christians in Iran noted that it is doubtful whether it would make a difference for the authorities if the convert is baptized. Middle East Concern source considered that a baptism, which is documented, could alert the authorities and prove to be problematic.

Recent Trial Cases Related to
House Churches and Converts

Christian converts are typically not charged with apostasy; convert cases are usually considered as national security matters59 which are handled by the Revolutionary Court. A source added that the authorities perceive activities related to conversion as political activities.

Death penalty in cases related to conversion is not a common punishment. A Western embassy highlighted that the implementation of the death penalty in Iran is related to drug and murder cases, and more rarely to high-profile political cases. A Western embassy noted that there has not been issued a death sentence for conversion the last 10 years.

The authorities are not filing cases against converts, and no one in Iran has been arrested solely because of a conversion, a Western embassy stated. Middle East Consultancy Service added that there is no legislation on apostasy in the *Penal Code*, however, many converts are prosecuted.

Organizers of house churches might risk accusations of "Crimes against God" which would carry the death penalty, a source stated. However, the source did not know of any cases where this accusation has resulted in actual execution of the accused.

As regards prosecution of house church members, one source stated that it would probably only be the leader of the House Church, while another source said that this goes both for low profile cases and for house church leader.

Pre-2018, State Monitoring Online Activities of Iranian Converts[503]

Inside Iran[504]

Amnesty International technologist Claudio Guarnieri and Collin Anderson, an independent cyber researcher, who have been studying Iranian hacking activities for several years, provide the following overview in a report published in August 2016:

> [S]ince the propagandic defacements of international communications platforms and

---

[503] Austrian Red Cross. Austrian Centre for Country of Origin and Asylum Research and Documentation, "Iran: Capacity and Methods of Authorities to Monitor Online Activities and Religious Activities of Iranians Living Abroad," January 11th, 2018 (http://www.refworld.org/docid/5943a56e4.html, retrieved: September 8th, 2019)

[504] *Ibid.* Also, extensive information on Iranian authorities' efforts for internet control and can be found in the following reports: Guarnieri, Claudio/ Anderson, Collin: Iran and the Soft War for Internet Dominance, August 2016 (https://iranthreats.github.io/us-16-Guarnieri-Anderson-Iran-And-The-Soft-War-ForInternet-Dominance-paper.pdf)

political dissident sites conducted by an
organization describing itself as the 'Iranian
Cyber Army' beginning in late 2009, Iranian
actors have been attributed in campaigns of
intrusions and disruptions of private companies,
foreign government entities, domestic
opposition, regional adversaries and international
critics. [...] Civil society and political opponents
are a primary target of Iranian intrusion
campaigns [...].

Our research incurs classic issues applicable to all reports on intrusion campaigns, primarily questions of attribution and intent. The end objective of particular CNO [Computer Network Operations] activities is not always discernable based on the tactics used or the data accessed, as the end implications of the disclosure of particular information is often distant and concealed from even the target. Where such intent is made evident, the reasons for Iranian intrusion campaigns range from retaliatory campaigns against adversaries, as a result of identifiable grievances, to surveillance of domestic opposition in support of the Islamic Republic establishment. Iranian intrusion sets appear to be interested in a broad field of challenges to the political and religious hegemony of the Islamic Republic. Previous reports on Iranian campaigns have referred to the targeting of Iranian dissidents, however, in practice those targeted range from reformists operating within the establishment from inside of Iran to violent extremist organizations outside.

Therefore, "Iranian CNO activities should be considered as a tool in the context broader state activities and policies, including offline events."[505]

The March 2017 USDOS country report on human rights practices 2016, which covers events of 2016, reports that the Iranian authorities "monitored private online communications" and "collected personally identifiable information in connection with citizens' peaceful expression of political, religious, or ideological opinion or beliefs."[506]

The same report refers to the Basij 'Cyber Council' and the Cyber Police (FATA) as examples of state organizations involved in "targeted citizens' activities on social networking websites officially banned":

> Government organizations, including the Basij
> 'Cyber Council, 'the Cyber Police, and the Cyber
> Army, which observers presumed to be
> controlled by the IRGC, monitored, identified,
> and countered alleged cyber threats to national
> security. These organizations especially targeted
> citizens' activities on social networking websites
> officially banned by the Committee in Charge of
> Determining Offensive Content, such as

---

[505] Guarnieri/Anderson, August 2016, pp. 1-2
[506] USDOS, March 3rd, 2017, section 2a

Facebook, Twitter, YouTube, and Flickr, and
reportedly harassed persons who criticized the
government or raised sensitive social
problems.[507]

A brief summary of the objectives of the Cyber
Police (FATA), an institution created in 2011,
can be found on the organization's undated
website:

> The purpose of establishing cyber police is to
> secure cyber space, to protect national and
> religious identity, community values, legal liberty,
> national critical infrastructure against electronic
> attacks, to preserve interests and national
> authority in cyberspace and to assure people in
> all legal affairs such as economic, social and
> cultural activities in order to preserve national
> power and sovereignty. Cyber police of Islamic
> Republic of Iran was established in 2011 based
> on internal and international standards in order
> to prevent, investigate and combat cybercrime.[508]

The Freedom House Freedom on the Net 2016
report of November 2016, which covers
developments from June 2015 up to May 2016,
gives the following overview of efforts by the
Iranian state to monitor cyberspace:

> The online sphere is heavily monitored by the
> state in Iran. In preparation for elections to the
> legislature and Assembly of Experts, Iran's
> deputy interior minister for security announced a
> new 'Elections Security Headquarters' would be

---

[507] *Ibid.*
[508] FATA, undated

established 'to monitor cyberspace.' Similarly, the IRGC [Islamic Revolutionary Guards Corps] launched a military exercise named 'Eghtedare Sarallah' in September 2015, which included the monitoring of social media activities. In June 2015, Iran's Cyber Police (FATA) created a new unit for monitoring computer games.

It remains unclear how the authorities can technically monitor the content of messages on foreign social networks, given that some apps encrypt their messages. However, all platforms and content hosted in Iran are subject to arbitrary requests by various authorities to provide more information on their users. Local equivalents of international platforms do not guarantee an adequate level of protection for users, which may explain users' hesitancy to adopt domestic platforms. An August 2015 survey of 904 Iranian Internet users found that they felt less comfortable using Iranian social networks.

In a troubling development, the Supreme Council on Cyberspace announced in May 2016 that all foreign messaging apps must move all data on Iranian users to servers located within the country. The order seemed targeted at Telegram, used by some 20 million Iranians, which has been under increased pressure by the authorities over the past year. Storing data on local servers would make it easier for the authorities to compel the company to hand over data on government critics and censor unfavorable views.[509]

---

[509] Freedom House, November 2016

Freedom House goes on to note with regard to the legal status of encryption:

> The legal status of encryption in Iran is somewhat murky. Chapter 2, Article 10 of the Computer Crimes Law prohibits 'concealing data, changing passwords, and/or encoding data that could deny access of authorized individuals to data, computer and telecommunication systems.' This could be understood to prohibit encryption, but enforcement is not common. Nonetheless, the Iranian authorities have periodically blocked encrypted traffic from entering the country through international gateways, particularly during contentious moments such as elections.[510]

The March 2017 USDOS report provides details on government measures taken with regard to the above-mentioned Telegram messaging application:

> An estimated 20 million Iranians use the online messaging application Telegram, which has security features that make the content of users' communications more difficult to be read by a third party. CPJ [Committee to Protect Journalists] nevertheless reported in June that users were at risk of being monitored, as had happened with other similar applications in the past. Iran's Supreme Council of Cyberspace announced on May 29 [2016] that Telegram had one year to move all of its data to servers inside Iran or risk being closed entirely. Telegram users in Iran continued to be harassed for content posted through its servers. According to local

---

[510] *Ibid.*

media reports, the Iranian Cyber Police arrested three Telegram channels administrators on August 9 [2016] for publishing material 'insulting religious sanctities.'"[511]

An August 2016 article of the Reuters news agency reports that over a dozen Telegram accounts belonging to "political activists involved in reformist movements and opposition organizations" have been hacked:

> Iranian hackers have compromised more than a dozen accounts on the Telegram instant messaging service and identified the phone numbers of 15 million Iranian users, the largest known breach of the encrypted communications system, cyber researchers told Reuters. The attacks, which took place this year and have not been previously reported, jeopardized the communications of activists, journalists and other people in sensitive positions in Iran, where Telegram is used by some 20 million people, said independent cyber researcher Collin Anderson and Amnesty International technologist Claudio Guarnieri, who have been studying Iranian hacking groups for three years. [...]

> Telegram's vulnerability, according to Anderson and Guarnieri, lies in its use of SMS text messages to activate new devices. When users want to log on to Telegram from a new phone, the company sends them authorization codes via SMS, which can be intercepted by the phone company and shared with the hackers, the

---

[511] USDOS, March 3rd, 2017, section 2a

researchers said. Armed with the codes, the hackers can add new devices to a person's Telegram account, enabling them to read chat histories as well as new messages. [...]

The Telegram hackers, the researchers said, belonged to a group known as Rocket Kitten, which used Persian-language references in their code and carried out 'a common pattern of spearphishing campaigns reflecting the interests and activities of the Iranian security apparatus.' Anderson and Guarnieri declined to comment on whether the hackers were employed by the Iranian government. Other cyber experts have said Rocket Kitten's attacks were similar to ones attributed to Iran's powerful Revolutionary Guards. The researchers said the Telegram victims included political activists involved in reformist movements and opposition organizations. They declined to name the targets, citing concerns for their safety. 'We see instances in which people ... are targeted prior to their arrest,' Anderson said. 'We see a continuous alignment across these actions.'

The researchers said they also found evidence that the hackers took advantage of a programing interface built into Telegram to identify at least 15 million Iranian phone numbers with Telegram accounts registered to them, as well as the associated user IDs.

That information could provide a map of the Iranian user base that could be useful for future attacks and investigations, they said. [...]

While Facebook and Twitter are banned in Iran, Telegram is widely used by groups across the political spectrum. They shared content on Telegram 'channels' and urged followers to vote

ahead of Iran's parliamentary elections in
February 2016. [...]

Amir Rashidi, an Internet security researcher at
the New York-based International Campaign for
Human Rights in Iran, has worked with Iranian
hacking victims. He said he knew of Telegram
users who were spied on even after they had set
passwords.[512]

In a May 2015 press release, Article 19, a
London-based human rights NGO focusing on
defending and promoting freedom of expression
and information, notes that "Operation
Ankaboot" (or "Spider"), "a surveillance
operation", is "believed to have been launched in
the fall of 2014 to identify and root out
Facebook pages and activities that spread
'corruption' and western-inspired lifestyles". The
operation was acknowledged by the IRGC in
January 2015:

Operation Ankaboot was acknowledged by
officials on January 31st, 2015, when the IRGC
Center for Investigation of Organized Cyber
Crimes, a subsidiary of the IRGC Cyber Defense
Command, put out a press release to inform the
public about the shutting down of 130 Facebook
pages, the arrest of 12 and detainment of 24
individuals.[513]

---

[512] Reuters, August 2nd, 2016
[513] Article 19, May 14th, 2015

The March 2017 USDOS report mentions that the government's operations "Spider I" and "Spider II" have led to the arrest of [e]ight online models" and the closure of an "unannounced number of online Instagram, Telegram, and Facebook pages in May 2016 "for 'immoral content' after images were posted that did not adhere to government-sanctioned dress requirements" (USDOS, March 3rd, 2017, section 2a).The May Article 19 press release notes with regard to the Iranian authorities' online monitoring capabilities:

> Beyond anecdotal evidence, documenting and confirming evidence of surveillance and monitoring of social media has proved difficult. However, at times, officials have publicly stated that they are actively monitoring Iranian citizens' activities on both blocked and unblocked websites and platforms. For instance, in September of 2014, The Chief of Iran's Cyber Police (FATA), warned the public about FATA's ability to monitor messaging applications such as Viber and WhatsApp. This announcement was made subsequent to the arrest of a number of Viber users who were targeted based on the exchange of 'inappropriate content.' While not offering conclusive evidence of surveillance, public statements by officials acknowledging surveillance activities does work to perpetuate concern, if not fear over whether the government's activities and capacity to monitor online activity, in particular social media. [...]
>
> Following the press release announcing Operation Ankaboot, Mostafa Alizadeh, a cyber-expert with the IRGC explained that the IRGC

can monitor all social networks, and those who
have deemed these platforms a safe place should
reconsider, as they are being watched. However,
from a technical perspective, the possibility of
this level of surveillance and scale of probing
remains unverifiable [...].[514]

An older query response of the Immigration and
Refugee Board of Canada (IRB) of January 2014
refers to several sources as saying that Iran's
authorities "monitor online activities [...]
including online activities outside of Iran". The
query response quotes a professor of political
science and public policy at York University
(Canada) as saying that "all Iranian websites are
closely monitored by the regime". The query
response also quotes a professor of modern
Middle Eastern history at the University of
Toronto with research experience in Iran as
indicating that Iranian authorities are "very
active' in cyber-monitoring, including monitoring
e-mail and online conversations". Meanwhile, the
IRB, with reference to the Director of the UK-
based NGO Small Media and the history
professor, notes that the authorities do not
monitor all online activities of Iranians:

> The Director of Small Media indicated that
> Iranian authorities do not have the technical
> capacity to conduct 'blanket monitoring,' which
> means that they do not follow all Iranian citizens'

---

[514] *Ibid.*

online activities (14 Jan. 2014). Similarly, the
Professor of history indicated that the
government does not seem to monitor all online
activities (Professor of History 13 Jan. 2014).[515]

Small Media, a UK-based NGO providing digital
research, training and advocacy solutions to civil
society actors who assist groups at risk, notes in
an older September/October 2013 article that
"[g]enerally, Iranian organizations", including the
cyber police [FATA], have had "problems
securing access to skilled workers and technical
resources". As a result, the article states, FATA
has been using "unconventional methods" to
identify and track down persons online, including
"acts of manipulation on social networking
sites":

> One of the most popular methods used by
> FATA is the creation of fake Facebook profiles,
> through which they may encourage other users to
> divulge personal information. Over the course of
> an investigation, a FATA agent can collect
> numerous pieces of information about a user
> from their social network accounts, linking them
> together to build a completer and more accurate
> image of the user.[516]

The same report further notes with regard to
FATA's capabilities:

> FATA's Central Unit has always shared the latest

---

[515] IRB, January 20th, 2014
[516] Small Media, September/October 2013, p. 3

technical research on surveillance and
enforcement methods with other FATA offices
around the country. In addition, this unit
attempts to locate loopholes and zero-day
vulnerabilities in Iranian computer systems and
software, in an effort to prevent security
weaknesses from being exploited. Besides this
Central Unit, FATA is also composed of a
number of more specialist sections, with the
Technical Department being one of them. Here,
a number of technical workers receive regular
training regarding Internet and computer
networks and security issues (though it should be
noted that most staff at FATA are not
technically-trained). Regardless, FATA claims
that its activities are incredibly far-ranging, with
FATA's chief in Kerman Province, Kambiz
Esmaeili, stating that the organization monitors
all activity on websites, blogs and forums on a
24/7 basis.[517]

A November 2015 article of *Al-Monitor*, an
online news platform focusing on coverage of
the Middle East, notes that "Iran's security
apparatus has been accumulating the skills and
expertise to limit the security risks presented by
social media ever since the protests in the
aftermath of the disputed 2009 presidential
election". The article goes on to state that the
government has acquired expertise in "data-
mining techniques, enabling it to find potential
troublemakers who use the web as a tool for

---

[517] Small Media, *ibid.*, pp. 3-4

stirring political unrest."[518]

A January 2015 Small Media report quotes analysts as saying that the authorities have been using Deep Packet Inspection (DPI) technology since the disputed 2009 presidential election to "analyze email content and track browsing history" of Internet users.[519]

In a July 2015 report, Article 19 describes the infiltration of Internet groups as a method commonly used by Iranian authorities:

> Infiltrating online groups is a commonly used strategy by the authorities. They use a variety of methods to ascertain the offline identities of individuals such as moderators or administrators of online groups. The methods employed vary, depending on the platform. Facebook, for instance, has been the platform the authorities have most commonly used. Methods employed in order to gather information and personal data have included the following:
>
> - Creating fake online identities to make friend requests;
> - Writing provocative comments or messages to encourage responses in order to trap the conversant. This style of entrapment is known as an 'agent provocateur';
> - Monitoring the public interactions of users to identify and flag trends. This includes

---

[518] *Al-Monitor*, November 8th, 2015
[519] Small Media, *supra*. p. 27

> using other group members to gather
> intelligence on specific individuals.[520]

Citing an Iranian web provider, a 2016 article of the CHRI notes that "strict censorship and 'security' laws" compel Internet service providers (ISPs) to "expose their customers' information and online activities":

> Iranian Internet service providers are particularly handicapped by strict censorship and 'security' laws that expose their customers' information and online activities. 'Since a few years ago, web hosting companies have been forced to cooperate with Internet monitoring agencies and as a result they can order the removal of any content,' said the web provider, speaking on condition of anonymity. [...] Deleting information from a website requires web hosting companies to violate privacy agreements so that state agencies can access the server's information bank. Internet providers are thus unable to protect customer data.[521]

The same report points to several patterns of online behaviour among Iranian Internet users that put them at risk of being monitored by the state. These include a tendency of not using the Blind Carbon Copy (BCC) function when sending emails to multiple addressees (thus making the names and email addresses of all

---

[520] Article 19, July 2nd, 2015, p. 22
[521] CHRI, March 14th, 2016

persons on the mailing list visible to everyone, "including unreliable contacts"), the use of real names in online activities, and general unawareness of the way information shared on Facebook can be used against them by authorities (including a poor understanding of privacy settings on Facebook). With regard to Facebook, the report specifies that users' common vulnerabilities include "[a]llowing lists of friends to be visible to the public", "[d]istributing mass invitations to events" and "[c]reating open or public groups that allow anyone to join, enabling them to see the details of all group members and activities". The same report further points to some cases where users have been "identified through activity logs on public computers and printers in places such as university campuses or the workplace" and notes that Internet café computers also log their clients' personal information and browsing data". The report goes on to note that Internet Service Providers (ISPs) are obliged to provide information on subscribers to the authority as requested and points to possible risks in the use of Virtual Private Networks (VPNs) as a means of circumventing the filtering and blocking and websites:

> The findings of this report show that ISPs [Internet Service Providers] in Iran do not generally protect the personal information of their subscribers. In fact, Iranian ISPs are mandated by law to provide all information

about their subscribers as the authorities require. All ISPs are subject to strict control and regulations by the authorities and follow national policies on filtering and censorship. As a result, some Internet users take steps to access the Internet in ways that avoid the authorities' filtering and blocking of websites, such as setting up Virtual Private Networks (VPNs). VPN use is common as it is very easy to set up. However, the reliability of VPNs was sometimes called into question; one interviewee believed that his VPN – purchased online – was corrupt, claiming that the authorities had access to it. In some interrogations, the authorities claimed to have gathered information directly from users' VPNs which, whether true or false, decreased Iranians' trust in VPNs. Iranians do not always pay attention to the source of the VPNs, or the software used to run them, that they use to access filtered websites such as Facebook.

In some cases, the authorities established their own VPNs, enabling them to channel users' information through a monitored route, which made surveillance easy." (Article 19, 2 July 2015, pp. 22-25) The March 2017 USDOS report refers to Internet activists as saying that there is a lack of clarity as to whether or not the use of VPNs is illegal:

> The computer crimes law makes it illegal to distribute circumvention tools and virtual private networks, but the law is not clear whether the use of such tools is illegal, according to Internet

activists.[522]

Freedom House states in its Freedom on the Net 2016 report of November 2016 that "[t]he use of VPNs does not appear to be criminalized, unlike the selling or promoting of VPN use", indicating that "several individuals were arrested in late 2015 for promoting, selling, or training individuals to use circumvention tools" (Freedom House, November 2016).

A November 2016 article by Guarnieri and Anderson, which partly refers to information presented at "Black Hat" information security events, notes apparent attempts by Iranian authorities to collect IP addresses using so-called WebRTC protocols. These efforts appear to target political opposition activists and human rights activists:

> In late December, several domains were registered in the name of the Oshkosh Corporation, an American defense industrial firm with subsidiaries in Saudi Arabia. The activities of fictitious social media profiles further indicated a sustained interested in the company, and aligned with a broader campaign of espionage directed at the defense industrial base. The typographic domains impersonated internal VPN resources to obtain employee credentials to private network resources, such as email accounts and shared file servers. Based on common patterns and registration information,

---

[522] USDOS, March 3rd, 2017, section 2a

the Oshkosh Corporation domains appeared to
be maintained by Iranian actors – the same
group behind the Ghambar malware
documented at Black Hat that we believe to be
related to Cylance's Operation Cleaver. The
impersonation sites themselves contained
another function we had not seen amongst
Iranian actors previously – an attempt to
enumerate internal IP addresses in order to
conduct network reconnaissance. This
approached has continued to arise in subsequent
spearphishing attempts, including more banal
Google credential phishing sites targeting Iranian
dissidents, across different campaigns and
different groups.

While at first this tactic could be directed at
identifying security researchers, subsequent
campaign indicates a deeper purpose. The
WebRTC protocol was designed to enable
responsive real-time communications over the
Internet, and is instrumental in allowing
streaming video and conferencing applications to
run in the browser. In order to easily facilitate
direct connections between computers
(bypassing the need for a central server to act as
a gatekeeper), WebRTC provides functionality to
automatically collect the local and public IP
addresses of Internet users (ICE or STUN).
These functions do not require consent from the
user, and can be instantiated by sites that a user
visits without their awareness. The potential
privacy implications of this aspect of WebRTC
are well documented, and certain browsers have
provided options to limit its behavior."[523]

---

[523] Guarnieri/Collins, November 11th, 2016

The same article goes on to describe the context in which these intrusions have taken place, pointing to government censorship of social media platforms (and users' strategies of circumventing them) and to arrests of members of banned online communities such as 11 dissidents and religious activists and, more recently, of "modelling communities, artists, and other social groups engaged in activities persecuted by the hardline establishment":

> The Iranian government's aggressive censorship of social media platforms has inadvertently supported a culture of privacy amongst Internet users. In response to high publicized campaigns against online activists prior to and during the Green Movement, use of pseudonyms on social media is common in Iran. Individuals frequently use initials or locations as their profile names. Moreover, the necessary use of VPNs or circumvention services to bypass the government's filter has afforded an additional degree of protection against passive network surveillance. This also aligns with our direct observation that a significant portion of the Iranian activists compromised by the *Infy* malware campaign regularly used VPN services [...].

> Taken in the context of increased adoption of HTTPS, the government has little direct awareness of the content of certain Internet traffic. In absence of compliance by foreign technology companies to Iranian government requests, the use of anti-filtering tools and consistent maintenance of pseudonyms affords a meaningful degree of privacy to online activists

against identification by domestic security agencies. Quite simply, without intrusions or social engineering, the Iranian government has little visibility into who is participating in certain online communities – or whether they are even in the country.

The response from the government – notably the Islamic Revolutionary Guard Corps – has been highly-public arrests of members of prohibited online communities, such as dissidents or religious minorities. These arrests, given names such as Operation Spider, have intended to send a chilling message to the public that the state is watching online – even to exaggerate its technical capacities. While earlier campaigns targeted activists, in recent months, announced arrests have also included modelling communities, artists, and other social groups engaged in activities persecuted by the hardline establishment. The arrested are often forced to confess on television, delete their accounts, or turn them over to authorities, which are then taken over to post public warnings.

The Iranian Revolutionary Guard Corps has not disclosed investigatory techniques, unsurprisingly. In at least one case, an individual arrested had posted personal information on their profile and would have been easy to identify. However, based on records sourced from infrastructure of Iranian threat groups, it appears that intrusion groups (e.g. Flying Kitten) have engaged in spearphishing against the same sets of targets.

While the recording of internal IPs in spearphishing attempts against private companies

or other institutions could reasonably be
attributed to reconnaissance, in other
documentations cases, the sole purpose of an
engagement was to collect addresses of private
individual with no other action in the attack.
Taken in the context of the targeting of those
attempts, these incidents suggest that certain
Iranian groups appear to be leveraging privacy
issues with WebRTC toward de-anonymizing
social network users.[524]

The same article highlights the following cases
where human rights defenders have been
approached through their social media accounts,
apparently with the purpose of collecting IP
addresses:

> In one case, a social media profile with the name
> 'Maryam Javadifar' – which used pictures of DJ
> and model Mellisa Clarke – approached a human
> rights activist over Facebook. In a series of
> messages, Javadifar claimed that the individual's
> password was found online, on a site hidden
> behind an Iranian short URL service. The site
> (rinpid.com) promised visitors the ability to buy
> psychoactive drugs, sex products, and other
> items prohibited by the 'Islamic regime.'
> Although poorly implemented, with errors and
> failing to hide messages from the copied code,
> the sole function of that bait site is to collect
> visitor IP addresses and report them back to
> operators. The Javadifar profile is over two years
> old, and clearly fake. While Iranian threat actors
> are known for their sustained use of fictitious
> profiles, it is also notable that the Javadifar has
> demonstrated a clear interest in specifically

---

[524] Guarnieri/Collins, *ibid.*

targeting hundreds of political dissidents, primarily members of the Green Movement and Monarchists (supporters of the deposed royal family). [...]

The same approach would arise again targeting Human Rights Activists in Iran (HRA), a well-known human right organization with deep connections within the country. HRA has been repeatedly targeted by different Iranian threat groups, and was amongst those targeted in the early IRGC crackdowns. HRA was approached on one of its Telegram accounts by an unknown individual asking about reports that one of its administrators was arrested. The bait posed as an image (domain name: 'tntnet.ir') and was once again designed to collect IPs. Perhaps ironically, the IP collection site is based on code copied from a service intended to educate users on such leakages, IPLeak.net. After the approach failed, the attacker then modified the previous messages to clean up their tracks.[525]

The March 2017 USDOS report states that in Iran's "National Information Network", which is "intended to act like an 'intranet' system, with full content control and user identification", was launched in August 2016, according to local media reports (USDOS, March 3rd, 2017, section 2a).

A March 2016 Article 19 report elaborates on the National Information Network (referred to here

---

[525] *Ibid.*

as the "National Internet Project"), its relevance for monitoring Internet users and its status of implementation at the time of reporting:

> For years, there has been discussion amongst the Iranian Authorities of a 'national' or 'clean' Internet, while taking steps towards the completion of the 'National Internet Project'. This project aims to create a national, secure and 'clean' Internet, which would be hosted inside the country and have limited access to the content of the World Wide Web. Content within the National Internet would be blocked or filtered according to political, cultural or religious criteria, and its users' activity would be monitored. It was planned that the National Internet Project would be fully implemented by the end of 2015, in three major phases [...] Execution of this three-phase plan has already deviated considerably from expectations. From the onset, severe delays and disorganization have plagued the already daunting task. According to the latest government budget proposal, full implementation of the National Internet Project is not expected before 2019. However, there has been progress in certain areas of implementation, as an example, Iranian authorities celebrate the fact that 40 percent of the content visited by Iranian users is now hosted domestically. [...] The Iranian government has repeatedly stated its intention to monitor citizens through the National Internet.[526]

Reporters Sans Frontières (RSF) reports on the launch of the first phase of the National Information Network in August 2016:

---

[526] Article 19, March 29th, 2016, pp. 1-2

Two news agencies and several information websites have been blocked since 4 September, a week after the official unveiling of the 'National Information Network (NIN),' also known as 'Halal Internet,' while the Centre for Monitoring Organized Crime (a Revolutionary Guard offshoot) has reported the arrest of around 100 Internet users in recent weeks. [...] The first phase of NIN was formally celebrated on 27 August by several government officials including the first vice-president, the minister of communication and information technology and the secretary-general of the Cyberspace Supreme Council. However, they restricted their statements to the usual slogans and did not explain how this NIN will work and what consequences it will have for Iran's Internet users, who are officially estimated to number 30 million. [...] Communication minister Mahmoud Vaezi said, 'the National Information Network imposes no limits on Internet users' but this was contradicted by deputy minister Nasrolah Jahangard, who said: 'In the Network, all connections including mobile connections have identification; without identification, you will not be able to use the Network's services.' As well as such propaganda-style statements, the authorities cite the need for protection as justification for the network – protection against cyber-attacks, protection of the country's sensitive data and the personal data of individual users, and finally protection of Iranian society's 'morality.' In fact, this National Information Network can be likened to a big Intranet, in which content is controlled and all users are identified, an Intranet that can be completely disconnected from the World Wide Web when the authorities so decide.

> It is a personal Internet or 'Halal Internet' based on 'intelligent filtering.' [...] For the past year, different sections of the Revolutionary Guards have been announcing the dismantling and systematic arrest of networks of people who act 'against society's moral security,' 'modelling criminals' (those who have photos and videos of models) and those who 'insult religious beliefs.'[527]

A March 2017 report of the UN Special Rapporteur on the situation of human rights in the Islamic Republic of Iran to the UN Human Rights Council (HRC) mentions reports of intimidation and prosecution of "Internet users, bloggers and social media activists."[528]

Article 19 reported in July 2015:

> According to the findings of this study, ethnic and religious minority activists (the Baha'i's and the Dervishes more than others), as well as members of known political groups, are kept under constant offline and online surveillance. This is intended both to control and suppress those activities of members of these groups that may lead to their recognition, and it is often carried out by special units of the intelligence services dedicated to monitoring minority activists. Methods used by the authorities include continuous blocking of websites, as well as ordering hosting providers to remove data and stop providing services to particular groups.[529]

---

[527] RSF, September 6th, 2016
[528] HRC, March 6th, 2017, p. 13
[529] Article 19, *ibid.*, July 2nd, 2015, p. 24

Iranians Abroad

The query response of the Immigration and Refugee Board of Canada (IRB) of January 2014 refers to several sources as saying that Iran's authorities "monitor online activities [...] including online activities outside of Iran."[530]

A fact-finding-mission report of DIS, published in June 2014, refers to a non-governmental organization in Turkey as saying that Iranian Christian who come to Turkey "feel that they are at risk of surveillance by Iranian agents in Turkey."[531] The DIS quotes an international organization in Turkey as saying that there are reports saying that Iranian authorities have agents and informants in some churches in Turkey, although the source expressed uncertainty as to whether the Iranian authorities' have the capabilities to "monitor those who are visiting Turkey in order to get baptized, for example, in a systematic way". The DIS report states with reference to information provided by Amnesty International (AI)'s International Secretariat:

> Regarding risks to individuals who return to Iran
> after having received religious training in Turkey,

---

[530] IRB, January 20th, 2014
[531] DIS, June 23rd, 2014, p. 37

AIIS (Amnesty International Secretariat) said
that it was possible that Iranian security officials
were monitoring activities that take place in
Turkey. It was considered that generally, it is
probably easier to monitor what goes on in
Turkey due to the geographical proximity and
the ease with which Iranians can travel to
Turkey.[532]

The DIS report goes on to say with reference to
Elam Ministries, a UK-based Iranian Christian
group that engages in missionary work in Iran
and has a presence in Turkey:

Elam Ministries stated that the organization
knows of many cases of individuals who came
for training in Turkey who upon return to Iran,
were immediately arrested. Over 500 individuals
that were connected to Elam have been arrested
and interrogated for shorter or longer periods,
within the past three years, and within the past
year, the number has been about 200 individuals.
The reason behind this high number is that the
authorities have obtained quite a bit of
information about how the house churches
operate. It also seems that the Iranian authorities
have agents in Turkey that know of what work
Elam is doing there.[533]

The same report further notes with reference to
representatives of the Union Church in Istanbul
which aids asylum-seekers while their cases are
processed by the United Nations High
Commissioner for Refugees (UNHCR):

---

[532] DIS, *ibid.*, p. 39
[533] *Ibid.*

When asked what obstacles a convert to
Christianity faces in Iran, the representatives of
the Union Church considered that if a convert
returns to Iran, he or she lives in fear of being
discovered. [...] According to the source the
Iranian secret police are reported to be active in
Istanbul. Many Iranians who approach the
church are cautious and will often use a different
name from their own because they fear that news
of their contact with other believers will pass on
to Iran.[534]

General Summary

Demography

As of 2018, Iran has an estimated population of
83,024,745 million. 99.4 percent of the
population are Muslim (*Shia* 90-95 percent, *Sunni*
5-10 percent),[535] 0.3 percent are 'other' religions

---

[534] *Ibid.*, p. 40

[535] The **Sunni** and **Shiite** sects of Islam encompass a wide spectrum
of doctrine, opinion and schools of thought. The branches are in
agreement on many aspects of Islam, but there are considerable
disagreements within each. Both branches include worshipers who
run the gamut from secular to fundamentalist. Shiites consider Ali
and the leaders who came after him as imams. Most believe in a line
of 12 imams, the last of whom, a boy, is believed to have vanished in
the ninth century in Iraq after his father was murdered. Shiites
known as Twelvers anticipate his return as the Mahdi, or Messiah.
Because of the different paths the two sects took, Sunnis emphasize
God's power in the material world, sometimes including the public
and political realm, while Shiites value in martyrdom and sacrifice
(Harney, "How Do Sunni and Shia Islam Differ?" *supra.*) (Emphasis
added).

(including Zoroastrian, Jewish and Christian) and 0.4 percent of the population are an 'unspecified religion.' There are approximately 66,700 Protestant Christians in Iran, which represents about 25 percent of the Iranian Christian community. (There could roughly be between 130,000 and three million Christians and Christian converts in Iran).

Nature of a Republic

The *Constitution* of Iran defines the country as an Islamic Republic, with Ja'afari Shia Islam as its official state religion. The law prohibits Muslim citizens from changing or renouncing their religious beliefs. The only recognized conversions are from another religion to Islam. Converting to any other religion is called Apostasy. Apostasy from Islam is a crime punishable by death. Under the law, a child born to a Muslim father is considered to be Muslim.

Proscriptions for Non-Muslims

By law, non-Muslims may not engage in public persuasion or attempted conversion of Muslims. These activities are considered proselytizing and punishable by death. In addition, citizens who are not recognized as Christians, Zoroastrians, or Jews may not engage in public religious expression, such as worshiping in a church, or

wearing religious symbols such as a cross.
Members (people who were born non-Muslims)
of one of the recognized religious minorities
(Zoroastrians, Jews, and Christians) must register
with the authorities. Registration conveys certain
rights, including the use of alcohol for religious
purposes. Failure of churchgoers to register and
attendance at churches by unregistered
individuals may subject a church to closure and
arrest of its leaders by the authorities.

Armenians, Assyrians, Sabean-Mandaeans
Christians

Since the law prohibits citizens from converting
from Islam to another religion, the government
only recognizes the Christianity of citizens who
are Armenian or Assyrian or Sabean-Mandaeans
Christians. The reason is because the presence of
these groups in the country predates Islam.
People who can prove that they or their families
were Christian prior to the 1979 revolution, are
equally allowed, with restrictions, to practice
their religions. Individuals who convert to
Christianity are not recognized as Christians
under the law.

Those who convert to Christianity usually travel
abroad (Turkey, Armenia, Azerbaijan, West
Europe or Canada or the USA) in order to be

baptized. Iranians who get baptized abroad rarely reveal their names and some choose not to appear on camera for fear of reprisals from the Iranian authorities.

Escape to Turkey

In Turkey, there are no reliable statistics for converted Iranian cases. Iranian converts in Turkey usually get together at different churches for Sunday sermons and community-building. In general, however, there are thousands of Iranian asylum-seekers across Europe who are turning to Christianity. Christianity is making a comeback in Europe – and it's mostly thanks to Muslims.

House Churches are Illegal

House churches are common in Iran and their numbers are growing. Iranian Christians are witnessing one of the fastest growing underground church movements in the world. The increasing number of house churches show that they have space to operate, even though they are illegal in Iran. Due to the underground nature of these house churches, the structure is not uniform across the country. Some house churches are very informal and are simply a gathering of close family and friends on a regular or semi-regular basis for prayer, worship and bible reading. These may be very small groups (a couple of people, for example) or larger (a couple of dozen or more perhaps). Often house churches grow organically as new Christians share their new faith with family and friends. Many house churches will have no formal links with any other Christian groups. However, some house churches are part of house church 'networks' within a particular city or area, or some networks even span across a number of cities.

Some house churches have leaders who have been able to receive training and teaching from Christian ministries (either online or in person through residential courses provided outside of Iran), whilst other house church leaders may have had no opportunity to receive training at all. An increasing number of house churches have "Internet pastors" – where the pastor has had to flee the country due to persecution, they may continue to lead the church remotely via the internet. 'However, the pressure and persecution on house churches in Iran means there are an increasing number of isolated Christians in Iran.

The authorities are primarily targeting the house church leaders and secondary the members and converts. The typical pattern of targeting is by arresting and releasing the house church leaders, as the authorities want to weaken the house church. Ordinary members of house churches also risk arrest in a house church. However, they will be released again on the condition that they stay away from proselytizing. If they stop proselytizing, the authorities will stop gathering information about them. It is possible for an arrested convert to pay his/her way out of an arrest.

Whether a house church member is targeted also depends on his/her conducted activities and if he/she is known abroad. If a house church member is arrested for the first time, he/she will normally be released within 24 hours. If he/she has been detained in prison, he/she will receive his charge within 24 hours and come to court within ten days.

Small, self-contained house church congregations that maintain a low profile and do not seek to recruit new members are unlikely to attract adverse attention from authorities beyond monitoring and, possibly, low-level harassment. Members of larger congregations that do engage in proselytization and have connections to broader house church networks are more likely to face official repercussions, which may include arrest and prosecution. The leaders of such congregations are at particular risk in this regard.

Christians without Regular Contacts

There are also Christians who do not have regular contact with other Christians. In most cases, these isolated Christians mostly receive their teaching via Christian TV programs, which they can access by satellite. They may also receive teaching and encouragement and a form of fellowship via the Internet.

The Expansion Phenomenon

Iranian authorities define the organized house church movement to be a threat against national security. The reason is that they relate the movement's activities to political opposition activities. House church meetings are conducted in secret. The authorities fear the expansion of the house churches phenomenon in Iran. Official reports and the media in Iran have characterized house churches as illegal networks and Zionist propaganda institutions.

Informers and Infiltrators

The authorities use informers to infiltrate the house churches. The infiltrators are identified and selected by the authorities. To prevent infiltration and intervention, house churches organize themselves as a mobile group consisting of a small number of people. Prevention of external infiltration is difficult, as the authorities use informers who pretend to be converts. One source explained that it would be a strategy for the authorities to either monitor or arrest and release members of a house church to make an informant out of them. The authorities could use information on the person's background to put pressure on them. House churches are monitored by the authorities. If the authorities receive a report about a specific house church, a monitoring process will be initiated.

However, the authorities will not act immediately, as the authorities want to collect information about both the members and who is doing what in the community. Flourishing house churches are more in danger, as the authorities see these churches as a bigger threat. Whether the authorities will intervene depends on the activities of the house church and the size of the group. House churches are systematically raided. Online Monitoring

There has been a change in the authorities monitoring of social media and online activities. There is a widespread monitoring of telecommunication and electronic communication if a Christian has caught the interest of the authorities. Certain keywords serve as base for the electronic surveillance e.g. "church," "Jesus," "Christian," and "baptism."

As it is well-known that the authorities are tapping phones, the house members are cautious and turn off their phones long before they reach their meeting place. The IRGC scrutinizes churches and Christian religious practice.

Whatever You Do, Don't Talk

None of the three recognized minority religions are expected to proselytize or accept converts as members. Strict instructions not to minister to Iranians apply to the small number of Latin Catholic and Protestant churches in Tehran and elsewhere that cater to expatriates. The prohibition is enforced through bans on the use of Farsi in services; bans on Iranians attending non-Muslim religious facilities, including for non-religious events such as musical performances; and the regular contacting of churches by telephone by false potential converts in order to test the reactions of church officials to receiving such enquiries. Security officials reportedly monitor registered congregation centres to verify that services are not conducted in Farsi, and perform identity checks on worshippers to confirm that non-Christians or converts do not participate in services. Authorities have closed several churches in recent years for failing to comply with these restrictions, including churches that had existed prior to 1979.

Christians—along with the other two protected minorities, Zoroastrians and Jews—cannot publicly practice or advocate for their religion. Christians were under intense persecution. There is an ongoing crackdown on Christian converts. In the past several years, a number of informal house churches have been raided and their pastors or congregants detained. Iran can arrest as many as 100 Christians in a given week, amid a growing crackdown by the Islamic Republic. Many of those detained are converts to Christianity from a Muslim background, accused of "proselytizing." Once arrested, they have to report the history of their Christian activities and are told to cut contact with any Christian groups. It has become increasingly common for authorities to arrest worshippers, raid house churches, and confiscate Bibles. as the number of converts to Christianity increase, so the authorities place greater restrictions on churches. The restrictions are worse for churches seen to be attended by Christians who have converted from Islam. Not only that, but the government is asking unreasonably high bail amounts and seeing longer prison terms for Christians. Church leaders are put under pressure to leave the country or face an arrest.

Limited Liberties

Even constitutionally recognized non-Muslim
minorities, for example Armenian and Assyrian
Christians face official harassment, intimidation,
discrimination, arrests, and imprisonment.
Although, under the current Islamic regime,
citizens are, at least in theory, free to practice the
religion of their choice, and each religious
minority is guaranteed a seat in parliament, as
stipulated in Iran's *Constitution*. In practice,
however, whilst conversion to Islam is accepted
and encouraged, it is illegal to convert to a
different religion once one has identified as
Muslim. This is considered apostasy and harsh
penalties can apply. Apostasy is punishable by
death in certain cases. Apostasy has never been
codified in law in Iran. Apostasy charges are
rarely stated on court documents although
individuals are verbally charged, questioned,
intimidated and threatened with apostasy.

While apostasy and blasphemy cases are no
longer an everyday occurrence in Iran, authorities
continue to use religiously-based charges (such as
"Insulting Islam") against a diverse group of
individuals. In recent years, the group has
included Shi'a members of the reform
movement, Muslim-born converts to
Christianity, Baha'i, Muslims who challenge the

prevailing interpretation of Islam (particularly *Sufis*), and others who espouse unconventional religious beliefs (including members of recognized religious groups). Some religiously-based cases have clear political overtones, while other cases do seem to be primarily of a religious nature, particularly when connected to proselytization.

Against National Security

Almost all those who are arrested are arrested for actions against "national security," which is very broad. These arrests are unlawful. "National security" is the reason given for arrests; people are not arrested for apostasy. Although apostasy is punishable by death in Iran, the Islamic Republic has never codified the crime of apostasy. Instead, relying on the *Iranian Constitution*, the *Islamic Penal Code* authorizes the enforcement of certain Islamic laws known as *hodud* crimes even when the crime is not specifically mentioned in the *Criminal Code*. The Intelligence Services monitor, arrest and interrogate converts, and prosecutions are held before the Revolutionary Court.

Leaders of groups of Christian converts have been arrested, prosecuted and have received long prison sentences for "crimes against the national security. Many Christians had been prosecuted and either sentenced to imprisonment or were awaiting trial. Christians, particularly evangelicals and converts from Islam, continued to experience disproportionate levels of arrests and detention, and high levels of harassment and surveillance. Numerous Christians remained imprisoned at year's end on charges related to their religious beliefs. Prison authorities reportedly continued to withhold medical care from prisoners, including some Christians. The Iranian government continues to enforce the prohibition on proselytizing.

Authorities continue to arrest members of unrecognized churches for operating illegally in private homes or on charges of supporting and accepting assistance from "enemy" countries. Many arrests reportedly take place during police raids on religious gatherings and include confiscations of religious property. Christians who are arrested are subjected to severe physical and psychological mistreatment by authorities, which at times include beatings and solitary confinement. Numerous Christians remain incarcerated for actions related to religious practice, including using wine in certain services.

Security Risks

In general, the Iranian government regards religious pluralism beyond their control as a security risk. At times, there have been unexplained assassinations of pastors in Iran.

If a converted person uses the religion politically to, for instance, compare disadvantages of Islam with advantages of Christianity or another religion on social media, it could be a problem for them.

Proscription of Proselytization

International observers advise that Iranians who convert to Christianity outside the country are unlikely to face adverse attention from authorities upon return to Iran, provided they have not previously come to the attention of authorities for political activities conducted in Iran, maintain a low profile and do not engage in proselytization or political activities within the country.

A person who converts to Christianity inside Iran is thought to be less of a threat than a person who converts outside of Iran, who is likely to be thought of as an evangelist. The regime is very suspicious of contact with the outside world. The Iranian regime would not explore the validity of a person's conversion when they return to Iran. It would be accepted at face value. A "convert" who returns to Iran (even if the conversion is not recognized as genuine in the place of conversion such as the UK) may be forced to sign a commitment to return to Islam. This is likely to involve detention and interrogation. Some people leave the country again. Treatment varies from city to city and may not always involve detention.

Some people who have families, property or businesses return to Iran. Many of those who return go back as their families have had to put up large sums of money for their bail and if they do not go back their families will have to cover the bail money. Many people have to give house deeds to ensure the release of family members; the defendant does not want their family to lose property.

SELECTED WORKS CITED

1951 Refugee Convention; and the Protocol Relating to the Status of Refugees

ACCORD, "Iran: Query Response," June 14th, 2017

AIIA, "Study Tour Report," April 2018

Al-Monitor, November 8th, 2015

AMAR, August 2012

ANM, "Iranians become Christian in Serbia," October 18th, 2018

Annual Report of the U.S. Commission on International Religious Freedom, "Iran," April 2018

Article 18, "Interview with CPIT, UK Home Office," July 12th, 2017

Article 18/MEC/CSW/Open Doors, "Joint Report," January 2019

Article 19, May 14th, 2015

Assist News, "House Church Members in Iran Sentenced to Year in Prison," August 18th, 2018

Austrian Red Cross. Austrian Centre for Country of Origin and Asylum Research and Documentation, "Iran: Capacity and Methods of Authorities to Monitor Online

Activities and Religious Activities of Iranians Living Abroad," January 11th, 2018

Canada.ca, "Interim Federal Health Program Policy."

Canadian Council for Refugees, "Recognizing successes, acting for change."

CHRI, March 14th, 2016

Christian Post, October 16th, 2018

CIA World Factbook, "Iran –people and society,", last updated April 3rd, 2019

CPIN, "Country Policy and Information Note.

Iran: Christians and Christian converts," March 2020

CPIN, "Iran: Christians and Christian converts," March 2018

CSW, October 2nd, 2018

Denmark and Norway Feb. 20th, 2013

Denmark. Danish Immigration Services, "Iran. House Churches and Converts."

DFAT, "Country Information Report on Iran," June 7th, 2018

DIS, Update on the Situation for Christian Converts in Iran, June 2014
DIS-DRC, "Joint Report," February 2018

DW, "What it's like to be a Christian in Iran," January 25th, 2016

Economist, September 14th, 2012

Elam Ministries, email 2017

FATA, undated

Finnish Immigration Service, "Christian Converts in Iran," August 21st, 2015

Fox News, "Muslim converts breathe new life into Europe's Christian churches', March 21st, 2017

Freedom House, "Freedom in the World 2019," February 4th, 2019

Freedom House, November 2016

Global Security, September 7th, 2011

Guarnieri/Anderson, August 2016

Harney, John, *The New York Times*, "How Do Sunni and Shia Islam Differ?" January 3rd, 2016

HRWF, "Database," updated December 6th, 2018

ICHRI, 'The Cost of Faith ...' January 16th, 2013

IHRDC, July 30th, 2014

Iran Human Rights Documentation Center, "Apostasy in the Islamic Republic of Iran," July 30th, 2014

IRB, "Chapter 5 - Well-Founded Fear."

IRB, "Chapter 6 - State Protection."
IRB, "Claiming Refugee Protection - 4. Attending Your Hearing."

Landinfo, "Iran: Christian Converts and House Churches (1)," November 27th, 2017

Minority Rights Group International n.d.; FIDH July 25th, 2010

Mohabat News, "Over 100 Iranian Christians Arrested by Intelligence Officials," December 13th, 2018

MRG, July 2014

NPR, "Iranians are converting to Evangelical Christianity in Turkey," December 14th, 2018

Ontario.ca, "Apply for OHIP and get a health card."

Open Doors, 'Police Raid Church in Iran, 9 Christians Sentenced to Five Years," October 23rd, 2019

Open Doors, "Interview with CPIT, UK Home Office," August 8th, 2017

Open Doors, "Iran," undated

Open Doors, "World Watch List."

Pastor Feb. 24, 2014

Radio Farda, "Christian Convert Arrested in Tabriz Still in jail," February 14th, 2018

Radio Farda, "Iranian Intelligence Shuts Down Church, Removes Cross," May 26th, 2019

Research Directorate, Immigration and Refugee Board of Canada, Ottawa, "Iran: Teachings, Interpretations and Knowledge of Christianity among Non-ethnic Christians," March 18th, 2014

Reuters, August 2nd, 2016

RSF, September 6th, 2016

Rudaw, "Christian Converts Leave Iran for Turkey, Claiming Persecution," August 14th, 2017

S.K Akcapar, "Religious Conversions in Forced Migration," January 10th, 2019

Senior Researcher Feb. 21, 2014

Small Media, September/October 2013

Special Rapporteur on [...] Human Rights in the Islamic Republic of Iran, "Report," March 17th, 2017

The 2017 USSD IRF Report

The Independent, "Muslim refugees are Converting to Christianity in Germany," December 2016

The Telegraph, "Iran arrests more than 100 Christians', December 10th, 2018

UK Home Office, "Interview with Article 18, July 12th, 2017.

UK Home Office, "Interview with Elam Ministries," September 6th, 2017.

UK Home Office, "Interview with Open Doors," August 8th, 2017.

UN General Assembly, August 27th, 2014

UNHCR *Handbook on Procedures and Criteria for Determining Refugee Status*, Geneva, September 1979

US CRS, "Iran: Internal Politics and U.S. Policy and Options," March 6th, 2019

USCIRF, "2018 Annual Report," April 2018

USCIRF, "Iran 2017 Annual Report," 2017

USCIRF, April 30th, 2015

USDOS, March 3rd, 2017

USSD, "International Religious Freedom Report for 2017," May 29th, 2018

USSD, "International Religious Freedom Report for 2017," May 29th, 2018

World Watch Monitor, "Staggering Number of Christians Arrested – 114 in a Week', December 5th, 2018

World Watch Monitor, 'Iranian Christians Sentenced', October 2nd, 2018

World Watch Monitor, "Thousands' of Iranians claiming asylum in Europe," July 19th, 2017

USEFUL SOURCES

(Source: The IRB Website)[536]

12.

Religion

12.1
Title:
Iran. International Religious Freedom Report for 2021.

Source:
United States. Department of State.
Date of Document:
2 June 2022
URL:
https://www.state.gov/reports/2021-report-on-
international-religious-freedom/iran/
Accessed Date:
24 November 2022
12.2
Title:
Iran. United States Commission on International
Religious Freedom. 2022 Annual Report.

Source:
United States. Commission on International Religious
Freedom.
Date of Document:
April 2022
URL:
https://www.uscirf.gov/sites/default/files/2022-
04/2022%20Iran.pdf

---

[536] <https://irb.gc.ca/en/country-
information/ndp/Pages/index.aspx?pid=11708> accessed on
January 21st, 2023

Accessed Date:
24 November 2022
12.4
Title:
Rights Denied: Violations against ethnic and religious
minorities in Iran

Source:
Minority Rights Group International et al.
Date of Document:
13 March 2018
URL:
https://minorityrights.org/wp-
content/uploads/2018/03/Rights-Denied-Violations-
against-ethnic-and-religious-minorities-in-Iran.pdf
Accessed Date:
10 March 2020
12.5
Title:
Iran: The Situation of the Bahá'í Community
Source:
Norway. Norwegian Country of Origin Information
Centre, Landinfo.
Date of Document:
12 August 2016
URL:
https://landinfo.no/asset/3567/1/3567_1.pdf
Accessed Date:
25 January 2018
12.6
Title:
Situation and treatment of Erfan Keyhani [Erfan-e
Keyhani, Erfan-e Halgheh, Erfan Halgheh, Erfan
Halqeh, Erfan-e Halghe] practitioners and their family
members by society and the authorities (2019–March
2021)
Code:

IRN200459.E
Source:
Immigration and Refugee Board of Canada
Date of Document:
2 March 2021
URL:
https://irb-cisr.gc.ca/en/country-information/rir/Pages/index.aspx?doc=458302
Accessed Date:
12 March 2021
12.7
Title:
Teachings, interpretations and knowledge of Christianity among non-ethnic Christians.
Code:
IRN104787.E
Source:
Immigration and Refugee Board of Canada
Date of Document:
18 March 2014
URL:
http://irb-cisr.gc.ca/Eng/ResRec/RirRdi/Pages/index.aspx?doc=455192&pls=1
Accessed Date:
27 March 2014
12.8
Title:
Information about the Gonabadi dervishes, including their origin, history in Iran, leaders, ideology, practice; and the treatment of dervishes and their family members by society and authorities in Iran, including whether dervishes can practice thei...
Code:
IRN104957.E

Source:
Immigration and Refugee Board of Canada
Date of Document:
23 September 2014
URL:
http://irb-cisr.gc.ca/Eng/ResRec/RirRdi/Pages/index.aspx?doc=455524&pls=1
Accessed Date:
30 March 2015
12.9
Title:
The Bahá'ís of Iran: A Persecuted Community

Source:
Baha'i International Community
Date of Document:
January 2019
URL:
https://www.bic.org/sites/default/files/pdf/iran/overview_of_persecution-0119_2.pdf
Accessed Date:
10 March 2020
12.10
Title:
Iran: House Churches and Converts

Source:
Denmark. Danish Immigration Service.; Danish Refugee Council
Date of Document:
February 2018
URL:
https://www.nyidanmark.dk/-/media/Files/US/Landerapporter/Report---House-churches-and-Converts---220218.pdf?la=en-GB&hash=3A687E2BB8A90B45E253B94BE1AC49684E0A0375

Accessed Date:
16 January 2019
12.11
Title:
Apostasy in the Islamic Republic of Iran
Source:
Iran Human Rights Documentation Center
Date of Document:
30 July 2014
URL:
https://iranhrdc.org/apostasy-in-the-islamic-republic-of-iran/
Accessed Date:
12 January 2017
12.12
Title:
Iran: Freedom of Religion; Treatment of Religious and Ethnic Minorities. COI Compilation.
Source:
Austrian Red Cross. Austrian Centre for Country of Origin and Asylum Research and Documentation.
Date of Document:
September 2015
URL:
http://www.ecoi.net/file_upload/90_1443443478_accord-iran-coi-compilation-september-2015.pdf
Accessed Date:
12 January 2016
12.13
Title:
Iran: Capacity and Methods of Authorities to Monitor Online Activities and Religious Activities of Iranians Living Abroad
Code:
a-10098

Source:
Austrian Red Cross. Austrian Centre for Country of
Origin and Asylum Research and Documentation.
Date of Document:
12 June 2017
URL:
http://www.refworld.org/docid/5943a56e4.html
Accessed Date:
11 January 2018
12.14
Title:
Situation and treatment of atheists and irreligious people
by society and authorities, particularly in Tehran; state
protection available (2014-December 2015)
Code:
IRN105384.E
Source:
Immigration and Refugee Board of Canada
Date of Document:
23 December 2015
URL:
http://irb-
cisr.gc.ca/Eng/ResRec/RirRdi/Pages/index.aspx?doc=4
56293
Accessed Date:
25 January 2016
12.15
Title:
Country Policy and Information Note. Iran: Christians
and Christian converts. Version 7.0.

Source:
United Kingdom. Home Office.
Date of Document:
September 2022
URL:

https://www.gov.uk/government/publications/iran-country-policy-and-information-notes/country-policy-and-information-note-christians-and-christian-converts-iran-september-2022-accessible

Accessed Date:

24 November 2022

12.16

Title:

Iran: The Yaresan

Source:

Denmark. Danish Immigration Service.

Date of Document:

6 April 2017

URL:

https://www.ecoi.net/en/file/local/1408422/1226_149 4231887_notatyaresan6april2017docx.pdf

Accessed Date:

11 January 2018

12.17

Title:

Iran: Treatment of Atheists by State and non-State actors

Code:

a-10099

Source:

Austrian Red Cross. Austrian Centre for Country of Origin and Asylum Research and Documentation.

Date of Document:

12 June 2017

URL:

http://www.refworld.org/docid/5943a5dc4.html

Accessed Date:

11 January 2018

12.18

Title:

Four Baha'is Sentenced to Five Years in Prison for
Trying to Access Higher Education
Source:
Center for Human Rights in Iran
Date of Document:
14 October 2021
URL:
https://iranhumanrights.org/2021/10/four-bahais-
sentenced-to-five-years-in-prison-for-trying-to-access-
higher-education/
Accessed Date:
21 March 2022
12.19
Title:
Iran: Erfan-e Halgheh

Source:
Denmark. Danish Immigration Service.
Date of Document:
May 2019
URL:
https://nyidanmark.dk/-
/media/Files/US/Landenotater/Report_Iran_Erfan-
e_Halgheh_may_2019.pdf?la=da&hash=0A81698B6661
9ADC533B19840C528A934E5957CD
Accessed Date:
10 March 2020
12.20
Title:
Iran: menaces pesant sur les personnes converties

Source:
Swiss Refugee Council
Date of Document:
7 June 2018
URL:

https://www.osar.ch/fileadmin/user_upload/Publikatio
nen/Herkunftslaenderberichte/Mittlerer_Osten_-
_Zentralasien/Iran/180607-irn-konvertierte-f.pdf
Accessed Date:
10 March 2020
12.21
Title:
Whether Vipassana is practiced in Iran; treatment of
Vipassana practitioners by society and authorities (2016-
September 2018)

Code:
IRN106170.E
Source:
Immigration and Refugee Board of Canada
Date of Document:
17 September 2018
URL:
https://irb-cisr.gc.ca/en/country-
information/rir/Pages/index.aspx?doc=457592
Accessed Date:
30 March 2020
12.22
Title:
Iran: Christian converts and house churches (1) –
prevalence and conditions for religious practise

Source:
Norway. Norwegian Country of Origin Information
Centre, Landinfo.
Date of Document:
27 November 2017
URL:
https://landinfo.no/wp-content/uploads/2018/04/Iran-
Christian-converts-and-house-churches-1-prevalence-
and-conditions-for-religious-practice.pdf

Accessed Date:
10 March 2020
12.23
Title:
Iran: Christian converts and house churches (2) – arrests
and prosecutions

Source:
Norway. Norwegian Country of Origin Information
Centre, Landinfo.
Date of Document:
29 November 2017
URL:
https://landinfo.no/wp-content/uploads/2018/04/Iran-
Christian-converts-and-house-churches-2-arrests-and-
prosecutions.pdf
Accessed Date:
10 March 2020
12.24
Title:
Iran : Situation des derviches de l'ordre soufi Nematollahi
Gonabadi

Source:
France. Office français de protection des réfugiés et
apatrides.

Date of Document:
5 February 2019
URL:
https://www.ofpra.gouv.fr/sites/default/files/atoms/fil
es/1810_irn_derviches.pdf
Accessed Date:
25 March 2021
12.25
Title:
Living in the Shadows of Oppression: The Situation of
Christian Converts in Iran

Source:
Iran Human Rights Documentation Center
Date of Document:
12 August 2021
URL:
https://iranhrdc.org/living-in-the-shadows-of-oppression-the-situation-of-christian-converts-in-iran/
Accessed Date:
14 November 2022
12.26
Title:
Living Under Suppression: The Situation of Gonabadi Dervishes in Iran

Source:
Iran Human Rights Documentation Center
Date of Document:
6 March 2021
URL:
https://iranhrdc.org/living-under-suppression-the-situation-of-gonabadi-dervishes-in-iran/
Accessed Date:
25 March 2021
12.27
Title:
Situation and treatment of Christians by society and the authorities (2017–February 2021)
Code:
IRN200458.E
Source:
Immigration and Refugee Board of Canada
Date of Document:
9 March 2021
URL:

https://irb-cisr.gc.ca/en/country-information/rir/Pages/index.aspx?doc=458305
Accessed Date:
26 March 2021
12.28
Title:
Situation and treatment of Gonabadi dervishes and their family members by society and authorities, including whether dervishes can practice their faith in Iran (2018–February 2021)
Code:
IRN200460.E
Source:
Immigration and Refugee Board of Canada
Date of Document:
2 March 2021
URL:
https://irb-cisr.gc.ca/en/country-information/rir/Pages/index.aspx?doc=458303
Accessed Date:
26 March 2021
12.29
Title:
Iran: For religious minorities, biometric identity cards threaten to become a new tool for surveillance and discrimination
Source:
Minority Rights Group International
Date of Document:
October 2020
URL:
https://minorityrights.org/programmes/library/trends2020/iran/
Accessed Date:
8 December 2020
12.30
Title:

Iran : Arrestations et condamnations de chrétiens en juillet 2017
Source:
France. Office français de protection des réfugiés et apatrides.
Date of Document:
30 June 2021
URL:
https://www.ofpra.gouv.fr/sites/default/files/atoms/fil es/2106_irn_arrestations_chretiens_juillet_2017_153383 _web.pdf
Accessed Date:
21 March 2022
12.31
Title:
Le shirazisme
Source:
France. Office français de protection des réfugiés et apatrides.
Date of Document:
28 July 2020
URL:
https://www.ofpra.gouv.fr/sites/default/files/atoms/fil es/2007_irn_le_shirazisme.pdf
Accessed Date:
21 March 2022
12.32
Title:
Country update: Iran. Religious Freedom Conditions in Iran
Source:
United States. Commission on International Religious Freedom.
Date of Document:
August 2021

Author:
Scott Weiner
URL:
https://www.uscirf.gov/sites/default/files/2021-08/2021%20Iran%20Country%20Update.pdf
Accessed Date:
21 March 2022
12.33
Title:
Iran: Stop destruction of mass grave site and allow dignified burials of persecuted Baha'is
Source:
Amnesty International
Date of Document:
29 April 2021
URL:
https://www.amnesty.org/en/latest/news/2021/04/iran-stop-destruction-of-mass-grave-site-and-allow-dignified-burials-of-persecuted-bahais-2/
Accessed Date:
21 March 2022

APPENDIX I: Selected BOC Narratives (redacted)

Abraham

1. [Omitted]

2.Growing up, my mother was very strict Muslim woman. She insisted that we attend Quran classes, pray and always wear the hijab. So, in my family we always participated in Islamic ceremonies.

3.When I started school, in primary school, everyday we were required to maintain all the traditions of the Islamic religion. We read the Quran, prayed and followed all the Islamic orders given to us.

4.In ██████████████, I entered into college. At college, Islam was relaxed, specifically at ████ University. Here for the first, I time learned about other religions, including Christianity. But I had no opportunity to follow the Christians because of fear of being persecuted. But it was very fascinating to know that other people followed other gods.

5.In the summer ████████████████████
████████████████████████████
████████████████████████████
████████████████████████████
████████████████████████████
████████████████████████████
████████████████████████████

████████████ On many occasions he spoke to me about the Bible and he read passages from the book he had with him. This greatly attracted my attention and made me very interested in Christianity.

6.Upon my return to Iran, I visited a church in downtown Tehran and seriously considered converting. But I was extremely scared and everyone I talked to discouraged me and warned me of serious consequences. I then got a piece from the Bible and started to secretly reading it.

7.On ████████████████████████████████
████████████████████████████████████
████████████████████ I discovered that he was secretly associated with the Ministry of Intelligence and the Revolutionary Guard Corps (or "Sepah").

8.[Omitted].

9.████████████████████████████████████.

10.████████████████████████████████████
███████ I did not know what the reason was, but ██ constantly argued with me, hit me and left the house. A few months later, one of the family friends informed me that ██ had taken another wife without my permission.

████████████████████████████████████
████████████████████████████████████
████████████████████████████████████

12. On ███████████, we divorced.

███I first visited Canada in ███████ for only less than one month. At that I had no fear of persecution in Iran. Therefore, I went back to Iran. ████████████████████████████

14.[Omitted].

15.When I refused to go along with this, ███ constantly harassed me at my place of work to the extent that I lost my job. ███ even tried this harassment tactic where I lived so that the landlord would be forced to evacuate me.

16.After these events, I changed my job ███████████ ██████████ ██████ I visited many churches and posted my pictures on social media. ███ used this to threaten to have me arrested and perhaps executed for the suspicion of changing my religion.

17.[Omitted].

18.My first brush with the police happened on ████ ████████. It was my ████ birthday. I had arranged for a birthday party for him and we were busy celebrating. Around 10:00 PM the police came to my house and said that someone had reported that we were spreading Christianity. We were all shocked and explained that we were only having a birthday party. Since then, I had been under police surveillance.

19. [Omitted].

20. On ▮▮▮▮▮▮▮▮, the police invaded my house in the presence of my son and began to search everywhere in the house. They did not tell me what they were looking for. After sometimes, they left.

21. About five days after that invasion, I received a call from the police to attend at ▮▮▮▮▮▮ ▮▮▮▮▮▮ for further interrogations.

22. On ▮▮▮▮▮▮▮▮, it was Iranian New Year and we had celebrations at my home. Suddenly, the police showed up and went straight ▮▮▮▮▮

████████████████████

where the Bible was securely hidden

23. I decided that the best way was to run away from Iran and flee to a safer place. I had a Canadian Visa already in my passport and I quickly ran to and entered Canada on █████████████

████████████████████

Abdulla

1. My name is ████████. I was born on ████ in a Muslim family in in Tehran, Iran.

████████████████████

■And we have been talking about Islam and
Christianity and differences and similarities of
them.

3.After I finished my studies, I returned to Iran in
██ and with the connections I had with my
University ████████████████████████
████████ I found some of them in Iran and we
often set up some times to meet each other at
restaurants and we talked about our jobs and
business in Iran. In late ███, in one of these
meetings, I met ████ who came to the
restaurant with one of my friends. I found him a
very polite and decent person and after a while
our relationship became stronger and I told him
about my background and living history ■

███████ And I was told him about ██████ and brief knowledge of Christianity. ██████ then confided in me that he was a recent convert to Christianity.

4.████ and I set up some specific times to talk about Christianity and the teachings of Jesus Christ. ████████████████████████████

██Considering the dangers and threats newly converted Christians face in Iran, I kept my connection with my Christian friends with more precaution. ████████████████████████

6.In the evening of ███████████, I went to pick up █████ and two of us went to the event location. When we were on the way to the event address, ████ called ████ and informed him of some of the participants of the ceremony who had been worried about my presence in that event and when we arrived at the event location, ██████ asked me to wait in the car until he got to the house and talked to other participants of ceremony about me attending the ceremony. It took about ten minutes ███████ did not come back. After a while I noticed one van and two Peagout 405 entered the area and I saw some men in plainclothes raided the house and two of them came to my car and started to ask some questions about my personal information and what I was doing there. Then they took my phone and identity.

7. After a while they took all the participants out of the house with harshness and we were all forced to go to their vans in handcuffs. After less than 1-hour driving, we reached a semiofficial building without any portals. They put me in a separate small room and after a while a guy came to take photos of me.

8. [Omitted].

9. I told them I just brought my friend ████ to that place and I didn't know any of them. At last after a couple of hours of interrogation, they released me that night. They asked me to be in access and inform them anything I found out in this regard and they told me I would be under their supervision. I was very sad of the incident that day and I did not have any news from ████.

████████████████████████████████
████████████████████████████████
████████████████████████████████
████████████████████████████████

11. [Omitted].

12. The fear of being captured caused me not to connect to any of my faithful friends for about two years but because of my heart interest in Christianity and the effects that Jesus Christ had in my life (granting my prayers by Jesus when I prayed for my uncle who was suffering from cancer and he got cured after a while. He also granted my prayers for myself to finding a good job in ██████ industry which is my major). I always tried to find a way to be in my faithful friend community again. This word of Jesus Christ that the church is His body and the members of the church are His organs and the importance of being gathered in church (any place that faithful Christians gather) in Christianity, always caused me to twinge. This is the reason why I always prayed to rejoin with my friends again.

13. [Omitted].

14. The following week I went to one of these prayer ceremonies in ██████ house in ██████. I met three converted Christians namely ██████ ████████████████████████ We were altogether five people and we all prayed and wished peace for everyone at the end and I was so happy for joining prayer ceremony again.

15. These ceremonies were held each week and in one of these ceremonies in ██████ house on ██████ ██████, I testified and declared my faith in Jesus Christ.

18. After passing two hours, the prayers ceremony finished. I was talking in the room on my phone when suddenly I heard women screaming in loud voices and I understood that the security officials had raided Mohamad's house and, panicking, I went on the balcony and jumped off the wall to the yard of next door neighbor and I escaped from the yard's door which had access to the next street. For the experience of being captured and the fact that I was already under their supervision, I was worried to be captured.

19.I had a very bad nightmare that night and the feeling of fear and stress overcame me again. In the early morning of ██████████ before I went to work, my doorbell rang with rough knocking on my door. When I opened the door fearfully, three of security officials raided my home and two of them started to search all cupboards and drawers in my room and even in the kitchen. After searching my writing desk drawers, they found some prayer texts and some printed materials from the Holy Bible. They took all the texts and also my cellphone and my Ids and handcuffed me and then brought me to a building after 1-hour drive.

██ In that building, they put me in a small room and after a while a man came and took me to another room for interrogation. ████████████████

21.He told me that my friends who had been captured in ██████████ house said I was the who persuaded them to join these ceremonies. He said after finding the printed prayers in my house my guilt became heavier. They told me I should be kept in captivity for some days for acting against national security and joining in illegal groups.

Eventually I got released after six days after giving the written commitment. I was told to be an informant in order to tell on all my friends. That was the condition of my release.

22.The day after when I went to work at ███████ ████, the security department of ████████ called me and when I went to their office and met one of the staff who called me in his office, he informed me with a bad tune of voice that I was not a proper person to work for them because of my beliefs and I was fired. When I went home that day, I was very sad for losing my desired job and for all the incidents that had happened to me and I asked Jesus Christ to help me.

23.[Omitted].

24.At first, I wanted to claim for refugee earlier, but I had no friends here in Canada to help me how. I searched the Internet while living at a hotel. It took a couple of days to complete the forms and required information about my past living.

25. [Omitted].

Thyron

1.My name is ████████████. I was born on ████████████████████████. I have a Bachelor's Degree in ████████████████████. I am married and my wife's name is ████████████ and she was born on ████████████████ Iran. We have

two children, █████████████████████████
██
██
███████████████████████████.

██I was born in a religious Muslim family. I was born
a Muslim. My father is a very religious person and
in addition to that, he is an employee at
████████████ State Department. He always
threatened me because of my liberal thinking,████
██
██
██
████████████████████.

3.I was not a religious person. But I wanted to know
more about religions before I committed to one,
although my father kept forcing me to continue
in Islam. So, I discussed Islam and other religions
with my friends called ████████████████████
███████████████████████████████████. I
remember whenever we talked about Islam, it
was about questions why the Islamic groups like
Taliban, ISIS and other Jihad groups were violent
and cruel and killing other people.

4.In around ████████████, I got accustomed with
█████████████████████. He introduced himself as the
█████ of ████████ Church at ██████████████
██████.
When he noticed that I was not interested in
Islam, he told me a little bit about Christianity. I

313

got curious to know more, so he invited me to his home church where six people met. These six people I came to know as ███████████████████ ████████████████████████████████ ████████████████████████████████ ████████████████████████████████ ████████████████.

5.For some months, we had weekly meetings on Thursdays at one of friend's home ████████ ████████████████████████████████ ████████████████████████████████ ██████████████████ I got more interested in Christianity.

6.On or around ████████████, I told the matter of my interest in Jesus to one of my friends called ██████████. He got so angry and shouted at me that I was doing apostate to Islam and to the government. He warned me if arrested, I would be severely punished.

7.On or around ████████████, I received a summons from a State branch at ████████████ ████. In fact, I was summoned because ██████████ had made a claim against me. He had told the police that I had confessed to him my interest in Christianity and that I was promoting it to other people. ████████████████████████ ████████████████████████████████ ████████████████.

█I was so scared, so I denied everything. I made a commitment not to do anything regarding

Christianity. ████████████████████
████████████████████████████████
███████████████████

9.But after three years, in ████, I felt the need to pray
and fellowship with other Christians. All that
three years, I felt so lonely and as if something
was missing in me. So, I went near a church and
waited for ██████ to come to church. As soon
as I saw him, I went and told him all my story to
him. He took my hand and brought me inside the
church. He told me to trust in Jesus, as he would
save me. So, after that I started going to the
secret home churches again. This time, I was very
careful not to be seen by anyone who worked for
the State. In fact, from anyone I did not know.

10.[Omitted].

11.[Omitted].

12.But suddenly, on ████████████, my ██
told me that agents had attacked one of
██████ secret home churches while they were
holding their meeting. They arrested all the
people there. ████████████████████
████████████████████████████████
███████████████████

13.[Omitted]

██ I know I will be tortured and killed if I return to
Iran by the State forces. ███████████████

████████████████████████████

Anderson

1.My name is ████████████████. I was born ██ ████████ in Tehran, Iran. As a child my parents moved to ████ Town, near ████ City, ██████████ Province, Iran. ████ is predominantly an ████-speaking town. I grew up speaking ████ as a family language and mother-tongue. However, for official purposes, such as TV, education, I continued to adhere to Persian language.

2.█████████████████████████████ ████████████████ I was an inquisitive and curious person. My many questions mainly related to political and religious issues. I could not accept, for example, saying prayers in Arabic when my mother-tongue was ████. I also questioned the validity of violence as a means of obtaining peace, which is predominant in Islam.

3.[Omitted]

4.After some time, as a student, I became a member of the association of students. I participated in the activities of combating racial discrimination of ████-speaking people in Iran and granting them their rights.

5.█████████████████████████ I was involved in publishing statement about ████ speaking rights;

publishing publication called ███ Magazine. This
magazine, published ███ University, focussed
on ███ issues – such as cultural, social, and
other issues – concerned with the welfare of the
███-speaking Iranians. ██████████

██████████████████████████

6. On ██████████, in the *Weekly* newspaper, the
official Iranian newspaper, which was a Friday
edition of the *Weekly*, a caricature of insulting the
███-speaking people of Iran was published.

7. Seeing this cartoon in the Council at Saturday, ███
████████, in collaboration with a number of
friends, such as ████████████
██████████, we decided to issue a letter to
condemn this act.

8. [Omitted]

[Omitted]

9. On ████████████████████
███████, in front of the university's
headquarters, we arranged protests against racism
and the promotion of the rights of ███-
speaking people of Iran.

10. Many students participated in the protests. On
████████████, the protests in ███
were widespread and got national attention.

11.Unfortunately, this demonstration was met with violence by security forces of the Iranian Revolutionary Guards (IRGs).

12.[Omitted]

13.Many demonstrators were arrested in most ████-speaking cities, and many were killed and wounded.

14.Two days later, ████████████. when I went outside the university, I was arrested by two plainclothes men.

15. [Omitted]

16.The two men took me to the black car and leaned over my head and closed my eyes. They were insulting me. ██.

17.Later, I learned that they had arrested me because I was the ring-leader of the student protests.

18. [Omitted].

19.This was terrible and horrifying to me. I did not know where I was ██

20. [Omitted].

21. [Omitted].

22. [Omitted].

23. [Omitted].

24. [Omitted].

25. I was arrested for two days without facilities in the same room.

26. [Omitted].

■ After two days, they fired me and kicked me to another room where they threatened me that if I was arrested again, I would not be alive again.

28. [Omitted].

■ A few days later, the security guard at the university contacted me and summoned me. ■

30. [Omitted].

31. [Omitted]

32.Due to participation in these protests and the fact that the security forces took pictures of the demonstrators, they did not approve of me for any research placement or job. All my applications were being rejected. █████████████

33. With basically no rights ████████████ ████████████ I easily became suspicious of the Islamic religion even further. This dejection is what made me to easily choose to change my attitude ████████████ I decided to change religion from Islam to Christianity.

34. [Omitted].

35. [Omitted].

36. [Omitted].

37. [Omitted].

38. But the classes I attended were done secretly. I was told not to show my belief openly or I would be in trouble with the authorities.

39. [Omitted].

40. [Omitted].

41. [Omitted].

42. I learned from my family that ██████ had disappeared, and nobody knew his whereabout.

43. Then on █████████████, I came to learn through an E-mail from my brother, █████, in Iran that the security forces had arrested ██ The officers had attacked my father's house and searched it thoroughly, and had found all my ██████ documents and files on my computers and CDs, which they confiscated.

44. [Omitted].

45. [Omitted].

46. If I return to Iran, I will be detained and persecuted or even killed. [Omitted].

Amatijan

1. My name is ██████████. I was born on ██████ ██████ Iran. I was born a Muslim. My family is very religious and I grew up in an Islamic religious environment. My family carried on a normal Islamic life, with its traditions and customs. I always thought that my family was a little bit too religious, as unlike in many of friends' homes, in ours, we were forced to do ceremonies almost every week. My family

sacrificed animals annually as well to appease the Imams. We participated in a ceremony annually were we had to hurt ourselves. I hated this ceremony, but as long as I lived under my parents' house, I was required to participate in it. So, I always inquired in myself, "Are there no other ways of getting close to God without hurting ourselves?"

2. On ███████, I married my ██████, ████████ ███████████ was born on ███████████. My hope was that ██████, like me, hated the ceremonies and superstitions. I found out that like me, her parents were very traditionalists – they engaged in many superstitions. ███████, too, did not like these traditional superstitions. ██████ and ██████ ████████████████████████████████████

We started looking for a way we could be religious without being too superstitious. We did not find such a way, so, we continue being Muslims but not being too extreme.

█ I worked in ███████████ department. My job was to ███████████. I lived in ███████ Iran with my ████ at that time. One of the persons I had become acquainted with was a person by the named ██████████ ██ ████████████████████████████

4. As I kept my acquaintance with ████████, I started to observe that he was different. His behaviour, manners, character and speech were different, in a good way. He was humble, kind and only used good language. In short, I saw that he did not like

to make trouble. He was very helpful to other people, and whenever I spoke with █████████ ████████.

5. At the end of ████████████ we invited ████████ and his family to our home. Our talk was more about work and life routines. When I talked about the calm and positive feelings of ████████████ and his help to the visitors, his wife said that this calmness and a sense of affection, he disclosed that his faith is rooted in Mysticism.

6. My wife and I were very shocked. We had never heard of Mysticism before until that time. So, we asked some questions, such as what Mysticism was. ████████ said that according to Mystic beliefs, their attitudes toward life were based on the knowledge of the Gnostic Ring. He explained that the Gnostic Ring brings life's calmness and purpose to life.

7. This led us to become interested in this attitude and way of life. And when they saw our passion, they offered me and ████████ the opportunity to participate in the ritual classes and invited us to their group.

8. We first participated in the session of the Gnostic Ring on ███████████████ and after hearing the explanation, I was more interested in participating in classes and continuing on this path. The sense of peace and calmness and the meaning of the Gnostic Ring we encountered, just informed us of our end of search. We believed that we had

found the way of peace we had been looking for. We decoded to become participants in Mysticism.

9.These classes were held every weekday on ███████ ███████ in the home of each member of the group. So, we were on a rotational schedule.

10.After attending these classes for about <u>half</u> a year, we had better life day-by-day and we felt that our heart beliefs were directed towards positive energy of an observed life.

11.At one of these classes on █████████, where the classroom was in our home, we started as usual at about ████ pm, and █████████, the Master of the group, began talking.

12.After about an hour, plainclothes agents from the Judiciary arrived at the house, entering our apartment in the tower at Damon on the Island of ████.

13.All nine (9) people of us gathered there were arrested. Without any explanation, we were taken by these to an undisclosed place along with our books, pamphlets and CDs related to the course.

14.They then interrogated and then mistreated and insulted us. They forced us to confess that we had anti-religious activities and had Shiite Imams.

███████████████████████████
████████████████████████████

████████████████████████████████
████████████████████████████

17.We traveled to Tehran in ███████████, for
   visiting our family for two weeks.

██████████████████████████████
████████████████████████

19.████████████████████████████
   ████████████████████████████
   ████████████████████████████

20.████████████████████████████
   ████████████████████████████
   ████████████████████████████

21.In the meantime, the security forces increased, and
   anti-riot forces attacked the protesters by
   motorcycles and cars.

22.Unfortunately, in this attack and the clash, one of
   the bomber-riders attacked us and struck me
   from behind and threw me down on the ground.

23.█████, my wife, tried to come to my rescue, but she was also hit by the same agent on her face.

24.Blood from the face of █████ oozed out.

25.With the help of two people, we sent █████ to █████ Hospital to cure on █████ █.

26.████████████████████████████████
████████████████████████████████
████████████████████████████████
█████████.

27.Given the psychological conditions of █████ and the fact that there were usually many trips to Asia and Europe, we decided to take Canada's visa. After applying for a Visa in █████
█████ to spend Iranian New Year holiday in Canada.

28.Before we could leave for Canada, on █████
█████ a class meeting was held at our home where my ████, █████, and her █████, █████, also attended in our house.

29.My sister's █████ (█████) is a religious and pro-Iranian-government man. As soon as he saw our class, he started to verbally abuse the people attending, including █████ and I.

████████████████████████████████
████████████████████████████████

31.Our class was closed on that day. This caused a controversy ███████████████████████

32.As it turned out, ██████████████, took things personal and seriously and went ahead and reported us to the Iranian Revolutionary Guard.

███████████████████████████

34.████████ I did not hesitate, we had already been warned not to be found practicing ████████. So, we immediately left Iran, and we arrived in Canada on ██████████████.

35.We are now wanted in Iranian by the state officials. There is nowhere to run to in Iran. We could not go to any other town to hide because the state security forces control the entire country. ███████████████████████

Sometimes the Iranian government kill people like us for committing what it calls Apostacy.

36.We cannot return to Iran. If we do, we will be arrested at the border/airport and detained and tried and imprisoned or killed. [Omitted].

Bobina

1.My name is ███████████. I was born in a very
   religious and conservative Islamic family on ██
   ███████. I was born a Muslim. I graduated with a
   ███████████████████████████████████
   ███████████████████████████████████
   ███████████████████████████████████
   ███████████████████████████████████
   ███████████████████████████████████
   ███████████████████████████████████
   ███████████████████████████████████
   ███████████████████████████████████
   ███████████████████████████████████

2. █████████████████████████████████████
   ███████████████████████████████████████
   █████████████.

3. [Omitted].

4. For several years I, ███████████ and my family
   lived in Iran in very difficult situations with fear
   and scare about losing our lives. We were always
   followed by intelligent service ████████████
   ██████. And this is how our story of coming to
   Canada to seek for refugee protection developed:

5.In █████, my ███████████████, was tortured severely
   by University Islamic ████████ members, while
   he was reading and reviewing Christianity papers
   with his friend ███████████. Regrettably, he
   was also fired from university within three weeks,

after three years of university study. But he was not arrested. They took note that he was reading Christian materials.

6. [Omitted].

7. [Omitted].

█In ████████████████████ suggested that I meet a friend of his called ██████████. He was a Christian. He was an Armenian and was born into Christianity. I knew him because he was my ████████████ friend at the university. ██

9. [Omitted].

10. [Omitted].

█After attending some of the meetings, it was also my turn to host the meeting. So, ████████ ████, it was arranged that one of those meetings to be held in our home. But unfortunately, between ████████████████, the intelligent service agents rushed into our home, arrested all people in home and took all books, materials, papers and personal computer. ████████████

████████████████████████████

12. [Omitted].

13. My ████████ was taken in a blindfold to an undisclosed location where he was interrogated

████████████████████████████

14. They released him just after taking commitment from him to cooperate with them. [Omitted].

15. [Omitted].

16. [Omitted].

17. [Omitted].

18. [Omitted].

Brian

1. I am ████████████. I was born ████████ in Iran. I was born in Muslim family. During the Fall of ████, I met a classmate by the name of ████████████

in Tehran. We became close slowly and gradually. After few months later, ▮ talked to me about ▮ religion and how ▮ changed it and joined Christianity. [Omitted].

2. I learned that Christianity was not just a religion for me but it was a way to know the true God and his Son Jesus Christ who died for my sins.

3. ▮ introduced me to her friends all of whom were new Christians. Their group leader was ▮ ▮. The group had 10 members. We always met to pray and talk about Jesus Christ. And we read the Gospels.

4. At the end of ▮, I was working in ▮. During one of the lunches, I discussed with one of my colleagues, because I bought a sandwich from one of Christian stores. He insulted Christians and Jesus. I tried to calm him down and tell him that he is wrong but he attacked me.

▮ Two days later, the company Security called me. When I went to the office, two men were waiting for me and introduced themselves as coming from the Iranian Revolutionary Guard (IRG). Then they commanded me to follow them for interrogation. When I protested, they handcuffed me and put me in the gray car with black window glasses and then blindfolded me. I did not know where they took me. After about an hour, we arrived at a military barrack. Then they put me in a lockup. I was there for one day without food or company. They locked me up in a very cold tiny place. Then they interrogated me for hours. They wanted to know if I had changed my religion from Islam to Christianity. I denied the allegations. Then they tortured me. They forced me to sign documents and make false statements. I refused to do all that, but they overpowered me.

6. [Omitted].
7.[Omitted].

8.[Omitted].

9. But on ████████████, a friend of mine by the name of ██████ emailed me and told me that ██████ was arrested and that they were looking for me. ██. If I return to Iran, I will be arrested.

10.[Omitted].

Bismarck

1.My name is ████████████████. I was born on ████████████ Iran. I was born in a typical Muslim family with all the trappings and traditions of pure Islam. I continued following all the rules and practices of Islam for as long as I can remember. On ████████████████████████████████

███████████████████████████.

2.This is how my journey towards change of religion
from staunchly Islamic to Christianity happened.
███████████████████████ one of my
childhood friends, came from a Christian family.
We knew each other when we were just children
in early childhood school. And we did not see
each other again until when we met again in
███████████████████████

3.[Omitted].

4. This was my starting point with Christianity. At
this party, I found out that Christianity stands for
kindness and calmness and inner peace.
Christianity means helping other people. At this
party, I also found that there were fundamental
differences between Islam and Christianity.

5.[Omitted].

6.[Omitted].

7.[Omitted].

8.[Omitted]

9.I asked: Why a Christian would pray for Muslims
and ask God to protect and bless them with good
health when they were busy killing Christians?
And she answered me: "Because Jesus Christ and
the Holy Spirit require all humanity to live in

peace and tranquility." And, "Because Jesus Christ died for all of these people. We all have to strive for calmness, friendship and health and peace, and to live together in harmony," she added.

10.[Omitted].

11.[Omitted].

12.████ replied: 'I've been going to the 'house church' secretly for a long time and I was about to tell you about it but I didn't know how to begin; I planned on changing religion a long time ago."

13.[Omitted].

14.[Omitted].

15.[Omitted].

16.[Omitted].

17.[Omitted].

18.[Omitted].

19. [Omitted].

20.[Omitted].

21.[Omitted].

22.[Omitted].

23.Because my business was thriving, I did not have any intentions or plan of not returning to Iran, either. I was doing very fine in Iran and I wanted to continue to do so.

24.[Omitted].

25. [Omitted].

26. [Omitted].

27.[Omitted].

28.[Omitted].

29.███████████████████

30.[Omitted].

31. [Omitted].

32. [Omitted].

33. [Omitted].

34.[Omitted].

35.[Omitted].

36. [Omitted].

37.[Omitted].

38. ███ told me to destroy all my Christian videos and photos immediately. By this time, we had removed every Christian symbol from our house.

39. [Omitted].

40. [Omitted].

41. [Omitted].

42. [Omitted].

43. [Omitted].

44. After returning from Canada, Colonel ███ called me again and demanded the rest of the money, saying that, "I have more evidence against you which I have not given yet to the police."

45. [Omitted].

46. [Omitted].

47. [Omitted].

48. [Omitted].

49. On ███, I got all my family and escaped from Iran, fearing that our lives could be in danger, although our lawyer had assured me that there was no danger at that time. But I was not decided on whether to claim for refugee because all my means of economic survival remained in Iran. I planned on finding a way to return to Iran without my family in order to collect my money from my debtors.

50. [Omitted].

51. Unfortunately, on ███████████████, along ████████ Street, I saw Colonel ████████, and I am sure he also saw me. [Omitted].

52. We have left everything in Iran and run to Canada. ███████████████████████████████████
██
██
██
████████████████████████████████████

Davinia

1. I am ████████████████. I was born in an Islamic religious family in Iran on ████████████. I have been a Muslim since birth. I was always reminded in the family if you were away from Islam and if you changed your religion, you would be apostate and punished with death. I always wondered why there was no place for research and freedom of religion in Islam. I heard a response every time that my understanding is low and I should not think about the depth of Islam and I should not be curious about this because it ultimately leads to disbelief. When I was █ years old in ████, in a mosque in Tehran, at the meeting of the Shiite (Shia') Imams, the orator explained that Shia' Imams are not sinful. I asked a question that if I do not sin, will I be innocent and can I be an Imam? When the

Imams were a child, did they not sin at all? The lecturer answered me that he would respond to me after the ceremony, but instead of answering my questions, I was arrested by security agents and was taken to an unknown location. I was there for 72 hours. I was beaten and ordered not to ask such questions in public ever again.

2. Due to the inequalities in Islam, I no longer had any interest in the religion of Islam. For a while, I studied and searched other religions and their sacred books. I discovered Christianity was simple and complete and free of violence. In Christianity, men and women were treated equally and they had equal rights. I also found that in Christianity, there was no prohibition except in the case of inhuman treatment.

3. In ▮▮▮, my ▮▮▮▮▮▮▮▮▮▮, had came to our house. He worked in ▮▮▮ City, where he was married and settled. After speaking with him, I realized that he had converted to Christianity many years ago. When he understood I had the desire to learn more about Christianity, he started to share with me the meaning of Christianity. ▮▮

▮After meeting with ▮▮▮▮▮▮▮▮, he had started meetings at his home and invited me to attend these meetings. I was led to Christ and became a Christian. ▮▮▮▮▮▮▮▮▮▮▮▮▮▮▮▮▮

█████████████████████████████
█████████████████████████████
█████████████████████████

5.In █████, at a meeting at █████ home in Tehran, █████ the Iranian Revolutionary Guard (IRG) officers attacked █████ home and we were arrested and taken to █████ Tehran.

█After █ days of arrest, I finally was sentenced to █ lashes and eventually released by commitment.

█████████████████████████████
█████████████████████████████
███████████████████

7. [Omitted].

8. [Omitted]

9. On █████████████, the Revolutionary Guard officers attacked the house of █████████ and arrested him and all their Christian followers. Fortunately, I was not there at that time. I immediately left █████ and ran to Tehran. The day after, my ████, informed me that the officers had gone to my house to arrest me. They had checked my house and threatened my ███ that █ discloses to them my whereabouts. █ refused that did not know where I was. So, because of my previous warning and beating, I

was in imminent danger of being killed if I was caught.

10.Since I already had a VISA to Canada and Canada has religious freedom, I did not hesitate to come here. [Omitted].

Dorothy

1.My name is ▮▮▮▮▮▮▮▮ and I am a ▮▮▮▮▮ doctor. ▮▮▮▮▮▮▮▮▮▮▮▮▮▮▮▮▮▮▮▮ ▮▮▮▮▮▮▮▮▮▮▮▮▮▮▮▮▮▮▮▮▮▮ ▮▮▮▮▮▮▮▮▮▮▮▮▮▮▮▮▮▮▮▮▮▮ ▮▮▮▮▮▮▮▮▮▮▮▮▮▮▮▮▮▮▮▮▮▮ ▮▮▮▮▮▮▮▮▮▮▮▮▮▮▮▮▮▮▮▮▮▮ ▮▮▮▮▮▮▮▮▮▮▮▮▮▮▮▮▮▮▮▮▮▮ ▮▮▮▮▮▮▮▮▮▮▮▮▮▮▮▮▮▮▮▮▮▮ ▮▮▮▮▮▮▮▮▮▮▮▮▮▮▮▮▮▮▮▮▮▮ ▮▮▮▮▮▮▮▮▮▮▮▮▮▮▮▮▮▮▮▮▮▮.

2.When I was barely ▮▮▮▮▮▮▮ years old, I got my first arrest. I was surprised to be charged with an inappropriate dress code because I left some of my hair showing. After that, I got several arrests for such things as mundane as laughing on the street. The last time I was arrested was in ▮▮▮▮▮ ▮▮▮ for alleged demonstration. ▮▮▮▮▮▮▮▮▮▮▮▮▮▮▮▮▮▮▮▮▮▮▮▮▮▮▮▮ ▮▮▮▮▮▮▮▮▮▮▮▮▮▮▮▮▮▮▮▮▮▮▮▮▮▮▮▮ ▮▮▮▮▮▮▮▮▮▮▮▮▮▮▮▮▮▮▮▮▮▮▮▮▮▮▮▮ ▮▮▮▮▮▮▮▮▮▮▮▮▮▮▮▮▮▮▮▮▮▮▮▮▮▮▮▮ ▮▮▮▮▮▮▮▮▮▮▮▮▮▮▮▮▮▮▮▮▮▮▮▮▮▮▮▮ ▮▮▮▮▮▮▮▮▮▮▮▮▮.

3. On other occasions, I got arrested because the IRG thought that my dress code was not in compliance with Islamic Shariah Law. [Omitted].

4.My story of how I changed my religion from Islam to Christianity begins with my sister ███. Together we had hired a part-time babysitter for my children. To our surprise, this babysitter, whose name was ███, was a Christian. [Omitted].

5.[Omitted].

6.[Omitted].

7.After a while, my ███████ got a warning letter ████████. The letter required her to report for court to answer charges for changing religion. ████████████████████ the same warning letter for me to our private office in Tehran.

8. Right now, I am a wanted person in Iran. I am afraid of returning to Iran for fear that upon arrival I will be arrested, imprisoned or even be killed as I did not attend court to defend myself. [Omitted].

Addendum

9.[Omitted].

Davina

1. I am ████████████████. I was born on ████████████████ I was born a Muslim in the Islamic Republic of Iran. I am a █████. My █████████ name is █████████████; he was born on ████████████████. He is a ████████████ ██████████████████████████████████████ ██████████████████████████████████████ ██████████████████████████████████████ ██████████████████████████████████████

2. Governments of the Islamic Republic of Iran put too much pressure on their own nationals, especially on women. Without the husband's permission, getting a passport and leaving the country is not possible; it doesn't matter if a woman has attained to a higher education or has a recognizable status in society. In other words, there is no equality for women in Iran.

3. [Omitted]

4. [Omitted].

5. In ████, I discovered that she secretly had meetings for religious newcomers. I joined those meetings. In these meetings, my faith in Jesus Christ grew, [Omitted].

6. [Omitted].

7.I was afraid they might come to my home and that is why I fled my home because I knew I was going to be in trouble. Luckily, I had already a valid visa in my passport [Omitted].

8. I got my plane ticket to Canada and I left the country on the same night, ███████████. [Omitted].

9. I believe that when I return to Iran, I will immediately be arrested, detained and possibly tried without delay and even be executed if I am found guilty. [Omitted].

10.[Omitted].

Addendum

11.[Omitted].

Imelda

1.My name is ███████████████. I was born on ███████████ Iran. I was born in a Muslim family; I am currently ███████ ████████████████.

2.███████████████████ I

met a colleague and new friend by the name of
█████████ who practiced [Omitted].

3.[Omitted].

4. [Omitted].

5. This ideology is not only extremely popular in Iran,
but it has grown in popularity across the world.
In Iran however, individuals are not privy to the
most basic human rights. Those of which include
the freedom to follow and believe in whichever
faith or religion you believe in. Unlike the laws of
Canada, citizens in Iran live in constant fear of
the government. How people who belong to this
practice are treated in Iran is as follows.
[Omitted].

6. [Omitted].

7. [Omitted].

8.Then, one of the officers began shouting at me to
comply with his instructions or I would have to
suffer severe consequences. As I had just seen
several people beaten to the point of
unconsciousness in this building, I agreed to
enter the interrogation room without any
difficulty because I did not want to risk getting
beaten to death by these officers. When I entered
the room I was immediately yelled at to sign a
declaration that I will not continue to follow
█████████████ by force I signed the
declaration because I knew if I did not, not only
would my life be at risk, but so would the lives of
my children and my ███. They then took us with
a van to a military field (Sepah). In this military

field we were forced into one small room with forty other detainees and were demanded to stay in that room and to sleep there until the next day. There was nothing but the cement floor in this room; we did not have access to bathrooms, food or water. The forty or so of us were forced to sleep on the ground, many of us forced to sleep upright until the next day. The following morning, they took us for a second interrogation. During this second interrogation they told us that those of us who follow and practice the faith of ███████████ are committing treason to the government of Iran and the country by following a religion that is not Islam. They then proceeded to tell me that anyone who stops practicing Islam in Iran and is an Iranian citizen must be sentenced to execution by law. They then told me that if I were to be arrested once more, that I would be sentenced to execution. After this interrogation, at 5pm we were placed once more in another van and taken away from the military field (Sepah) all the while I had been blindfolded. During this period from the moment I had been arrested to this moment I had not even a sip of water, I was hungry, hurt, threatened, thirsty and fearing for my life. In the van, we were taken to the south of Tehran and dropped off at a random location on the street.

9.[Omitted].

10.[Omitted].

11.[Omitted].

12.I knew that it was only a matter of time before I
would be arrested again, this time however I
wouldn't be dropped off after a few days of
interrogations and hunger in the middle of the
street in Tehran, this time would be very
different, I would be more likely than not
detained indefinitely awaiting my execution.
[Omitted].

13. [Omitted].

14.[Omitted].

15.[Omitted].

Festus

1.My name is ████████████ Sadjadi. I was born
on ████████ 1969 at my grandfather's home in
████, Iran. I was born in an Islamic family; I was
born a Muslim. My father's name is ████
████. He was born on ████████ 1938 in ████,
Iran. He has been a Muslim from birth like I was.
My mother's name is ████████████
████████████, and she was born on February
3ʳᵈ, 1948. I have ████ siblings; one male and four
females. On March 16ᵗʰ, 1995, I married
Fereshteh Zarandi; she was born on April 6ᵗʰ,
1971. We have two children: Negisadat Sadjadi is
our first born; she was born on February 5ᵗʰ, 1997
in Tehran, Iran. Our second and last born is
Seyedsaman Sadjadi; and he was born on June 1ˢᵗ,
2005.

2.When I was born, in those years, my father
travelled frequently to other countries, especially
the border towns in the north and northeastern
parts of Iran. My father's trips were usually
business in nature. He was the chief bread-winner
for the family and a very devoted Muslim. He
demanded that we all adhere strictly to Islamic
teachings and traditions. We did.

3. Yazd is a strict Islamic city. It is full of pious
Muslims who demanded true adherence to strict
Islamic traditions. My father did not want his
children to grow up there, although he was a
Muslim himself, he wanted us to practice Islam
his way – a modified or non-strict form of Islam.

4.In January 1970, my father bought a shop in
Tehran, Iran and moved there with my mother.
He became an appliance salesman in the Yusef
Abad District of Tehran. Since he was acquainted
with foreign languages, many foreigners and
embassies were his client. In those years, Yusef
Abad was one of Tehran's best neighborhoods,
and many Christians and Jewish people lived
there.

5.My indirect exposure to Christian and Jewish values
started here, in my neighborhood. I was the first
child of my family and my father was very eager
to have me follow his footsteps in his business.
As early as eight years old, especially during the
summer months, I was close to my father and I
understood how he conducted business with
Christians and Jews. His business was basically
my business, too. He made me meet so many

Christians and Jews. But my father largely dealt with them in business. He still maintained that we adhere to a strict Islamic way of life. Indirectly, however, I was getting more and more interested in Christianity and the Jewish religions.

6. [Omitted].

7. Between 1995 and 2002, I joined and worked for a Bhutan Company. There at Bhutan, I met a friend called Rafik Babakhan, who later became one of my best friends for various reasons. One of the reasons he became my best friend was because we always supported each other at work and even during after-work hours. We went through hard times and sometimes we celebrated together – like attending his children and mine's birthdays and so on. But more importantly, it was strange that we were close and yet he was a Christian and I was still a Muslim.

8. [Omitted].

9. Honestly, this was the first time we began to realize how loving Christianity is, that someone can do what Christ did for bad people. We were very encouraged because, for some years, I had observed Rafiq's behaviour; he was calm, peaceful and eager to accept everybody. That's how we had formed a close friendship even when we had different religious beliefs. Now we knew and understood the secret to his peaceful and kind lifestyle.

10. Rafiq also told us about attending Church. Despite our interest in attending his Church, we could not attend his church because we were afraid of other

Muslims reporting us to the authorities.
[Omitted].

11. ██████ suggested to us that we could attend secret
meetings at his home and he also made us aware
that there were many people like us who were
converts from the Islamic religion and that they
met in secret homes. So, we came to his home
and heard him talk about God and Christ, and we
pretended that we were only there for business or
family arrangements as we did in the past.

12. [Omitted].

13. [Omitted].

██ At the end of ████, I made a resolution to attend
Church more often. ████████████████████████
██
██
████████████████████████

15. These two visits to the Church caused me trouble.
I have no idea how someone had noticed me
entering and leaving the Christian Church and
they had told the police.

16. [Omitted].

17. Although I stopped attending the Church in
secret, I continued to go from home to home
churches. I was advised not to attend the same
home church twice or in a row as neighbours or
bad friends could know what was happening and
report me. ████████████████████████████████

2018, I attended very few home churches because I was aware that the authorities were watching my movements.

18.[Omitted].

19.[Omitted].

20.On ▮▮▮▮▮▮▮▮▮▮, my ▮▮▮ called me that there was a summon for me to appear before the court. The summon stated that I should appear on ▮▮▮▮▮▮▮▮▮ to answer charges. I did not go to Iran to attend the court because I knew what they would do to me. Upon arrival at the airport, I would be arrested, probably tried without justice and imprisoned or killed.

21.[Omitted].

22.[Omitted].

Herold

My name is ▮▮▮▮▮▮▮▮▮▮▮▮▮. I was born on ▮▮▮▮▮▮. I am married to ▮▮▮▮▮▮▮. We have two sons. ▮▮▮▮▮▮▮▮▮▮▮▮▮

I was born a Muslim in Iran, in a typical Islamic family. I was subjected to mandatory courses by my family and the teaching system of my country. I had to be forced to go to mosque by my mother during my growing up.

During my teenage years, I increasingly became interested in other religions. I began speaking to people from other religions. In the ███████████, when I was ██ years old, I became familiar with a friend whose name was ██████████. After being in contact for some time with ████, gradually, I realized that he had the same situation in the past so, he tried to make me familiar with Christian friends and their beliefs. It was very difficult at first, but because of their speech and their kind behaviour, I began to see how humble and loving Christians were.

███████████████████████████████████

███████████████████████████████████ I began to learn that there was only one way to God the Father and it was through our Lord Jesus Christ, but I scared because of the crackdown by Iranian forces on those who convert from Islam to Christianity.

Around my ████ birthday, I decided to leave my city ██████. I immigrated to Tehran, but my relation with ████ continued.

█████

, I became acquainted with a Christian whose name was ████████. He was one of my customers

█████

██████████████████████████████████████
██████████████████████████████████████
██████████████████████████████████ I invited them to
my workshop to see the Holy Cross.

Unfortunately, in the ███████████ after introducing
Christianity to a friend by the name of █████████
he also introduced it to another friend called █████
████ found out that I was influenced by Christians and
he called me and threatened me. █████████████████
██████████████████████████████████████
██████████████████████████████████████
█████████████████████████████████
███████████████████████████████

During all this time, I was under Interrogation ███████
██████████████████████████████████████
██████████████████████████████████████
██████████████████████████████████████
██████████████████████████████████ by the
Islamic Revolutionary Guard.

██████████████████████████████████████
██████████████████████████████████████
██████████████████████████████████████
██████████████████████████████████████
███████████████████████████████

It had never been our intention to leave Iran for good or to seek for refugee protection anywhere else. We knew we were under surveillance in Iran,

When I came back to Iran from accompanying my family to Canada, I was still being monitored by security forces

We immediately got tickets on A█████████, and left
Iran secretly on █████████████████████████████████

███
███
███
███
███████████████████████████████████

Addendum

.[Omitted]

Jason

1. My name is ████████████████████████████
████████████████████ in the Islamic
Republic of Iran. I was born a Muslim.
[Omitted].

2. [Omitted].

3. [Omitted].

4. [Omitted].

5. [Omitted].

6. The critical event that that brought so much pain
to our family happened on ███████████. We

had gathered at our ███████ 's house with other relatives to watch a broadcast television program about Islam.

7. My ████ began to dispute the topics that were being broadcast, and he said that the beliefs were false. He yelled that the message on TV was totally false, and he did not believe in it.

8. [Omitted] All the other relatives present were extremists with the exception of our family. ███████ took advantage of this event and began to inflict pain and suffering upon us.

9. All the other relatives there immediately and without pause disowned us and decided to disconnect from us.

10. [Omitted].

11. [Omitted].

12. We had no option but to leave ██████. We went to live in another small city called ██████.

13. In the city of ██████, after a while I found friends and since we were in the Armenian neighborhood of ██████, most of my friends and neighbours were Christians.

14. In the liberal ██████, our relationship with the new neighbours and new friends was friendlier and cordial. The people there respected us and treated us with kindness.

15. The single most important thing that influenced by attitudes towards Christianity was this change we now experienced in ███████.

16. Around the first week of ██████████████, I attended one Christian Party organized by the Christians. I was invited by the family of ██████ to this celebration. I heard the Gospel of Jesus Christ for the first time in my life at this party in ████████████████.

17. [Omitted].

18. [Omitted].

19. [Omitted]. I found peace, harmony and confidence in following Jesus Christ.

20. [Omitted].

21. There were Christian meetings every week, and each member was required to have a meeting in their home on a rotation basis. I understand that this was done to avoid the Iranian authorities who were arresting those who were born Muslims and they converted after a certain age.

22. On ████████████████, the meeting was to be held at my ██████ home. There were other people who attended and described themselves as Christian brothers and sisters. What we all did not know was that they were plain clothed police officers.

23. [Omitted].

24. They took us to an unknown place. They accused us of apostasy and said that we were out of religion and that we should be punished. [Omitted].

25. [Omitted].

26. [Omitted].

27. After a few hours of interrogation, they released us on bail, and they warned us not to have any contact with Christians.

28. [Omitted].

29. All of us were taken to an undisclosed location. The officers had closed our eyes and handcuffed us.

30. [Omitted].

31. After a few days, they put papers in front of me and forcibly forced me to sign.

32. [Omitted].

33. There was no longer any security in Iran, neither for me or my family.

34. [Omitted].

35. On ▮▮▮▮▮▮▮▮▮▮, I was offered temporary residence in Turkey.

36. [Omitted].

37. Since Turkey is bordered by Iran and has had good relations with Iran, it sometimes cooperates with the Iranian government in arresting and re-arresting people and sending them back to Iran. So, I still was not safe in Turkey.

38. [Omitted].

39. [Omitted].

40. [Omitted].

41. [Omitted].

42. [Omitted]

43. [Omitted].

44. [Omitted].

45. Given that I was being chased by people every day in Turkey, I realized that I was also one of the people the government was targeting. █████████ they decided to run to the United Nations High Commission for Refugees (UNHCR) in Turkey for their own protection as well. That's how I came to Canada and my parents claimed for UNHCR refugee protection right in Turkey.

46.[Omitted].

47.[Omitted].

48. [Omitted].

Morison

1. My name is ███████████████. I was
   born on ████████████████, Iran. I
   graduated in ████████████
   from ████████ University. I also do freelance
   ████████ on the side. I obtained my Canadian
   Visa on ████████ and entered Canada on
   ████████████ The reason for leaving Iran at
   that time was because of the summon from court
   that I had received. Some of my friend and I were
   arrested by the Basij because of our conversion to
   Christianity.

2. [Omitted].

3. [Omitted].

4. My change to Christianity was not unexpected. I
   had been looking for meaning to life ever since I
   saw how Islam treated me and my family,
   especially my father. I did not want to continue in
   the same religion any longer. I had been born a
   Muslim, so, simply changing religion was not an
   easy option.

5. But my chance came in ████. It happened after I
   had visited Georgia, after 2 years graduating from

university. In Georgia, I visited ███████ ███████ churches in Tbilisi. I was so impressed by their spirituality and serenity, so that I decided to research more about nature of Christianity.

6. After returning to Iran, I went several times to ████ Church in ████████ St., Tehran. But because it raised curiosity to the people who had known that I was born a Muslim, ██████ ████████████████████████████.

7. [Omitted].

8. [Omitted].

9. [Omitted].

10. [Omitted].

11. [Omitted].

12. [Omitted].

13. On ████████████, I received a summons from the Iranian court. Since I had a Canadian Visa, I decided to leave Iran and come to Canada. ██

14. After arriving Canada, I felt completely free to go to church (████████████) from first days and started learning more about Christianity.

15. [Omitted].

APPENDIX II: RPD Rules[537]

Under the
IMMIGRATION AND REFUGEE PROTECTION ACT

Interpretation

1 The following definitions apply in these Rules.

•*Act* means the *Immigration and Refugee Protection Act*. (*Loi*)

•*Basis of Claim Form* means the form in which a claimant gives the information referred to in Schedule 1. (*Formulaire de fondement de la demande d'asile*)

•*contact information* means, with respect to a person,

•**(a)** the person's name, postal address and telephone number, and their fax number and email address, if any; and

•**(b)** in the case of counsel for a claimant or protected person, if the counsel is a person referred to in any of paragraphs 91(2)(a) to (c) of the Act, in addition to the information referred to in paragraph (a), the name of the body of which the counsel is a member and the membership identification number issued to the counsel. (*coordonnées*)

---

[537] Refugee Protection Division Rules, SOR/2012-256

•*Division* means the Refugee Protection Division. (*Section*)

•*officer* means a person designated as an officer by the Minister under subsection 6(1) of the Act. (*agent*)

•*party* means,

> •(a) in the case of a claim for refugee protection, the claimant and, if the Minister intervenes in the claim, the Minister; and

> •(b) in the case of an application to vacate or to cease refugee protection, the protected person and the Minister. (*partie*)

•*proceeding* includes a conference, an application or a hearing. (*procédure*)

•*registry office* means a business office of the Division. (*greffe*)

•*Regulations* means the *Immigration and Refugee Protection Regulations*. (*Règlement*)

•*vulnerable person* means a person who has been identified as vulnerable under the *Guideline on Procedures with Respect to Vulnerable Persons Appearing Before the IRB* issued under paragraph 159(1)(h) of the Act. (*personne vulnérable*)

•*working day* does not include Saturdays, Sundays or other days on which the Board offices are closed. (*jour ouvrable*)

Communicating with the Division

2 All communication with the Division must be directed to the registry office specified by the Division.

Information and Documents to Be Provided
Claims for Refugee Protection

Fixing date, time and location of hearing

- **3 (1)** As soon as a claim for refugee protection is referred to the Division, or as soon as possible before it is deemed to be referred under subsection 100(3) of the Act, an officer must fix a date, time and location for the claimant to attend a hearing on the claim, within the time limits set out in the Regulations, from the dates, times and locations provided by the Division.

  Date fixed by officer

  (2) Subject to paragraph 3(b), the officer must select the date closest to the last day of the applicable time limit set out in the Regulations, unless the claimant agrees to an earlier date.

  Factors

  (3) In fixing the date, time and location for the hearing, the officer must consider

  - **(a)** the claimant's preference of location; and

  - **(b)** counsel's availability, if the claimant has retained counsel at the time of referral and the officer has been informed that counsel will be available to attend a hearing on one of the dates provided by the Division.

(4) The officer must

    ◦**(a)** notify the claimant in writing by way of a notice to appear

        ▪**(i)** of the date, time and location of the hearing of the claim; and

        ▪**(ii)** of the date, time and location of any special hearing on the abandonment of the claim under subrules 65(2) and (3);

    ◦**(b)** unless the claimant has provided a completed Basis of Claim Form to the officer in accordance with subsection 99(3.1) of the Act, provide to the claimant the Basis of Claim Form; and

    ◦**(c)** provide to the claimant information in writing

        ▪**(i)** explaining how and when to provide a Basis of Claim Form and other documents to the Division and to the Minister,

        ▪**(ii)** informing the claimant of the importance of obtaining relevant documentary evidence without delay,

- **(iii)** explaining how the
  hearing will proceed,

- **(iv)** informing the claimant
  of the obligation to notify
  the Division and the
  Minister of the claimant's
  contact information and
  any changes to that
  information,

- **(v)** informing the claimant
  that they may, at their
  own expense, be
  represented by legal or
  other counsel, and

- **(vi)** informing the claimant
  that the claim may be
  declared abandoned
  without further notice if
  the claimant fails to
  provide the completed
  Basis of Claim Form or
  fails to appear at the
  hearing.

(5) After providing to the claimant the
information set out in subrule (4), the officer
must without delay provide to the Division

- **(a)** a written statement indicating how
  and when the information set out in
  subrule (4) was provided to the
  claimant;

o**(b)** the completed Basis of Claim Form for a claimant referred to in subsection 99(3.1) of the Act;

o**(c)** a copy of each notice to appear provided to the claimant in accordance with paragraph (4)(a);

o**(d)** the information set out in Schedule 2;

o**(e)** a copy of any identity and travel documents of the claimant that have been seized by the officer;

o**(f)** a copy of the notice of seizure of any seized documents referred to in paragraph (e); and

o**(g)** a copy of any other relevant documents that are in the possession of the officer.

(6) The officer must provide to the claimant a copy of any documents or information that the officer has provided to the Division under paragraphs (5)(d) to (g).

- **4 (1)** The claimant must provide their contact information in writing to the Division and to the Minister.

Time limit

(2) The claimant's contact information must be received by the Division and the Minister no later than 10 days after the day on which the claimant receives the information provided by the officer under subrule 3(4).

Change to contact information

(3) If the claimant's contact information changes, the claimant must without delay provide the changes in writing to the Division and to the Minister.

Information concerning claimant's counsel

(4) A claimant who is represented by counsel must without delay, on retaining counsel, provide the counsel's contact information in writing to the Division and to the Minister and notify them of any limitations on the counsel's retainer. If that information changes, the claimant must without delay provide the changes in writing to the Division and to the Minister.

Declaration — counsel not representing or advising for consideration

5 If a claimant retains counsel who is not a person referred to in any of paragraphs 91(2)(a) to (c) of the Act, both the claimant and their counsel must without delay provide the information and declarations set out in Schedule 3 to the Division in writing.

Basis of Claim Form

Claimant's declarations

- **6 (1)** The claimant must complete a Basis of Claim Form and sign and date the declaration set out in the form stating that

    o**(a)** the information given by the claimant is complete, true and correct; and o**(b)** the claimant understands that the declaration is of the same force and effect as if made under oath.

Form completed without interpreter

(2) If the claimant completes the Basis of Claim Form without an interpreter's assistance, the claimant must sign and date the declaration set out in the form stating that they can read the language of the form and understand what information is requested.

Interpreter's declaration

(3) If the claimant completes the Basis of Claim Form with an interpreter's assistance, the interpreter must sign and date the declaration in the form stating that

o**(a)** they are proficient in the language and dialect, if any, used, and were able to communicate effectively with the claimant;

o**(b)** the completed Basis of Claim Form and all attached documents were interpreted to the claimant; and

o**(c)** the claimant indicated that the claimant understood what was interpreted.

Providing Basis of Claim Form — inland claim

- **7 (1)** A claimant referred to in subsection 99(3.1) of the Act must provide the original and a copy of the completed Basis of Claim Form to the officer referred to in rule 3.

Providing Basis of Claim Form — port of entry claim

(2) A claimant other than a claimant referred to in subsection 99(3.1) of the Act must provide the original and a copy of the completed Basis of Claim Form to the Division.

Documents to be attached

(3) The claimant must attach to the original and to the copy of the completed Basis of Claim Form a copy of their identity and travel documents, genuine or not, and a copy of any other relevant documents in their possession. The claimant does not have to attach a copy of a document that has been seized by an officer or provided to the Division by an officer.

Documents obtained after providing Basis of Claim Form

(4) If the claimant obtains an identity or travel document after the Division has received the completed Basis of Claim Form, they must provide two copies of the document to the Division without delay.

Providing Basis of Claim Form — port of entry claim

(5) The Basis of Claim Form provided under subrule (2) must be

> o**(a)** received by the Division within the time limit set out in the Regulations, and

o**(b)** provided in any of the following ways:

> ▪**(i)** by hand,
>
> ▪**(ii)** by courier,
>
> ▪**(iii)** by fax if the document is no more than 20 pages long, unless the Division consents to receiving more than 20 pages, or
>
> ▪**(iv)** by email or other electronic means if the Division allows.

Original Basis of Claim Form

(6) A claimant who provides the Basis of Claim Form by fax must provide the original to the Division at the beginning of the hearing.

Application for extension of time

- **8 (1)** A claimant who makes an application for an extension of time to provide the completed Basis of Claim Form must make the application in accordance with rule 50, but the claimant is not required to give evidence in an affidavit or statutory declaration.

Time limit

(2) The application must be received by the Division no later than three working days before the expiry of the time limit set out in the Regulations.

Application for medical reasons

REFUGEE PROTECTION IN CANADA

(3) If a claimant makes the application for medical reasons, other than those related to their counsel, they must provide, together with the application, a legible, recently dated medical certificate signed by a qualified medical practitioner whose name and address are printed or stamped on the certificate. A claimant who has provided a copy of the certificate to the Division must provide the original document to the Division without delay.

Content of certificate

(4) The medical certificate must set out the particulars of the medical condition, without specifying the diagnosis, that prevent the claimant from providing the completed Basis of Claim Form in the time limit referred to in paragraph 7(5)(a).

Failure to provide medical certificate

(5) If a claimant fails to provide a medical certificate in accordance with subrules (3) and (4), the claimant must include in their application

- **(a)** particulars of any efforts they made to obtain the required medical certificate, supported by corroborating evidence;

- **(b)** particulars of the medical reasons for the application, supported by corroborating evidence; and

- **(c)** an explanation of how the medical condition prevents them from providing the completed Basis of

Claim Form in the time limit referred to in paragraph 7(5)(a).

Providing Basis of Claim Form after extension granted

(6) If an extension of time is granted, the claimant must provide the original and a copy of the completed Basis of Claim Form to the Division in accordance with subrules 7(2) and (3), no later than on the date indicated by the Division and by a means set out in paragraph 7(5)(b).

Changes or additions to Basis of Claim Form

- **9 (1)** To make changes or add any information to the Basis of Claim Form, the claimant must

  o **(a)** provide to the Division the original and a copy of each page of the form to which changes or additions have been made;

  o **(b)** sign and date each new page and underline the changes or additions made; and

  o **(c)** sign and date a declaration stating that

    ▪ **(i)** the information given by the claimant in the Basis of Claim Form, together with the changes and additions, is complete, true and correct, and

    ▪ **(ii)** the claimant understands that the declaration is of

the same force and effect
as if made under oath.

Time limit

(2) The documents referred to in subrule (1)
must be provided to the Division without delay
and must be received by it no later than 10 days
before the date fixed for the hearing.

Conduct of a Hearing

Standard order of questioning

- **10 (1)** In a hearing of a claim for refugee
  protection, if the Minister is not a party, any
  witness, including the claimant, will be questioned
  first by the Division and then by the claimant's
  counsel.

  **Order of questioning — Minister's
  intervention on exclusion issue**

  (2) In a hearing of a claim for refugee protection,
  if the Minister is a party and has intervened on an
  issue of exclusion under subrule 29(3), any
  witness, including the claimant, will be questioned
  first by the Minister's counsel, then by the
  Division and then by the claimant's counsel.

  **Order of questioning — Minister's
  intervention not on exclusion issue**

  (3) In a hearing of a claim for refugee protection,
  if the Minister is a party but has not intervened
  on an issue of exclusion under subrule 29(3), any
  witness, including the claimant, will be questioned
  first by the Division, then by the Minister's
  counsel and then by the claimant's counsel.

Order of questioning — application to vacate or cease refugee protection

(4) In a hearing into an application to vacate or to cease refugee protection, any witness, including the protected person, is to be questioned first by the Minister's counsel, then by the Division and then by the protected person's counsel.

Variation of order of questioning

(5) The Division must not vary the order of questioning unless there are exceptional circumstances, including that the variation is required to accommodate a vulnerable person.

Limiting questioning of witnesses

(6) The Division may limit the questioning of witnesses, including a claimant or a protected person, taking into account the nature and complexity of the issues and the relevance of the questions.

Oral representations

(7) Representations must be made orally at the end of a hearing unless the Division orders otherwise.

Oral decision and reasons

(8) A Division member must render an oral decision and reasons for the decision at the hearing unless it is not practicable to do so.

Information and Documents to Be Provided (continued)
Documents Establishing Identity and Other Elements of the Claim

Documents

11 The claimant must provide acceptable documents establishing their identity and other elements of the claim. A claimant who does not provide acceptable documents must explain why they did not provide the documents and what steps they took to obtain them.

Application to Vacate or to Cease Refugee Protection

Contact information

12 If an application to vacate or to cease refugee protection is made, the protected person must without delay notify the Division and the Minister in writing of

- •**(a)** any change in their contact information; and

- •**(b)** their counsel's contact information and any limitations on the counsel's retainer, if represented by counsel, and any changes to that information.

Declaration — counsel not representing or advising for consideration

13 If a protected person retains counsel who is not a person referred to in any of paragraphs 91(2)(a) to (c) of the Act, both the protected person and their counsel must without delay provide the information and declarations set out in Schedule 3 to the Division in writing.

Counsel of Record

Becoming counsel of record

- **14 (1)** Subject to subrule (2), as soon as counsel for a claimant or protected person agrees to a date for a proceeding, or as soon as a person becomes counsel after a date for a proceeding has been fixed, the counsel becomes counsel of record for the claimant or protected person.

Limitation on counsel's retainer

(2) If a claimant or protected person has notified the Division of a limitation on their counsel's retainer, counsel is counsel of record only to the extent of the services to be provided within the limited retainer. Counsel ceases to be counsel of record as soon as those services are completed.

Request to be removed as counsel of record

- **15 (1)** To be removed as counsel of record, counsel for a claimant or protected person must first provide to the person represented and to the Minister, if the Minister is a party, a copy of a written request to be removed and then provide the written request to the Division, no later than three working days before the date fixed for the next proceeding.

Oral request

(2) If it is not possible for counsel to make the request in accordance with subrule (1), counsel must appear on the date fixed for the proceeding and make the request to be removed orally before the time fixed for the proceeding.

Division's permission required

(3) Counsel remains counsel of record unless the request to be removed is granted.

Removing counsel of record

- **16 (1)** To remove counsel as counsel of record, a claimant or protected person must first provide to counsel and to the Minister, if the Minister is a party, a copy of a written notice that counsel is no longer counsel for the claimant or protected person, as the case may be, and then provide the written notice to the Division.

Ceasing to be counsel of record

(2) Counsel ceases to be counsel of record as soon as the Division receives the notice.

Language of Proceedings

Choice of language — claim for refugee protection

- **17 (1)** A claimant must choose English or French as the language of the proceedings at the time of the referral of their claim for refugee protection to the Division.

Changing language

(2) A claimant may change the language of the proceedings that they chose under subrule (1) by notifying the Division and the Minister in writing. The notice must be received by the Division and the Minister no later than 10 days before the date fixed for the next proceeding.

Choice of language — application to vacate or cease refugee protection

- **18 (1)** The language that is chosen under rule 17 is to be the language of the proceedings in any application made by the Minister to vacate or to cease refugee protection with respect to that claim.

Changing language

(2) A protected person may change the language of the proceedings by notifying the Division and the Minister in writing. The notice must be received by the Division and the Minister no later than 10 days before the date fixed for the next proceeding.

Interpreters

Need for interpreter — claimant

- **19 (1)** If a claimant needs an interpreter for the proceedings, the claimant must notify an officer at the time of the referral of the claim to the Division and specify the language and dialect, if any, to be interpreted.

Changing language of interpretation

(2) A claimant may change the language and dialect, if any, that they specified under subrule (1), or if they had not indicated that an interpreter was needed, they may indicate that they need an interpreter, by notifying the Division in writing and indicating the language and dialect, if any, to be interpreted. The notice must be received by the Division no later than 10 days before the date fixed for the next proceeding.

Need for interpreter — protected person

(3) If a protected person needs an interpreter for the proceedings, the protected person must notify the Division in writing and specify the language and dialect, if any, to be interpreted. The notice must be received by the Division no later than

10 days before the date fixed for the next proceeding.

Need for interpreter — witness

(4) If any party's witness needs an interpreter for the proceedings, the party must notify the Division in writing and specify the language and dialect, if any, to be interpreted. The notice must be received by the Division no later than 10 days before the date fixed for the next proceeding.

Interpreter's oath

(5) The interpreter must take an oath or make a solemn affirmation to interpret accurately.

Designated Representatives

Duty of counsel or officer to notify

- **20 (1)** If counsel for a party or if an officer believes that the Division should designate a representative for the claimant or protected person because the claimant or protected person is under 18 years of age or is unable to appreciate the nature of the proceedings, counsel or the officer must without delay notify the Division in writing.

Exception

(2) Subrule (1) does not apply in the case of a claimant under 18 years of age whose claim is joined with the claim of their parent or legal guardian if the parent or legal guardian is 18 years of age or older.

Content of notice

(3) The notice must include the following information:

- o**(a)** whether counsel or the officer is aware of a person in Canada who meets the requirements to be designated as a representative and, if so, the person's contact information;

- o**(b)** a copy of any available supporting documents; and

- o**(c)** the reasons why counsel or the officer believes that a representative should be designated.

Requirements for being designated

(4) To be designated as a representative, a person must

- o**(a)** be 18 years of age or older;

- o**(b)** understand the nature of the proceedings;

- o**(c)** be willing and able to act in the best interests of the claimant or protected person; and

- o**(d)** not have interests that conflict with those of the claimant or protected person.

Factors

(5) When determining whether a claimant or protected person is unable to appreciate the nature of the proceedings, the Division must consider any relevant factors, including o**(a)** whether the person can understand the reason for the proceeding and can instruct counsel;

o**(b)** the person's statements and behaviour at the proceeding;

o**(c)** expert evidence, if any, on the person's intellectual or physical faculties, age or mental condition; and

o**(d)** whether the person has had a representative designated for a proceeding in another division of the Board.

Designation applies to all proceedings

(6) The designation of a representative for a person who is under 18 years of age or who is unable to appreciate the nature of the proceedings applies to all subsequent proceedings in the Division with respect to that person unless the Division orders otherwise.

End of designation — person reaches 18 years of age

(7) The designation of a representative for a person who is under 18 years of age ends when the person reaches 18 years of age unless that representative has also been designated because the person is unable to appreciate the nature of the proceedings.

Termination of designation

(8) The Division may terminate a designation if the Division is of the opinion that the representative is no longer required or suitable and may designate a new representative if required.

Designation criteria

(9) Before designating a person as a representative, the Division must

> o**(a)** assess the person's ability to fulfil the responsibilities of a designated representative; and

> o**(b)** ensure that the person has been informed of the responsibilities of a designated representative.

Responsibilities of representative

(10) The responsibilities of a designated representative include

> o**(a)** deciding whether to retain counsel and, if counsel is retained, instructing counsel or assisting the represented person in instructing counsel;

> o**(b)** making decisions regarding the claim or application or assisting the represented person in making those decisions;

> o**(c)** informing the represented person about the various stages and procedures in the processing of their case;

> o**(d)** assisting in gathering evidence to support the represented person's case and in providing evidence and, if

necessary, being a witness at the hearing;

o**(e)** protecting the interests of the represented person and putting forward the best possible case to the Division;

o**(f)** informing and consulting the represented person to the extent possible when making decisions about the case; and

o**(g)** filing and perfecting an appeal to the Refugee Appeal Division, if required.

Disclosure of Personal Information

Disclosure of information from another claim

- **21 (1)** Subject to subrule (5), the Division may disclose to a claimant personal and other information that it wants to use from any other claim if the claims involve similar questions of fact or if the information is otherwise relevant to the determination of their claim.

Notice to another claimant

(2) If the personal or other information of another claimant has not been made public, the Division must make reasonable efforts to notify the other claimant in writing that

o**(a)** it intends to disclose the information to a claimant; and

o**(b)** the other claimant may object to that disclosure.

Request for disclosure

(3) In order to decide whether to object to the disclosure, the other claimant may make a written request to the Division for personal and other information relating to the claimant. Subject to subrule (5), the Division may disclose only information that is necessary to permit the other claimant to make an informed decision.

Notice to claimant

(4) If the personal or other information of the claimant has not been made public, the Division must make reasonable efforts to notify the claimant in writing that

> o**(a)** it intends to disclose the information to the other claimant; and

> o**(b)** the claimant may object to that disclosure.

Information not to be disclosed

(5) The Division must not disclose personal or other information unless it is satisfied that

> o**(a)** there is not a serious possibility that disclosing the information will endanger the life, liberty or security of any person; or

> o**(b)** disclosing the information is not likely to cause an injustice.

Information from joined claims

(6) Personal or other information from a joined claim is not subject to this rule. If claims were once joined but were later separated, only personal or other information that was provided before the separation is not subject to this rule.

Specialized Knowledge

Notice to parties

22 Before using any information or opinion that is within its specialized knowledge, the Division must notify the claimant or protected person and, if the Minister is present at the hearing, the Minister, and give them an opportunity to

> •**(a)** make representations on the reliability and use of the information or opinion; and

> •**(b)** provide evidence in support of their representations.

Allowing a Claim Without a Hearing

Claim allowed without hearing

23 For the purpose of paragraph 170(f) of the Act, the period during which the Minister must notify the Division of the Minister's intention to intervene is no later than 10 days after the day on which the Minister receives the Basis of Claim Form.

Conferences

Requirement to participate at conference

- **24 (1)** The Division may require the parties to participate at a conference to fix a date for a proceeding or to discuss issues, relevant facts and any other matter to make the proceedings fairer and more efficient.

Information or documents

(2) The Division may require the parties to give any information or provide any document, at or before the conference.

Written record

(3) The Division must make a written record of any decisions and agreements made at the conference.

Notice to Appear

Notice to appear

- **25 (1)** The Division must notify the claimant or protected person and the Minister in writing of the date, time and location of the proceeding.

Notice to appear for hearing

(2) In the case of a hearing on a refugee claim, the notice may be provided by an officer under paragraph 3(4)(a).

Date fixed for hearing

(3) The date fixed for a hearing of a claim or an application to vacate or to cease refugee protection must not be earlier than 20 days after the day on which the parties receive the notice referred to in subrule (1) or (2) unless

○**(a)** the hearing has been adjourned or postponed from an earlier date; or

○**(b)** the parties consent to an earlier date.

Exclusion, Integrity Issues, Inadmissibility and Ineligibility

Notice to Minister of possible exclusion before hearing

- **26 (1)** If the Division believes, before a hearing begins, that there is a possibility that section E or F of Article 1 of the Refugee Convention applies to the claim, the Division must without delay notify the Minister in writing and provide any relevant information to the Minister.

Notice to Minister of possible exclusion during hearing

(2) If the Division believes, after a hearing begins, that there is a possibility that section E or F of Article 1 of the Refugee Convention applies to the claim and the Division is of the opinion that the Minister's participation may help in the full and proper hearing of the claim, the Division must adjourn the hearing and without delay notify the Minister in writing and provide any relevant information to the Minister.

Disclosure to claimant

(3) The Division must provide to the claimant a copy of any notice or information that the Division provides to the Minister.

Resumption of hearing

(4) The Division must fix a date for the resumption of the hearing that is as soon as practicable,

> o**(a)** if the Minister responds to the notice referred to in subrule (2), after receipt of the response from the Minister; or

o**(b)** if the Minister does not respond to that notice, no earlier than 14 days after receipt of the notice by the Minister.

Notice to Minister of possible integrity issues before hearing

- **27 (1)** If the Division believes, before a hearing begins, that there is a possibility that issues relating to the integrity of the Canadian refugee protection system may arise from the claim and the Division is of the opinion that the Minister's participation may help in the full and proper hearing of the claim, the Division must without delay notify the Minister in writing and provide any relevant information to the Minister.

Notice to Minister of possible integrity issues during hearing

(2) If the Division believes, after a hearing begins, that there is a possibility that issues relating to the integrity of the Canadian refugee protection system may arise from the claim and the Division is of the opinion that the Minister's participation may help in the full and proper hearing of the claim, the Division must adjourn the hearing and without delay notify the Minister in writing and provide any relevant information to the Minister.

Integrity issues

(3) For the purpose of this rule, claims in which the possibility that issues relating to the integrity of the Canadian refugee protection system may arise include those in which there is o**(a)** information that the claim may have been made under a false identity in whole or in part;

o**(b)** a substantial change to the basis of the claim from that indicated in the Basis of Claim Form first provided to the Division;

o**(c)** information that, in support of the claim, the claimant submitted documents that may be fraudulent; or

o**(d)** other information that the claimant may be directly or indirectly misrepresenting or withholding material facts relating to a relevant matter.

Disclosure to claimant

(4) The Division must provide to the claimant a copy of any notice or information that the Division provides to the Minister.

Resumption of hearing

(5) The Division must fix a date for the resumption of the hearing that is as soon as practicable,

o**(a)** if the Minister responds to the notice referred to in subrule (2), after receipt of the response from the Minister; or

o**(b)** if the Minister does not respond to that notice, no earlier than 14 days after receipt of the notice by the Minister.

Notice of possible inadmissibility or ineligibility

- **28 (1)** The Division must without delay notify the Minister in writing and provide the Minister with any relevant information if the Division believes that

  o**(a)** a claimant may be inadmissible on grounds of security, violating human or international rights, serious criminality or organized criminality;

  o**(b)** there is an outstanding charge against the claimant for an offence under an Act of Parliament that is punishable by a maximum term of imprisonment of at least 10 years; or

  o**(c)** the claimant's claim may be ineligible to be referred under section 101 or paragraph 104(1)(c) or (d) of the Act.

Disclosure to claimant

(2) The Division must provide to the claimant a copy of any notice or information that the Division provides to the Minister.

Continuation of proceeding

(3) If, within 20 days after receipt of the notice referred to in subrule (1), the Minister does not notify the Division that the proceedings are suspended under paragraph 103(1)(a) or (b) of the Act or that the pending proceedings respecting the claim are terminated under section 104 of the Act, the Division may continue with the proceedings.

Intervention by the Minister

Notice of intention to intervene

- **29 (1)** To intervene in a claim, the Minister must provide

    o **(a)** to the claimant, a copy of a notice of the Minister's intention to intervene; and

    o **(b)** to the Division, the original of the notice, together with a written statement indicating how and when a copy was provided to the claimant.

Contents of notice

(2) In the notice, the Minister must state

    o **(a)** the purpose for which the Minister will intervene;

    o **(b)** whether the Minister will intervene in writing only, in person, or both; and

    o **(c)** the Minister's counsel's contact information.

Intervention — exclusion clauses

(3) If the Minister believes that section E or F of Article 1 of the Refugee Convention may apply to the claim, the Minister must also state in the notice the facts and law on which the Minister relies.

Time limit

(4) Documents provided under this rule must be received by their recipients no later than 10 days before the date fixed for a hearing.

Claimant or Protected Person in Custody

Custody

30 The Division may order a person who holds a claimant or protected person in custody to bring the claimant or protected person to a proceeding at a location specified by the Division.

Documents
Form and Language of Documents

Documents prepared by party

- **31 (1)** A document prepared for use by a party in a proceeding must be typewritten, in a type not smaller than 12 point, on one or both sides of 216 mm by 279 mm (8 ½ inches x 11 inches) paper.

  ## Photocopies

  (2) Any photocopy provided by a party must be a clear copy of the document photocopied and be on one or both sides of 216 mm by 279 mm (8 ½ inches x 11 inches) paper.

  ## List of documents

  (3) If more than one document is provided, the party must provide a list identifying each of the documents.

  ## Consecutively numbered pages

(4) A party must consecutively number each page of all the documents provided as if they were one document.

Language of documents — claimant or protected person

- **32 (1)** All documents used by a claimant or protected person in a proceeding must be in English or French or, if in another language, be provided together with an English or French translation and a declaration signed by the translator.

Language of Minister's documents

(2) All documents used by the Minister in a proceeding must be in the language of the proceeding or be provided together with a translation in the language of the proceeding and a declaration signed by the translator.

Translator's declaration

(3) A translator's declaration must include translator's name, the language and dialect, if any, translated and a statement that the translation is accurate.

Disclosure and Use of Documents

Disclosure of documents by Division

- **33 (1)** Subject to subrule (2), if the Division wants to use a document in a hearing, the Division must provide a copy of the document to each party.

Disclosure of country documentation by Division

(2) The Division may disclose country documentation by providing to the parties a list of those documents or providing information as to where a list of those documents can be found on the Board's website.

Disclosure of documents by party

- **34 (1)** If a party wants to use a document in a hearing, the party must provide a copy of the document to the other party, if any, and to the Division.

Proof that document was provided

(2) The copy of the document provided to the Division must be accompanied by a written statement indicating how and when a copy of that document was provided to the other party, if any.

Time limit

(3) Documents provided under this rule must be received by their recipients no later than

- o**(a)** 10 days before the date fixed for the hearing; or

- o**(b)** five days before the date fixed for the hearing if the document is provided to respond to another document provided by a party or the Division.

Documents relevant and not duplicate

35 Each document provided by a party for use at a proceeding must

•**(a)** be relevant to the particular proceeding; and

•**(b)** not duplicate other documents provided by a party or by the Division.

Use of undisclosed documents

36 A party who does not provide a document in accordance with rule 34 must not use the document at the hearing unless allowed to do so by the Division. In deciding whether to allow its use, the Division must consider any relevant factors, including

•**(a)** the document's relevance and probative value;

•**(b)** any new evidence the document brings to the hearing; and

•**(c)** whether the party, with reasonable effort, could have provided the document as required by rule 34.

Providing a Document

General provision

37 Rules 38 to 41 apply to any document, including a notice or request in writing.

Providing documents to Division

• **38 (1)** A document to be provided to the Division must be provided to the registry office specified by the Division.

Providing documents to Minister

(2) A document to be provided to the Minister must be provided to the Minister's counsel.

Providing documents to person other than Minister

(3) A document to be provided to a person other than the Minister must be provided to the person's counsel if the person has counsel of record. If the person does not have counsel of record, the document must be provided to the person.

How to provide document

39 Unless these Rules provide otherwise, a document may be provided in any of the following ways:

- **(a)** by hand;

- **(b)** by regular mail or registered mail;

- **(c)** by courier;

- **(d)** by fax if the recipient has a fax number and the document is no more than 20 pages long, unless the recipient consents to receiving more than 20 pages; and

- **(e)** by email or other electronic means if the Division allows.

Application if unable to provide document

- **40 (1)** If a party is unable to provide a document in a way required by rule 39, the party may make an application to the Division to be allowed to provide the document in another way or to be excused from providing the document.

Form of application

(2) The application must be made in accordance with rule 50.

Allowing application

(3) The Division must not allow the application unless the party has made reasonable efforts to provide the document to the person to whom the document must be provided.

When document received by Division

- **41 (1)** A document provided to the Division is considered to be received by the Division on the day on which the document is date-stamped by the Division.

When document received by recipient other than Division

(2) A document provided by regular mail other than to the Division is considered to be received seven days after the day on which it was mailed. If the seventh day is not a working day, the document is considered to be received on the next working day.

Extension of time limit — next working day

(3) When the time limit for providing a document ends on a day that is not a working day, the time limit is extended to the next working day.

Original Documents

Original documents

- **42 (1)** A party who has provided a copy of a document to the Division must provide the original document to the Division

   ○**(a)** without delay, on the written request of the Division; or

   ○**(b)** if the Division does not make a request, no later than at the beginning of the proceeding at which the document will be used.

Documents referred to in paragraph 3(5)(e) or (g)

(2) On the written request of the Division, the Minister must without delay provide to the Division the original of any document referred to in paragraph 3(5)(e) or (g) that is in the possession of an officer.

Additional Documents

Documents after hearing

- **43 (1)** A party who wants to provide a document as evidence after a hearing but before a decision takes effect must make an application to the Division.

Application

(2) The party must attach a copy of the document to the application that must be made in accordance with rule 50, but the party is not required to give evidence in an affidavit or statutory declaration.

Factors

(3) In deciding the application, the Division must consider any relevant factors, including

   ○**(a)** the document's relevance and probative value;

  o**(b)** any new evidence the document brings to the proceedings; and

  o**(c)** whether the party, with reasonable effort, could have provided the document as required by rule 34.

Witnesses

Providing witness information

- **44 (1)** If a party wants to call a witness, the party must provide the following witness information in writing to the other party, if any, and to the Division:

  o**(a)** the witness's contact information;

  o**(b)** a brief statement of the purpose and substance of the witness's testimony or, in the case of an expert witness, the expert witness's brief signed summary of the testimony to be given;

  o**(c)** the time needed for the witness's testimony;

  o**(d)** the party's relationship to the witness;

  o**(e)** in the case of an expert witness, a description of the expert witness's qualifications; and

  o**(f)** whether the party wants the witness to testify by means of live telecommunication.

Proof witness information provided

(2) The witness information provided to the Division must be accompanied by a written statement indicating how and when it was provided to the other party, if any.

Time limit

(3) Documents provided under this rule must be received by their recipients no later than 10 days before the date fixed for the hearing.

Failure to provide witness information

(4) If a party does not provide the witness information, the witness must not testify at the hearing unless the Division allows them to testify.

Factors

(5) In deciding whether to allow a witness to testify, the Division must consider any relevant factors, including

o**(a)** the relevance and probative value of the proposed testimony; and

o**(b)** the reason why the witness information was not provided.

Requesting summons

- **45 (1)** A party who wants the Division to order a person to testify at a hearing must make a request to the Division for a summons, either orally at a proceeding or in writing.

Factors

(2) In deciding whether to issue a summons, the Division must consider any relevant factors, including o**(a)** the necessity of the testimony to a full and proper hearing;

o**(b)** the person's ability to give that testimony; and

o**(c)** whether the person has agreed to be summoned as a witness.

Using summons

(3) If a party wants to use a summons, the party must

o**(a)** provide the summons to the person by hand;

o**(b)** provide a copy of the summons to the Division, together with a written statement indicating the name of the person who provided the summons and the date, time and place that it was provided by hand; and

o**(c)** pay or offer to pay the person the applicable witness fees and travel expenses set out in Tariff A of the *Federal Courts Rules*.

Cancelling summons

- **46 (1)** If a person who is summoned to appear as a witness wants the summons cancelled, the person must make an application in writing to the Division.

Application

(2) The person must make the application in accordance with rule 50, but is not required to give evidence in an affidavit or statutory declaration.

Arrest warrant

- **47 (1)** If a person does not obey a summons to appear as a witness, the party who requested the summons may make a request to the Division orally at the hearing, or in writing, to issue a warrant for the person's arrest.

Written request

(2) A party who makes a written request for a warrant must provide supporting evidence by affidavit or statutory declaration.

Requirements for issue of arrest warrant

(3) The Division must not issue a warrant unless

- **(a)** the person was provided the summons by hand or the person is avoiding being provided the summons;

- **(b)** the person was paid or offered the applicable witness fees and travel expenses set out in Tariff A of the _Federal Courts Rules_;

- **(c)** the person did not appear at the hearing as required by the summons; and

- **(d)** the person's testimony is still needed for a full and proper hearing.

Content of warrant

(4) A warrant issued by the Division for the arrest of a person must include directions concerning detention or release.

Excluded witness

48 If the Division excludes a witness from a hearing room, no person may communicate to the witness any evidence given while the witness was excluded unless allowed to do so by the Division or until the witness has finished testifying.

Applications
General

General provision

49 Unless these Rules provide otherwise,

> •**(a)** a party who wants the Division to make a decision on any matter in a proceeding, including the procedure to be followed, must make an application to the Division in accordance with rule 50;

> •**(b)** a party who wants to respond to the application must respond in accordance with rule 51; and

> •**(c)** a party who wants to reply to a response must reply in accordance with rule 52.

How to Make an Application

Written application and time limit

- **50 (1)** Unless these Rules provide otherwise, an application must be made in writing, without delay, and must be received by the Division no later than 10 days before the date fixed for the next proceeding.

Oral application

(2) The Division must not allow a party to make an application orally at a proceeding unless the party, with reasonable effort, could not have made a written application before the proceeding.

Content of application

(3) Unless these Rules provide otherwise, in a written application, the party must

> o**(a)** state the decision the party wants the Division to make;

> o**(b)** give reasons why the Division should make that decision; and

> o**(c)** if there is another party and the views of that party are known, state whether the other party agrees to the application.

Affidavit or statutory declaration

(4) Unless these Rules provide otherwise, any evidence that the party wants the Division to consider with a written application must be given in an affidavit or statutory declaration that accompanies the application.

Providing application to other party and Division

(5) A party who makes a written application must provide o**(a)** to the other party, if any, a copy of the application and a copy of any affidavit or statutory declaration; and

o**(b)** to the Division, the original application and the original of any affidavit or statutory declaration, together with a written statement indicating how and when the party provided a copy to the other party, if any.

How to Respond to a Written Application

Responding to written application

- **51 (1)** A response to a written application must be in writing and

    o**(a)** state the decision the party wants the Division to make; and

    o**(b)** give reasons why the Division should make that decision.

Evidence in written response

(2) Any evidence that the party wants the Division to consider with the written response must be given in an affidavit or statutory declaration that accompanies the response. Unless the Division requires it, an affidavit or statutory declaration is not required if the party who made the application was not required to give evidence in an affidavit or statutory declaration, together with the application.

Providing response

(3) A party who responds to a written application must provide

o**(a)** to the other party, a copy of the response and a copy of any affidavit or statutory declaration; and

o**(b)** to the Division, the original response and the original of any affidavit or statutory declaration, together with a written statement indicating how and when the party provided a copy to the other party.

Time limit

(4) Documents provided under subrule (3) must be received by their recipients no later than five days after the date on which the party receives the copy of the application.

How to Reply to a Written Response

Replying to written response

- **52 (1)** A reply to a written response must be in writing.

Evidence in reply

(2) Any evidence that the party wants the Division to consider with the written reply must be given in an affidavit or statutory declaration that accompanies the reply. Unless the Division requires it, an affidavit or statutory declaration is not required if the party was not required to give evidence in an affidavit or statutory declaration, together with the application.

Providing reply

(3) A party who replies to a written response must provide

> o**(a)** to the other party, a copy of the reply and a copy of any affidavit or statutory declaration; and

> o**(b)** to the Division, the original reply and the original of any affidavit or statutory declaration, together with a written statement indicating how and when the party provided a copy to the other party.

Time limit

(4) Documents provided under subrule (3) must be received by their recipients no later than three days after the date on which the party receives the copy of the response.

Changing the Location of a Proceeding

Application to change location

- **53 (1)** A party may make an application to the Division to change the location of a proceeding.

Form and content of application

(2) The party must make the application in accordance with rule 50, but is not required to give evidence in an affidavit or statutory declaration.

Time limit

(3) Documents provided under this rule must be received by their recipients no later than 20 days before the date fixed for the proceeding.

Factors

(4) In deciding the application, the Division must consider any relevant factors, including

- o**(a)** whether the party is residing in the location where the party wants the proceeding to be held;

- o**(b)** whether a change of location would allow the proceeding to be full and proper;

- o**(c)** whether a change of location would likely delay the proceeding;

- o**(d)** how a change of location would affect the Division's operation;

- o**(e)** how a change of location would affect the parties;

- o**(f)** whether a change of location is necessary to accommodate a vulnerable person; and

- o**(g)** whether a hearing may be conducted by a means of live telecommunication with the claimant or protected person.

Duty to appear

(5) Unless a party receives a decision from the Division allowing the application, the party must appear for the proceeding at the location fixed and be ready to start or continue the proceeding.

Changing the Date or Time of a Proceeding

Application in writing

- **54 (1)** Subject to subrule (5), an application to change the date or time of a proceeding must be made in accordance with rule 50, but the party is not required to give evidence in an affidavit or statutory declaration.

Time limit and content of application

(2) The application must

- o**(a)** be made without delay;

- o**(b)** be received by the Division no later than three working days before the date fixed for the proceeding, unless the application is made for medical reasons or other emergencies; and

- o**(c)** include at least three dates and times, which are no later than 10 working days after the date originally fixed for the proceeding, on which the party is available to start or continue the proceeding.

Oral application

(3) If it is not possible for the party to make the application in accordance with paragraph (2)(b), the party must appear on the date fixed for the proceeding and make the application orally before the time fixed for the proceeding.

Factors

(4) Subject to subrule (5), the Division must not allow the application unless there are exceptional circumstances, such as

> o**(a)** the change is required to accommodate a vulnerable person; or

> o**(b)** an emergency or other development outside the party's control and the party has acted diligently.

Counsel retained or availability of counsel provided after hearing date fixed

(5) If, at the time the officer fixed the hearing date under subrule 3(1), a claimant did not have counsel or was unable to provide the dates when their counsel would be available to attend a hearing, the claimant may make an application to change the date or time of the hearing. Subject to operational limitations, the Division must allow the application if

> o**(a)** the claimant retains counsel no later than five working days after the day on which the hearing date was fixed by the officer;

> o**(b)** the counsel retained is not available on the date fixed for the hearing;

> o**(c)** the application is made in writing;

> o**(d)** the application is made without delay and no later than five working days after the day on which the hearing date was fixed by the officer; and

o**(e)** the claimant provides at least three dates and times when counsel is available, which are within the time limits set out in the Regulations for the hearing of the claim.

Application for medical reasons

(6) If a claimant or protected person makes the application for medical reasons, other than those related to their counsel, they must provide, together with the application, a legible, recently dated medical certificate signed by a qualified medical practitioner whose name and address are printed or stamped on the certificate. A claimant or protected person who has provided a copy of the certificate to the Division must provide the original document to the Division without delay.

Content of certificate

(7) The medical certificate must set out

o**(a)** the particulars of the medical condition, without specifying the diagnosis, that prevent the claimant or protected person from participating in the proceeding on the date fixed for the proceeding; and

o**(b)** the date on which the claimant or protected person is expected to be able to participate in the proceeding.

Failure to provide medical certificate

(8) If a claimant or protected person fails to provide a medical certificate in accordance with subrules (6) and (7), they must include in their application

> o**(a)** particulars of any efforts they made to obtain the required medical certificate, supported by corroborating evidence;
>
> o**(b)** particulars of the medical reasons for the application, supported by corroborating evidence; and
>
> o**(c)** an explanation of how the medical condition prevents them from participating in the proceeding on the date fixed for the proceeding.

Subsequent application

(9) If the party made a previous application that was denied, the Division must consider the reasons for the denial and must not allow the subsequent application unless there are exceptional circumstances supported by new evidence.

Duty to appear

(10) Unless a party receives a decision from the Division allowing the application, the party must appear for the proceeding at the date and time fixed and be ready to start or continue the proceeding.

New date

(11) If an application for a change to the date or time of a proceeding is allowed, the new date fixed by the Division must be no later than 10 working days after the date originally fixed for the proceeding or as soon as possible after that date.

Joining or Separating Claims or Applications

Claims automatically joined

- **55 (1)** The Division must join the claim of a claimant to a claim made by the claimant's spouse or common-law partner, child, parent, legal guardian, brother, sister, grandchild or grandparent, unless it is not practicable to do so.

Applications joined if claims joined

(2) Applications to vacate or to cease refugee protection are joined if the claims of the protected persons were joined.

Application to join

- **56 (1)** A party may make an application to the Division to join claims or applications to vacate or to cease refugee protection.

Application to separate

(2) A party may make an application to the Division to separate claims or applications to vacate or to cease refugee protection that are joined.

Form of application and providing application

(3) A party who makes an application to join or separate claims or applications to vacate or to cease refugee protection must do so in accordance with rule 50, but the party is not required to give evidence in an affidavit or statutory declaration. The party must also

- o**(a)** provide a copy of the application to any person who will be affected by the Division's decision on the application; and

- o**(b)** provide to the Division a written statement indicating how and when the copy of the application was provided to any affected person, together with proof that the party provided the copy to that person.

Time limit

(4) Documents provided under this rule must be received by their recipients no later than 20 days before the date fixed for the hearing.

Factors

(5) In deciding the application to join or separate, the Division must consider any relevant factors, including whether

- o**(a)** the claims or applications to vacate or to cease refugee protection involve similar questions of fact or law;

- o**(b)** allowing the application to join or separate would promote the efficient administration of the Division's work; and

- o**(c)** allowing the application to join or separate would likely cause an injustice.

Proceedings Conducted in Public

Minister considered party

- **57 (1)** For the purpose of this rule, the Minister is considered to be a party whether or not the Minister takes part in the proceedings.

Application

(2) A person who makes an application to the Division to have a proceeding conducted in public must do so in writing and in accordance with this rule rather than rule 50.

Oral application

(3) The Division must not allow a person to make an application orally at a proceeding unless the person, with reasonable effort, could not have made a written application before the proceeding.

Content of application

(4) In the application, the person must

- **(a)** state the decision they want the Division to make;

- **(b)** give reasons why the Division should make that decision;

- **(c)** state whether they want the Division to consider the application in public or in the absence of the public;

- **(d)** give reasons why the Division should consider the application in public or in the absence of the public;

o**(e)** if they want the Division to hear the application orally, give reasons why the Division should do so; and

o**(f)** include any evidence that they want the Division to consider in deciding the application.

Providing application

(5) The person must provide the original application together with two copies to the Division. The Division must provide a copy of the application to the parties.

Response to application

(6) A party may respond to a written application. The response must

o**(a)** state the decision they want the Division to make;

o**(b)** give reasons why the Division should make that decision;

o**(c)** state whether they want the Division to consider the application in public or in the absence of the public;

o**(d)** give reasons why the Division should consider the application in public or in the absence of the public;

o**(e)** if they want the Division to hear the application orally, give reasons why the Division should do so; and

o**(f)** include any evidence that they want the Division to consider in deciding the application.

Providing response

(7) The party must provide a copy of the response to the other party and provide the original response and a copy to the Division, together with a written statement indicating how and when the party provided the copy to the other party.

Providing response to applicant

(8) The Division must provide to the applicant either a copy of the response or a summary of the response referred to in paragraph (12)(a).

Reply to response

(9) An applicant or a party may reply in writing to a written response or a summary of a response.

Providing reply

(10) An applicant or a party who replies to a written response or a summary of a response must provide the original reply and two copies to the Division. The Division must provide a copy of the reply to the parties.

Time limit

(11) An application made under this rule must be received by the Division without delay. The Division must specify the time limit within which a response or reply, if any, is to be provided.

Confidentiality

(12) The Division may take any measures it considers necessary to ensure the confidentiality of the proceeding in respect of the application, including

> o**(a)** providing a summary of the response to the applicant instead of a copy; and

> o**(b)** if the Division holds a hearing in respect of the application,

>> ▪**(i)** excluding the applicant or the applicant and their counsel from the hearing while the party responding to the application provides evidence and makes representations, or

>> ▪**(ii)** allowing the presence of the applicant's counsel at the hearing while the party responding to the application provides evidence and makes representations, upon receipt of a written undertaking by counsel not to disclose any evidence or information adduced until a decision is made to hold the hearing in public.

Summary of response

(13) If the Division provides a summary of the response under paragraph (12)(a), or excludes the applicant and their counsel from a hearing in respect of the application under subparagraph (12)(b)(i), the Division must provide a summary of the representations and evidence, if any, that is sufficient to enable the applicant to reply, while ensuring the confidentiality of the proceeding having regard to the factors set out in paragraph 166(b) of the Act.

Notification of decision on application

(14) The Division must notify the applicant and the parties of its decision on the application and provide reasons for the decision.

Observers

Observers

- **58 (1)** An application under rule 57 is not necessary if an observer is a member of the staff of the Board or a representative or agent of the United Nations High Commissioner for Refugees or if the claimant or protected person consents to or requests the presence of an observer other than a representative of the press or other media of communication at the proceeding.

Observers — factor

(2) The Division must allow the attendance of an observer unless, in the opinion of the Division, the observer's attendance is likely to impede the proceeding.

Observers — confidentiality of proceeding

(3) The Division may take any measures that it considers necessary to ensure the confidentiality of the proceeding despite the presence of an observer.

Withdrawal

Abuse of process

- **59 (1)** For the purpose of subsection 168(2) of the Act, withdrawal of a claim or of an application to vacate or to cease refugee protection is an abuse of process if withdrawal would likely have a negative effect on the Division's integrity. If no substantive evidence has been accepted in the hearing, withdrawal is not an abuse of process.

Withdrawal if no substantive evidence accepted

(2) If no substantive evidence has been accepted in the hearing, a party may withdraw the party's claim or the application to vacate or to cease refugee protection by notifying the Division orally at a proceeding or in writing.

Withdrawal if substantive evidence accepted

(3) If substantive evidence has been accepted in the hearing, a party who wants to withdraw the party's claim or the application to vacate or to cease refugee protection must make an application to the Division in accordance with rule 50.

Reinstating a Withdrawn Claim or Application

Application to reinstate withdrawn claim

- **60 (1)** A person may make an application to the Division to reinstate a claim that was made by the person and was withdrawn.

Form and content of application

(2) The person must make the application in accordance with rule 50, include in the application their contact information and, if represented by counsel, their counsel's contact information and any limitations on counsel's retainer, and provide a copy of the application to the Minister.

Factors

(3) The Division must not allow the application unless it is established that there was a failure to observe a principle of natural justice or it is otherwise in the interests of justice to allow the application.

(4) In deciding the application, the Division must consider any relevant factors, including whether the application was made in a timely manner and the justification for any delay.

Subsequent application

(5) If the person made a previous application to reinstate that was denied, the Division must consider the reasons for the denial and must not allow the subsequent application unless there are exceptional circumstances supported by new evidence.

Application to reinstate withdrawn application to vacate or to cease refugee protection

- **61 (1)** The Minister may make an application to the Division to reinstate an application to vacate or to cease refugee protection that was withdrawn.

Form of application

(2) The Minister must make the application in accordance with rule 50.

Factors

(3) The Division must not allow the application unless it is established that there was a failure to observe a principle of natural justice or it is otherwise in the interests of justice to allow the application.

(4) In deciding the application, the Division must consider any relevant factors, including whether the application was made in a timely manner and the justification for any delay.

Subsequent application

(5) If the Minister made a previous application to reinstate that was denied, the Division must consider the reasons for the denial and must not allow the subsequent application unless there are exceptional circumstances supported by new evidence.

Reopening a Claim or Application

Application to reopen claim

- **62 (1)** At any time before the Refugee Appeal Division or the Federal Court has made a final determination in respect of a claim for refugee protection that has been decided or declared abandoned, the claimant or the Minister may make an application to the Division to reopen the claim.

Form of application

(2) The application must be made in accordance with rule 50 and, for the purpose of paragraph 50(5)(a), the Minister is considered to be a party whether or not the Minister took part in the proceedings.

Contact information

(3) If a claimant makes the application, they must include in the application their contact information and, if represented by counsel, their counsel's contact information and any limitations on counsel's retainer.

Allegations against counsel

(4) If it is alleged in the application that the claimant's counsel in the proceedings that are the subject of the application provided inadequate representation,

- o**(a)** the claimant must first provide a copy of the application to the counsel and then provide the original application to the Division, and

- o**(b)** the application provided to the Division must be accompanied by a written statement indicating how and when the copy of the application was provided to the counsel.

Copy of notice of appeal or pending application

(5) The application must be accompanied by a copy of any notice of pending appeal or any pending application for leave to apply for judicial review or any pending application for judicial review.

Factor

(6) The Division must not allow the application unless it is established that there was a failure to observe a principle of natural justice.

(7) In deciding the application, the Division must consider any relevant factors, including

      o**(a)** whether the application was made in a timely manner and the justification for any delay; and

      o**(b)** the reasons why

            ▪**(i)** a party who had the right of appeal to the Refugee Appeal Division did not appeal, or

            ▪**(ii)** a party did not make an application for leave to apply for judicial review or an application for judicial review.

Subsequent application

(8) If the party made a previous application to reopen that was denied, the Division must consider the reasons for the denial and must not allow the subsequent application unless there are exceptional circumstances supported by new evidence.

Other remedies

(9) If there is a pending appeal to the Refugee Appeal Division or a pending application for leave to apply for judicial review or a pending application for judicial review on the same or similar grounds, the Division must, as soon as is practicable, allow the application to reopen if it is necessary for the timely and efficient processing of a claim, or dismiss the application.

Application to reopen application to vacate or to cease refugee protection

- **63 (1)** At any time before the Federal Court has made a final determination in respect of an application to vacate or to cease refugee protection that has been decided or declared abandoned, the Minister or the protected person may make an application to the Division to reopen the application.

Form of application

(2) The application must be made in accordance with rule 50.

Contact information

(3) If a protected person makes the application, they must include in the application their contact information and, if represented by counsel, their counsel's contact information and any limitations on counsel's retainer, and they must provide a copy of the application to the Minister.

Allegations against counsel

(4) If it is alleged in the application that the protected person's counsel in the proceedings that are the subject of the application to reopen provided inadequate representation,

   o**(a)** the protected person must first provide a copy of the application to the counsel and then provide the original application to the Division, and

o**(b)** the application provided to the Division must be accompanied by a written statement indicating how and when the copy of the application was provided to the counsel.

Copy of pending application

(5) The application must be accompanied by a copy of any pending application for leave to apply for judicial review or any pending application for judicial review in respect of the application to vacate or to cease refugee protection.

Factors

(6) The Division must not allow the application unless it is established that there was a failure to observe a principle of natural justice.

(7) In deciding the application, the Division must consider any relevant factors, including

o**(a)** whether the application was made in a timely manner and the justification for any delay; and

o**(b)** if a party did not make an application for leave to apply for judicial review or an application for judicial review, the reasons why an application was not made.

Subsequent application

(8) If the party made a previous application to reopen that was denied, the Division must consider the reasons for the denial and must not allow the subsequent application unless there are exceptional circumstances supported by new evidence.

Other remedies

(9) If there is a pending application for leave to apply for judicial review or a pending application for judicial review on the same or similar grounds, the Division must, as soon as is practicable, allow the application to reopen if it is necessary for the timely and efficient processing of a claim, or dismiss the application.

Applications to Vacate or to Cease Refugee Protection

Form of application

- **64 (1)** An application to vacate or to cease refugee protection made by the Minister must be in writing and made in accordance with this rule.

Content of application

(2) In the application, the Minister must include

- **(a)** the contact information of the protected person and of their counsel, if any;

- **(b)** the identification number given by the Department of Citizenship and Immigration to the protected person;

o**(c)** the date and file number of any Division decision with respect to the protected person;

o**(d)** in the case of a person whose application for protection was allowed abroad, the person's file number, a copy of the decision and the location of the office;

o**(e)** the decision that the Minister wants the Division to make; and

o**(f)** the reasons why the Division should make that decision.

Providing application to protected person and Division

(3) The Minister must provide

o**(a)** a copy of the application to the protected person; and

o**(b)** the original of the application to the registry office that provided the notice of decision in the claim or to a registry office specified by the Division, together with a written statement indicating how and when a copy was provided to the protected person.

Abandonment

Opportunity to explain

- **65 (1)** In determining whether a claim has been abandoned under subsection 168(1) of the Act, the Division must give the claimant an

opportunity to explain why the claim should not
be declared abandoned,

> o**(a)** immediately, if the claimant is
> present at the proceeding and the
> Division considers that it is fair to do
> so; or

> o**(b)** in any other case, by way of a special
> hearing.

Special hearing — Basis of Claim Form

(2) The special hearing on the abandonment of
the claim for the failure to provide a completed
Basis of Claim Form in accordance with
paragraph 7(5)(a) must be held no later than five
working days after the day on which the
completed Basis of Claim Form was due. At the
special hearing, the claimant must provide their
completed Basis of Claim Form, unless the form
has already been provided to the Division.

Special hearing — failure to appear

(3) The special hearing on the abandonment of
the claim for the failure to appear for the hearing
of the claim must be held no later than five
working days after the day originally fixed for the
hearing of the claim.

Factors to consider

(4) The Division must consider, in deciding if the
claim should be declared abandoned, the
explanation given by the claimant and any other
relevant factors, including the fact that the
claimant is ready to start or continue the
proceedings.

Medical reasons

(5) If the claimant's explanation includes medical reasons, other than those related to their counsel, they must provide, together with the explanation, the original of a legible, recently dated medical certificate signed by a qualified medical practitioner whose name and address are printed or stamped on the certificate.

Content of certificate

(6) The medical certificate must set out

- o**(a)** the particulars of the medical condition, without specifying the diagnosis, that prevented the claimant from providing the completed Basis of Claim Form on the due date, appearing for the hearing of the claim, or otherwise pursuing their claim, as the case may be; and

- o**(b)** the date on which the claimant is expected to be able to pursue their claim.

Failure to provide medical certificate

(7) If a claimant fails to provide a medical certificate in accordance with subrules (5) and (6), the claimant must include in their explanation

- o**(a)** particulars of any efforts they made to obtain the required medical certificate, supported by corroborating evidence;

- o**(b)** particulars of the medical reasons included in the explanation, supported by corroborating evidence; and

o**(c)** an explanation of how the medical condition prevented them from providing the completed Basis of Claim Form on the due date, appearing for the hearing of the claim or otherwise pursuing their claim, as the case may be.

Start or continue proceedings

(8) If the Division decides not to declare the claim abandoned, other than under subrule (2), it must start or continue the proceedings on the day the decision is made or as soon as possible after that day.

Notice of Constitutional Question

Notice of constitutional question

- **66 (1)** A party who wants to challenge the constitutional validity, applicability or operability of a legislative provision must complete a notice of constitutional question.

Form and content of notice

(2) The party must complete the notice as set out in Form 69 of the *Federal Courts Rules* or any other form that includes

o**(a)** the party's name;

o**(b)** the Division file number;

o**(c)** the date, time and location of the hearing;

o**(d)** the specific legislative provision that is being challenged;

o**(e)** the material facts relied on to support the constitutional challenge; and

o**(f)** a summary of the legal argument to be made in support of the constitutional challenge.

Providing notice

(3) The party must provide

o**(a)** a copy of the notice to the Attorney General of Canada and to the attorney general of each province of Canada, in accordance with section 57 of the _Federal Courts Act_;

o**(b)** a copy of the notice to the Minister;

o**(c)** a copy of the notice to the other party, if any; and

o**(d)** the original notice to the Division, together with a written statement indicating how and when the copies of the notice were provided under paragraphs (a) to (c), and proof that they were provided.

Time limit

(4) Documents provided under this rule must be received by their recipients no later than 10 days before the day on which the constitutional argument is made.

Decisions

Notice of decision and reasons

- **67 (1)** When the Division makes a decision, other than an interlocutory decision, it must provide in writing a notice of decision to the claimant or the protected person, as the case may be, and to the Minister.

Written reasons

(2) The Division must provide written reasons for the decision together with the notice of decision

> o**(a)** if written reasons must be provided under paragraph 169(1)(d) of the Act;

> o**(b)** if the Minister was not present when the Division rendered an oral decision and reasons allowing a claim for refugee protection; or

> o**(c)** when the Division makes a decision on an application to vacate or to cease refugee protection.

Request for written reasons

(3) A request under paragraph 169(1)(e) of the Act for written reasons for a decision must be made in writing.

When decision of single member takes effect

- **68 (1)** A decision made by a single Division member allowing or rejecting a claim for refugee protection, on an application to vacate or to cease refugee protection, on the abandonment of a claim or of an application to vacate or to cease refugee protection, or allowing an application to withdraw a claim or to withdraw an application to vacate or to cease refugee protection takes effect

  o **(a)** if given orally at a hearing, when the member states the decision and gives the reasons; and

  o **(b)** if made in writing, when the member signs and dates the reasons for the decision.

When decision of three member panel takes effect

(2) A decision made by a panel of three Division members allowing or rejecting a claim for refugee protection, on an application to vacate or to cease refugee protection, on the abandonment of a claim or of an application to vacate or to cease refugee protection, or allowing an application to withdraw a claim or to withdraw an application to vacate or to cease refugee protection takes effect

  o **(a)** if given orally at a hearing, when all the members state their decision and give their reasons; and

  o **(b)** if made in writing, when all the members sign and date their reasons for the decision.

General Provisions

No applicable rule

69 In the absence of a provision in these Rules dealing with a matter raised during the proceedings, the Division may do whatever is necessary to deal with the matter.

Powers of Division

70 The Division may, after giving the parties notice and an opportunity to object,

- •**(a)** act on its own initiative, without a party having to make an application or request to the Division;

- •**(b)** change a requirement of a rule;

- •**(c)** excuse a person from a requirement of a rule; and

- •**(d)** extend a time limit, before or after the time limit has expired, or shorten it if the time limit has not expired.

Failure to follow rule

71 Unless proceedings are declared invalid by the Division, a failure to follow any requirement of these Rules does not make the proceedings invalid.

Repeals

72 [Repeal]

73 [Repeal]

Coming into Force

These Rules come into force on the day on which section 26 of the *Balanced Refugee Reform Act* comes into force, but if they are registered after that day, they come into force on the day on which they are registered.

SCHEDULE 1 (Rule 1)

Claimant's Information and Basis of Claim

Item	Information
1	Claimant's name.
2	Claimant's date of birth.
3	Claimant's gender.
4	Claimant's nationality, ethnic or racial group, or tribe.
5	Languages and dialects, if any, that the claimant speaks.
6	Claimant's religion and denomination or sect.
7	Whether the claimant believes that they would experience harm, mistreatment or threats if they returned to their country today. If yes, description of what the claimant expects would happen, including who would harm, mistreat or threaten them and what the claimant believes would be the reasons for it.
8	Whether the claimant or the claimant's family have ever experienced harm, mistreatment or threats in the past. If yes, a description of the harm, mistreatment or threats, including when it

Item	Information

occurred, who caused it, what the claimant believes are the reasons for it and whether similarly situated persons have experienced such harm, mistreatment or threats.

9   Whether the claimant sought protection or help from any authority or organization in their country. If not, an explanation of why not. If yes, the authority or organization from which the claimant sought protection or help and a description of what the claimant did and what happened as a result.

10   When the claimant left their country and the reasons for leaving at that time.

11   Whether the claimant moved to another part of their country to seek safety. If not, an explanation of why not. If the claimant moved to another part of their country, the reasons for leaving it and an explanation why the claimant could not live there or in another part of their country today.

12   Whether the claimant moved to another country to seek safety. If yes, details including the name of the country, when the claimant moved there, length of stay and whether the claimant claimed refugee protection there. If the claimant did not claim refugee protection there, an explanation of why not.

13   Whether minors are claiming refugee protection

Item	Information

with the claimant. If yes, whether the claimant is the minor's parent and the other parent is in Canada, or whether the claimant is not the minor's parent, or whether the claimant is the minor's parent but the other parent is not in Canada. If the claimant is not the minor's parent or if the claimant is the minor's parent but the other parent is not in Canada, details of any legal documents or written consent allowing the claimant to take care of the minor or travel with the minor. If the claimant does not have such documents, an explanation of why not.

14   If a child six years old or younger is claiming refugee protection with the claimant, an explanation of why the claimant believes the child would be at risk of being harmed, mistreated or threatened if returned to their country.

15   Other details the claimant considers important for the refugee protection claim.

16   Country or countries in which the claimant believes they are at risk of serious harm.

17   The country or countries in which the claimant is or has been a citizen, including how and when citizenship was acquired and present status.

18   Name, date of birth, citizenship and place and country of residence of relatives, living or dead, specifically the claimant's spouse, common-law partner, children, parents, brothers and sisters.

Item	Information
19	If the claimant or the claimant's spouse, common-law partner, child, parent, brother or sister has claimed refugee protection or asylum in Canada or in any other country — including at a Canadian office abroad or from the United Nations High Commissioner for Refugees — the details of the claim including the name of the person who made the claim, and the date, location, result of the claim and IRB file number or CIC client ID number, if any.
20	Whether the claimant applied for a visa to enter Canada. If yes, for what type of visa, the date of the application, at which Canadian office the application was made and whether or not it was accepted. If the visa was issued, the date of issue and the duration of the visa. If the application was refused, the date and reasons of refusal.
21	Claimant's contact information.
22	Whether the claimant has counsel and if so, details concerning counsel — including what counsel has been retained to do and counsel's contact information.
23	Claimant's choice of official language for communications with and proceedings before the Board.
24	Whether the claimant needs an interpreter during any proceeding, and the language and dialect, if

Item	Information
	any, to be interpreted.

SCHEDULE 2 (Paragraph 3(5)(d))

Information To Be Provided About the Claimant by an Officer

Item	Information
1	Name, gender and date of birth.
2	Department of Citizenship and Immigration client identification number.
3	If the claimant is detained, the name and address of the place of detention.
4	Claimant's contact information in Canada, if any.
5	Contact information of any counsel for the claimant.
6	Official language chosen by the claimant as the language of proceedings before the Board.
7	Date the claim was referred or deemed to be referred to the Division.
8	Section of the Act under which the claim is being referred.
9	Officer's decision about the claim's eligibility

Item	Information
	under section 100 of the Act, if a decision has been made.
10	The country or countries in which the claimant fears persecution, torture, a risk to their life or a risk of cruel and unusual treatment or punishment.
11	Whether the claimant may need a designated representative and the contact information for any proposed designated representative.
12	Whether the claimant needs an interpreter, including a sign language interpreter, during any proceeding, and the language and dialect, if any, to be interpreted.
13	If a claim of the claimant's spouse, common-law partner or any relative has been referred to the Division, the name and Department of Citizenship and Immigration client identification numbers of each of those persons.
14	When and how the officer notified the claimant of the referral of the claim to the Division.
15	Whether the claim was made at a port of entry or inside Canada other than at a port of entry.
16	Any other information gathered by the officer about the claimant that is relevant to the claim.

SCHEDULE 3 (Rules 5 and 13)

Information and Declarations — Counsel Not
Representing or Advising for Consideration

Item	Information
1	IRB Division and file number with respect to the claimant or protected person.
2	Name of counsel who is representing or advising the claimant or protected person and who is not receiving consideration for those services.
3	Name of counsel's firm or organization, if applicable, and counsel's postal address, telephone number, fax number and email address, if any.
4	If applicable, a declaration, signed by the interpreter, that includes the interpreter's name, the language and dialect, if any, interpreted and a statement that the interpretation is accurate.
5	Declaration signed by the claimant or protected person that the counsel who is representing or advising them is not receiving consideration and the information provided in the form is complete, true and correct.
6	Declaration signed by counsel that they are not receiving consideration for representing or advising the claimant or protected person and that the information provided in the form is complete, true and correct.

APPENDIX III:
Sample Christian Questions & Answers

Who is Jesus Christ?

Answer:

Jesus Christ is the promised Messiah, the Savior of mankind (people) from their sins and Hell fire. He is the Lord. He was born, so He is a Man. But because the power that caused His birth came from the Holy Spirit (God), He is also God. Jesus means "Savior."

Key Claims of Jesus Christ:

Jesus Christ claimed that He was from the beginning first as the Word and God: "In the beginning was the Word, and the Word was with God, and the Word was God."[538]

He claimed that He temporarily came to earth in the flesh, as a human being: "The Word became flesh and made his dwelling among us. We have seen his glory, the glory of the one and only Son, who came from the Father, full of grace and truth."[539]

He claimed, and others worshipped Him, as the Son of God: "Then those who were in the boat worshiped him, saying, 'Truly you are the Son of God.'"[540]

He claimed that He is the Way, the Truth and the Life, and that there is no other passage way to the Father

---

[538] John 1:1
[539] John 1:14
[540] Matthew 14:33

(God) except through Him: "I am the way and the truth and the life. No one comes to the Father except through me."[541]

He claimed that He was the Bread of Life: "I am the bread of life. He who comes to me will never go hungry, and he who believes in me will never be thirsty.'"[542]

He claimed that He was the Light of the World: "When Jesus spoke again to the people, he said, 'I am the light of the world. Whoever follows me will never walk in darkness, but will have the light of life.'"[543]

He claimed that He was the Vine: "I am the vine; you are the branches. If a man remains in me and I in him, he will bear much fruit; apart from me you can do nothing."[544]

He claimed that He was the Good Shepherd: "I am the good shepherd. The good shepherd lays down his life for the sheep."[545]

He claimed that He was the Door: "I am the door. If anyone enters by Me, he will be saved, and will go in and out and find pasture."[546]

He claimed that He was the Resurrection and the Life: "I am the resurrection and the life. He who believes in me will live, even though he dies; and whoever lives and believes in me will never die."[547]

---

[541] John 14:6
[542] John 6:35
[543] John 8:12
[544] John 15:5
[545] John 10:11
[546] John 10:9
[547] John 11:25-26

He claimed that He could forgive sins: "Then Jesus said to her, 'Your sins are forgiven.'"[548] And Jesus also gave the authority to His disciples to forgive sins: "If you forgive anyone's sins, their sins are forgiven; if you do not forgive them, they are not forgiven."[549]

Key Facts about Jesus Christ:

Jesus Christ died for humanity so that through Him they could be saved if they believe and confess Him. Jesus is the Son of God, "Whosoever shall confess that Jesus is the Son of God, God dwelleth in him, and he in God."[550]

As God's only begotten Son, Jesus Christ saves those who believe in Him, "For God so loved the world, that he gave his only begotten Son, that whosoever believeth in him should not perish, but have everlasting life."[551]

Through Jesus Christ, God's love is revealed, "In this was manifested the love of God toward us, because that God sent his only begotten Son into the world, that we might live through him."[552]

Jesus Christ gives eternal life, "And I give unto them eternal life; and they shall never perish, neither shall any man pluck them out of my hand. My Father, which gave them [to] me, is greater than all; and no man is able to pluck them out of my Father's hand. I and my Father are one."[553]

---

[548] Luke 7:48
[549] John 20:23
[550] 1 John 4:15
[551] John 3:16
[552] 1 John 4:9
[553] John 10:28-30

God, the Creator, is the Father of Jesus Christ, "Blessed
be God, even the Father of our Lord Jesus Christ, the
Father of mercies, and the God of all comfort; Who
comforteth us in all our tribulation, that we may be able
to comfort them which are in any trouble, by the comfort
wherewith we ourselves are comforted of God."[554]

Only through Jesus Christ is there salvation for the entire
human race, "Be it known unto you all, and to all the
people of Israel, that by the name of Jesus Christ of
Nazareth, whom ye crucified, whom God raised from the
dead, even by him doth this man stand here before you
whole. This is the stone, which was set at naught of you
builders, which is become the head of the corner. Neither
is there salvation in any other: for there is none other
name under heaven given among men, whereby we must
be saved."[555]

Jesus Christ is the beginning and the end of the Christian
faith, "Looking unto Jesus the author and finisher of our
faith; who for the joy that was set before him endured
the cross, despising the shame, and is set down at the
right hand of the throne of God."[556]

Jesus Christ heals those who believe in Him, "But he was
wounded for our transgressions, he was bruised for our
iniquities: the chastisement of our peace was upon him;
and with his stripes we are healed."[557]

Anyone who confesses (acknowledges and admits) Jesus
Christ and believes in their hearts that God rose Him
from the dead, they are saved and spared from Hell fire,

[554] 2 Corinthians 1:3-4
[555] Acts 4:10-12
[556] Hebrews 12:2
[557] Isaiah 53:5

"That if thou shalt confess with thy mouth the Lord Jesus, and shalt believe in thine heart that God hath raised him from the dead, thou shalt be saved."[558]

Christ is the demonstration of God's love, "And walk in love, as Christ also hath loved us, and hath given himself for us an offering and a sacrifice to God for a sweetsmelling savor."[559]

Jesus Christ and the Father are one, "Verily, verily, I say unto you, He that receiveth whomsoever I send receiveth me; and he that receiveth me receiveth him that sent me."[560]

Jesus Christ, like the Father, is the same always, "Jesus Christ the same yesterday, and today, and forever."[561]

Jesus Christ is God in the flesh, "And the Word was made flesh, and dwelt among us, (and we beheld his glory, the glory as of the only begotten of the Father,) full of grace and truth,"[562] and, "Let this mind be in you, which was also in Christ Jesus: Who, being in the form of God, thought it not robbery to be equal with God: But made himself of no reputation, and took upon him the form of a servant, and was made in the likeness of men: And being found in fashion as a man, he humbled himself, and became obedient unto death, even the death of the cross."[563]

---

[558] Romans 10:9
[559] Ephesians 5:2
[560] John 13:20
[561] Hebrews 13:8
[562] John 1:14
[563] Philippians 2:5-8

Jesus Christ is the conqueror of death, "O death, where is thy sting? O grave, where is thy victory? The sting of death is sin; and the strength of sin is the law. But thanks be to God, which giveth us the victory through our Lord Jesus Christ."[564]

Jesus Christ prayed for all believers, "Wherefore he is able also to save them to the uttermost that come unto God by him, seeing he ever liveth to make intercession for them."[565]

Jesus Christ made believers the light of the world, "Ye are the light of the world. A city that is set on a hill cannot be hid. Neither do men light a candle, and put it under a bushel, but on a candlestick; and it giveth light unto all that are in the house. Let your light so shine before men, that they may see your good works, and glorify your Father which is in heaven."[566]

Jesus Christ has the name above all names, "Wherefore God also hath highly exalted him, and given him a name which is above every name: That at the name of Jesus every knee should bow, of things in heaven, and things in earth, and things under the earth; And that every tongue should confess that Jesus Christ is Lord, to the glory of God the Father."[567]

Jesus Christ is God's glory incarnate, "Jesus saith unto her, Said I not unto thee, that, if thou wouldest believe, thou shouldest see the glory of God?"[568]

---

[564] 1 Corinthians 15:55-57
[565] Hebrews 7:25
[566] Matthew 5:14-16
[567] Philippians 2:9-11
[568] John 11:40

Jesus Christ was the promised Savior, "For unto us a child is born, unto us a son is given and the government shall be upon his shoulder: and his name shall be called Wonderful, Counsellor, The Mighty God, The Everlasting Father, The Prince of Peace."[569]

Jesus Christ died and rose again for all the world, "For I delivered unto you first of all that which I also received, how that Christ died for our sins according to the scriptures; And that he was buried, and that he rose again the third day according to the scriptures."[570]

Jesus Christ holds everlasting dominion, "I saw in the night visions, and, behold, one like the Son of man came with the clouds of heaven, and came to the Ancient of Days, and they brought him near before him. And there was given him dominion, and glory, and a kingdom, that all people, nations, and languages, should serve him: his dominion is an everlasting dominion, which shall not pass away, and his kingdom that which shall not be destroyed."[571]

Jesus Christ is the pioneer of the Christian faith, "Fixing our eyes on Jesus, the pioneer and perfecter of faith. For the joy set before him he endured the cross, scorning its shame, and sat down at the right hand of the throne of God."[572]

Key Summaries:

1. Who is Jesus' heavenly father?

---

[569] Isaiah 9:6
[570] 1 Corinthians 15:3-4
[571] Daniel 7:13-14
[572] Hebrews 12:2

Answer: God, the Father

    2. What is the name of Jesus' mother?

Answer: Mary, the Virgin

    3. Was Mary a virgin when she had Jesus?

Answer: Yes.

    4. How did a virgin have a baby?

Answer:

God, through the power of the Holy Spirit, came upon her.

    5.What did Joseph want to do with Mary when he discovered that she was pregnant?

Answer:

He had a dream that Mary's Son would be the savior of the world.

    6. In which town was Jesus Christ born?

Answer: Bethlehem.

    7. Where did Joseph take Mary to live, and then when His life was threatened, to hide?

Answer: Nazareth; Egypt

    8. Who is John the Baptist?

Answer:

Jesus Christ' cousin who was born six months before
Jesus. He preached repentance and baptized people in
River Jordan. When Jesus approached him, he said that
he did not want Jesus to be baptized by him, saying that
he was not even worth to untie Jesus' shoes. John lived in
the desert (wilderness). He wore a camel-hair garment
and a leather belt. And he ate only honey and wild
locusts.

9. Who is John the Baptist's mother and father?

Answer: Mother: Elizabeth
Father: Zachariah

10. Who wanted Jesus Christ to die?

Answer:

The Jews – the Pharisees and teachers of the law.

11. Did Jesus perform miracles?

Answer: Yes.

12. Name some of the miracles?

Answer:

- Turning water into wine
- Walking on water
- Calming the wind (storm)
- Feeding 5000 people
- Giving sight to blind people

- Raising the dead to life

13. What is the name of the Roman Governor who permitted Jesus to be killed?

Answer: Pontius Pilate.

14. Who was King Herod?

Answer:

The *de facto* king imposed upon the Jews by the Romans. He wanted the three *Maji* (the wisemen from the East) to tell him about Jesus so he could kill Jesus.

15. Who was Herodias?

Answer:

She was King Herod's sister-in-law and Herod was having a sexual affair with her. She asked Herod for the head of John the Baptist after her daughter danced before Herod and was asked to name a gift.

16. What is a Sabbath?

Answer:

The seventh-day of the week, Saturday. It was a day of rest because on that day God had rested from creating the heavens and the earth.

17. What is water baptism?

Answer:

Being immersed in water as a sign of death and resurrection. Believers in Jesus Christ may undergo the waters of baptism as a formal process of being entered into Church membership. Spiritually, it is a Christian ritual which ushers believers into what is called the "Body of Christ." There are many methods of conducting the baptismal service. Some prefer a complete immersion in water as a symbol of dying and resurrecting to others who sprinkle water. Some Christian groups prefer to baptize babies to others who only baptize those who have an understanding of what baptism means. To the later, lessons may be taken just before baptism. In both cases, many Christian groups offer a certificate of baptism as a formal and legal piece of evidence of membership either in the local church or in the universal Body of Christ.

18. Did John baptize with water or with the Holy Spirit?

Answer: Water.

19. What did John say Jesus was going to baptize people with?

Answer: The Holy Spirit and fire.

20. Was Jesus Christ baptized in water?

Answer: Yes.

21. Who baptized Jesus Christ in water?

Answer: John the Baptist

22. In which river did John baptize Jesus?

Answer: In the River Jordan.

23. What happened at Jesus' baptismal ceremony?

Answer:

John saw Jesus coming. John did not want to baptize Jesus because John knew that Jesus was God and that John did not count himself worthy to baptize his creator. But Jesus told John to continue baptizing Him in order to fulfil all righteousness. At that time, while in the flesh and before His death and resurrection, Jesus was still under the Law of Moses and all its ceremonies. This, further, proved that Jesus was also a Man, not just God. Then God the Holy Spirit, in the form of a dove, came upon Jesus and John heard a voice from Heaven saying, "This is my beloved Son in whom I am well pleased."

24. Around what age was Jesus when he was crucified?

Answer: He was 33 years old.

25. Who betrayed Jesus?

Answer: Jesus was betrayed by Judas Iscariot.

26. For how many pieces of silver was Jesus betrayed (sold)?

Answer:

For 30 pieces of silver. Judas was, later, overcome with guilt for betraying Jesus. He threw the 30 silver coins into the temple. The Jewish leaders used the 30 pieces of silver to buy a field from a potter. Judas hanged himself (committed suicide) in that same field.

27.How many disciples did Jesus have?

Answer: 12.

28. What were the names of Jesus' disciples?

Answer: Andrew
Bartholomew (Nathaniel)
James Alpheus
James Zebedee
John Zebedee
Judas Alpheus
Judas Iscariot
Matthew Levi
Philip
Simon Peter
Thaddaeus (Jude)
Thomas Didymus

29. Which disciple rejected Jesus three times, and which one doubted Him?

Answer: Simon Peter (rejected Jesus)
Thomas (doubted Jesus)

30. Name the garden Jesus prayed in three times before he went to the cross.

Answer: Gethsemane

31. How many days was Jesus dead?

Answer: 3 days

32. Who was Lazarus?

Answer:

Jesus' cousin who had been dead for four days.

33. Who were Lazarus' two sisters?

Answer: Martha and Mary

34. What did Jesus say at Lazarus' grave?

Answer:

Jesus went to his tomb and said "Lazarus, come forth"?

35. What is the meaning of Salvation.

Answer:

Salvation means that a person has believed in Jesus Christ as their personal Lord and Savior by repenting of their sins, believing and confessing that Jesus Christ is Lord, and accepting the free gift of Eternal Life, which is Christ. This is usually done by confessing or professing with the mouth and by a strong internal witness of the personal spirit that one has rejected the evil world and accepted the promise of an everlasting life after death. This process may also be termed, "Conversion."

36. What is Sin?

Answer:

Sin is both a state and a condition. All humans are presumed to be in a state of sin; they are born in sin according to the Bible:

"Behold, I was brought forth in iniquity,
And in sin my mother conceived me."[573]

But sin is also a condition; people may deliberately choose to sin (disobedience):

"The one who sins is the one who will die. The child will not share the guilt of the parent, nor will the parent share the guilt of the child. The righteousness of the righteous will be credited to them, and the wickedness of the wicked will be charged against them."[574]

Sin is defined in the Bible, as the transgression (violation or breaking) of the law:

"Whosoever committeth sin transgresseth also the law: *for sin is the transgression of the law*."[575]

In short, Sin is when someone knows the good they must do but, rather, choose to do the bad or evil. The Bible mentions many varieties of sins (or works of the flesh), including: "...sexual immorality, impurity, sensuality, idolatry, sorcery, enmity, strife, jealousy, fits of anger, rivalries, dissensions, divisions, envy, drunkenness, orgies, and things like these."[576]

---

[573] Psalm 51:5
[574] Ezekiel 18:20
[575] 1 John 3:4 (emphasis added)
[576] Galatians 5:19-21

However, there has been a modification to the definition of Sin under the law and the one under grace. Since the resurrection of Jesus Christ ushered in a new dispensation of grace (basically absence of law), Sin is no longer the breaking of the law, because there is no law to break. Under grace, everything is permitted: "'I have the right to do anything,' you say—but not everything is beneficial. 'I have the right to do anything'—but I will not be mastered by anything."[577] What is Sin, therefore, is anything that is not beneficial to you and to your neighbor. If what you do or say or your attitude is not beneficial to you or your neighbor, then doing it is Sin to you. Therefore, "If anyone, then, knows the good they ought to do and doesn't do it, it is sin for them."[578]

This means that, unlike in the Old Testament and in our legal systems where there was and there is a national, public deterrent system that classifies certain behaviors as wrongs (sins), under grace, such facility does not exist anymore. Sin is individualized. It is a matter of our hearts, of our consciences: "If our hearts condemn us, we know that God is greater than our hearts, and he knows everything."[579] In other words, if your heart condemns you, you have sinned, if it doesn't, you haven't sinned. Similarly, if what you contemplate to do or say or your attitude will make another person stumble, then don't do or say or behave it.[580] Ultimately, the only sin that takes people to Hell is because they do not or did not believe in Jesus.[581]

37. What is Forgiveness?

---

[577] 1 Corinthians 6:12
[578] James 4:17
[579] 1 John 3:20
[580] See also Romans 14:19-21
[581] See John 16:9

Answer:

Forgiveness is letting go of the wrongs others have done against you. In Christianity, it is mandatory and compulsory for every Christian to forgive others. It is also a condition of one's own forgiveness from God: "[Forgive and you shall be forgiven] For if you forgive other people when they sin against you, your heavenly Father will also forgive you."[582]

38. What is Redemption?
Answer:

Redemption is a system that was followed in slavery times. It was an act of buying back the property that one had lost or sold. To do so, a ramson was required. Thus, a former slave owner would redeem his former slave if they so wanted them very much.

In the Bible, with modification, this process was engaged in to save humanity from the clutches of sin and the devil. It is premised upon the ground that humanity sold its birthright for dominion and rule over God's creation to Satan. This happened in the Garden of Eden – when the first couple, Adam and Eve, succumbed to Satan (serpent)'s temptation to eat from the Tree of Knowledge of Good and Evil. When they did, they willingly sold their power and authority to Satan. God could not give that power and authority back to mankind because humanity gave it willingly to Satan. God needed a human agent to do so. But no human being was worthy

---

[582] Matthew 6:14

because they all had sinned.[583] Hence, God took the form of Man and paid with His own blood to redeem mankind. This process of Jesus Christ becoming flesh, living a sinless life, shedding His own blood and dying on the Cross, is called *Redemption*. In the end, it was the Man (Jesus Christ) who claimed back His power and authority by paying with His own life. Jesus Christ did not just die; He also rose again from the dead. By rising, Jesus Christ gave a strong witness to the redemption process and secured for humanity a permanent right over the dominion of the earth, as it was originally intended. Thus, everyone who believes in Jesus Christ will rise again from the dead in order to continue their rightful domination of the earth: "Here is a trustworthy saying: If we died with him, we will also live with him."[584]

39. What is Holy Communion?

Answer:

It is also called *The Last Supper* or the *Eucharist*. It was the last meal Jesus Christ had with His disciples. In it, Jesus Christ announced (proclaimed) a New Covenant which would be based upon His blood. Through it, He also ushered in the Church, the Body of Christ. Bread was broken, symbolizing Jesus' broken body, and wine was drunk, symbolizing Jesus' spilled blood. The Bible summarizes it, thus:

> For I received from the Lord Himself that [instruction] which I passed on to you, that the Lord Jesus on the night in which He was betrayed took bread; and when He had given thanks, He broke it and said, "This is (represents) My body, which is [offered as a

---

[583] See Romans 3:23
[584] 2 Timothy 2:11

sacrifice] for you. Do this in [affectionate]
remembrance of Me." In the same way, after
supper He took the cup, saying, "This cup is
the new covenant [ratified and established] in
My blood; do this, as often as you drink it, in
[affectionate] remembrance of Me." For every
time you eat this bread and drink this cup, you
are [symbolically] proclaiming [the fact of] the
Lord's death until He comes [again].

So, then whoever eats the bread or drinks the
cup of the Lord in a way that is unworthy [of
Him] will be guilty of [profaning and sinning
against] the body and blood of the Lord. But a
person must [prayerfully] examine himself
[and his relationship to Christ], and only when
he has done so should he eat of the bread and
drink of the cup. For anyone who eats and
drinks [without solemn reverence and heartfelt
gratitude for the sacrifice of Christ], eats and
drinks a judgment on himself if he does not
[b]recognize the body [of Christ].[585]

And Jesus Christ Himself gave a command that this
(Communion) should be done frequently in
remembrance of Him till His return: "…and when he
had given thanks, he broke it and said, 'This is my body,
which is for you; do this in remembrance of me….This
cup is the new covenant in My blood; do this, as often as
you drink it, in remembrance of Me.'"[586] Some Christian
groups (also called denominations) do this every Sunday
when they meet for mass; others do so occasionally
during their Church services.

---

[585] 1 Corinthians 11:23-29 (Amplified Bible)
[586] 1 Corinthians 11:24-25

40. What is Resurrection?

Answer:

This is one of the central tenets of the Christian faith and doctrine. It is the doctrine (creed) of rising back to life after death. Christians believe that Jesus Christ died and came back to life again by the power of the Holy Spirit. They also believe that since Jesus rose again from the dead, they will also be raised from the dead at the end of the age. Apostle Paul argues that, if the resurrection doesn't exist, Christianity doesn't exist, either: "And if Christ has not been raised, our preaching is useless and so is your faith."[587] The implication is that, there is a resurrection.

41. What is Rapture?

Answer:

Christian believers believe that when Jesus comes again for the second time, He will first "rapture," or take out of the earth in bodily form, all those who had died in faith and those who will be alive. This elation of believers in the air is called a Rapture. Apostle Paul declares it this way:

> For the Lord Himself will descend from
> heaven with a loud command, with the voice
> of an archangel, and with the trumpet of God,
> and the dead in Christ will be the first to rise.
> After that, we who are alive and remain will be
> caught up together with them in the clouds to
> meet the Lord in the air. And so we will always
> be with the Lord.[588]

---

[587] 1 Corinthians 15:14
[588] 1 Thessalonians 4:16-17

42. What is Revelation?

Answer:

In his old age, Apostle John, the beloved, was arrested and imprisoned on a Greek island called Patmos. John writes, "I, John, both your brother and companion in tribulation, was on the island that is called Patmos for the word of God and for the testimony of Jesus Christ."[589] It was during that time that John wrote the last book of the New Testament Bible called "Revelation." It is the further revelation of Jesus Christ and of the end days and of what will follow.

43. What is Repentance?

Answer:

Repentance means to turn away from sin. Biblically, this means to stop living an evil life and to begin living a righteous life. It is believed to be the first step into conversion.

44. What is a Trinity?

Answer:

Christians believe that God is a triune God – the Father, the Son (Jesus Christ) and the Holy Spirit. "But for us, there is one God, the Father, by whom all things were created, and for whom we live. And there is one Lord, Jesus Christ, through whom all things were created, and

---

[589] Revelation 1:9

through whom we live."[590] God is also the Spirit: "Now the Lord is the Spirit, and where the Spirit of the Lord is, there is freedom."[591] And these three are One: "May the grace of the Lord Jesus Christ, and the love of God, and the fellowship of the Holy Spirit be with you all."[592]

45. Who killed Jesus?

Answer:

The Romans did the actual killing. However, it was the Jews who demanded for His death.

46. Did the Jews accept Jesus as their Savior?

Answer:

There was mixed views among the Jews concerning the deity of Jesus Christ. Some, like among His own disciples, willingly accepted Him as the promised Messiah. However, some of the nobilities and the teachers of the law and the Pharisees, rejected Him as Messiah.

47. Who is Barabbas?

Answer:

The criminal the Jews asked to be released instead of Jesus.

48. What are the Beatitudes?

---

[590] 1 Corinthians 8:6
[591] 2 Corinthians 3:17
[592] 2 Corinthians 13:14

Answer:

The sermon on the mountain and the happy (blessed) attitudes. They are contained in these refrains:[593]

> Blessed are the poor in spirit,
>   for theirs is the kingdom of heaven.
> Blessed are those who mourn,
>   for they will be comforted.
> Blessed are the meek,
>   for they will inherit the earth.
> Blessed are those who hunger and thirst for righteousness,
>   for they will be filled.
> Blessed are the merciful,
>   for they will be shown mercy.
> Blessed are the pure in heart,
>   for they will see God.
> Blessed are the peacemakers,
>   for they will be called children of God.
> Blessed are those who are persecuted because of righteousness,
>   for theirs is the kingdom of heaven.
> Blessed are you when people insult you, persecute you and falsely say all kinds of evil against you because of me. Rejoice and be glad, because great is your reward in heaven, for in the same way they persecuted the prophets who were before you.

49. What is Heaven?

Answer:

---

[593] Matthew 5:3-12

The place of God's abode, and where the souls of the saints are expected to go. During the Old Testament, God revealed that Heaven was His throne: "This is what the LORD says: "Heaven is my throne, and the earth is my footstool. Where is the house you will build for me? Where will my resting place be?"[594] Jesus claimed that He came down from there: "For I have *come down from heaven*, not to do My own will, but the will of Him who sent Me."[595] The phrase, "come down from heaven,' has a connotation that Heaven is above, and the earth is below, and Hell is under the earth.

50. What is Hell?

Answer:

The place of torment and fire without end. Jesus Christ said that Hell was a place of torture: "Don't fear those who kill the body, rather fear Him who is able to destroy both soul and body in hell."[596]

51. How does one become a Christian?

Answer:

By grace (God's unmerited favor) through faith in Jesus Christ.[597] One must believe in their hearts and confess with their mouths that Jesus Christ is Lord. For "Everyone who calls on the name of the Lord will be saved."[598]

---

[594] Isaiah 66:1
[595] John 6:38 (emphasis added).
[596] Matthew 10:28; Matthew 5:29-30; 23:15,33; and Luke 10:15; 16:23
[597] Ephesians 2:8-9
[598] Romans 10:13

However, there is no formulae as to how different people become Christians. God is Sovereign, and in His sovereignty, He may accept people in different ways. The central belief for all who have ever believed in Jesus Christ and converted into Christianity is that they saw a need for their sins to be forgiven and they called upon Jesus Christ to save them. In short, they *believe* in Jesus Christ.

> 52. What are the fruits of being a converted Christian?

Answer:

The Bible has given a guidance on this, and it is included in what is known as the *Fruit of the Spirit*: "But the fruit of the Spirit is love, joy, peace, forbearance, kindness, goodness, faithfulness, gentleness, and self-control. Against such things there is no law."[599] The rendition "fruit" (singular) is supported by the New Living Translation of Matthew 7:16: "You can identify them by their *fruit*, that is, by the way they act. Can you pick grapes from thornbushes, or figs from thistles?"[600]

This may mean that a Christian produces one kind of a fruit with different parts. It may also mean that a Christian produces different kinds of fruits with different tastes. What is clear, however, is the fact that whatever a genuinely converted Christian produces is true, noble, right, pure, lovely, admirable, excellent or praiseworthy.[601]

---

[599] Galatians 5:22-23
[600] Emphasis added
[601] Philippians 4:8

A person who claims to have been genuinely converted to Christianity but who fails to produce the *fruit* or *fruits* as tabulated above, may put their Christianity in question, and, therefore, in doubt.

APPENDIX IV:
Refugee Hearing Preparation Questionnaire

Claimant Identification:

1.Name: ___; DOB: ___Nationality: _____

Religion/No Religion:_____ Current
Address:

_____

_____

_____

_____

Email: _____;Tel/Cell: _____

Basis of Claim (BOC):

2.Your claim arises in (check one):

Political Opinion [ ]
Religion [ ]
Race [ ]
Nationality [ ]
Membership in a particular social group/Non-State-Actors (gangs, tribe, clan, culture, etc.) [ ]
Spousal Abuse [ ]
Sexual Orientation [ ]

3.Do you know your story well?

_____

_____

4.Is there any need to update, amend or add to your story/narrative new information which recently came to your knowledge?

_____

_____

_____

Evidence:

5.Do you have relevant documents/evidence to support your claim/story? If so, list the documents (add more pages, if required):

_____

_____

_____

_____

_____

_____

_____

6.If you are submitting **affidavits**, are the signatures fresh?

_____

_____

_____

7.Do you have any **witness/es** to support your claim? If so, list their names and contact details. How do you think they will help you in the hearing? (*Add more pages if required*)

_____

_____

_____

_____

8.Are you reading your story/narrative every day? If
not, why?

_____
_____
_____
_____

Narrative Details:

9.Have you mastered/remembered all *dates, places,
events/time* or the *order* in which events
happened?

_____
_____
_____
_____
_____
_____

10.Do you have a hearing date (date to appear) yet, if
so, what is the date?

_____
_____

11.Have you remembered to submit all the relevant
documents and/or amendments to your BOC
narrative **at least 10 days before the hearing?**

_____
_____

12.Do you hold Green Card from the USA?

_____
_____

13.Did you pass through the USA to come to
Canada, if so, did you claim refugee there, if not,
why didn't you claim refugee protection or
asylum in USA? (*Add more pages if required*)

_____

_____

_____

_____

14.Is the information you provided on your
Visa/immigration application the same as you
gave in your **refugee application**? Have you
thoroughly checked forms, letters, online
account, if any, responses, and etc., to make sure
you haven't contradicted yourself in the
immigration/refugee application process?

_____

_____

_____

_____

_____

_____

15.Have you elected or are you thinking of using an
interpreter at the hearing, if so, in what language
and do you need any help?

_____

_____

_____

16.Are you comfortable answering questions in
shorter sentences?

_____

_____

17. Are you comfortable understanding **Canadian English accent?**

_____

_____

18. Are you comfortable looking the "Member" (adjudicator or decision-maker or "judge") in the eye when testifying?

_____

_____

_____

State of Mind:

19. Do you feel **stressed or depressed** thinking about your hearing?

_____

_____

20. Are you thinking you may be clinically depressed because of what you went through and may need the help of a **mental health professional?** If so, what help do you need?

_____

_____

_____

_____

_____

Complete Disclosure:

21. To the best of your ability and knowledge, have you told me everything I need to know about

your case? If there is anything else you want to tell me, please do so (*Add more pages if required*)

_____

_____

_____

_____

_____

_____

22. Is there any **information or documents** that are **not** in your possession but you believe they are relevant to supporting your claim? If so, can you obtain them in good time?

_____

_____

_____

_____

_____

_____

Representation:

23. Do you know the difference between an **advocate** (your representative) and **witness/Claimant** (yourself) in the hearing process? _____ **If not, note:** Your representative's role as **advocate** is to assist you present your case using questions based on your immigration documents and forms, refugee documents and forms, and evidence you provided. An advocate is not allowed to answer questions for you during the hearing. Your role as a **witness/Claimant** is to answer the questions truthfully, accurately and credibly by eliciting short, straightforward and pointed answers to the questioning your representative or the adjudicator, also known as the Member, will be

asking you. Do you have any concerns?

_____

_____

_____

_____

_____

_____

24. How often do you propose we meet or communicate in order to thoroughly prepare you for the hearing? (*Add more pages if required*)

_____

_____

_____

Expectations:

25. What are your **expectations**, and is there anything more you want your representative to do to help you better prepare for your hearing (other than meeting in person, when necessary, phone calls or email or other agreed upon forms of correspondence you may have agreed upon)? (*Add more pages if required*)

_____

_____

_____

_____

_____

_____

_____

_____

_____

_____
_____

Sign: (Claimant/s) _____; **Date**:
_____

Note: Attach a copy of your identity document,
preferably a Driver's License or Passport.

APPENDIX V:
Sample ICAC

INTEGRATED CLAIM ANALYSIS CENTRE (ICAC)
CHECKLIST TO IRB

UCI:
TBX-XXXXX

VPERSONAL INFORMATION

Date Found Eligible: 2019/10/03

Intake Office: Etobicoke IRCC (3296)

Original passport on file: ☒ Yes ☐ No

NAME OF PRINCIPAL APPLICANT:				
DATE OF BIRTH:				
COUNTRY OF BIRTH:	Iran			
COUNTRY(IES) OF CITIZENSHIP/NATIONALITY:	Iran			
IF NO COUNTRY OF NATIONALITY, THEN COUNTRY OF FORMER HABITUAL RESIDENCE:				
COUNTRY(IES) OF ALLEGED PERSECUTION:	Iran			
CLAIM TYPE(S)	Category: Religion	Type: Christian	Remarks: Conversion to Christianity.	
	Category:	Type:	Remarks:	

SCHEDULING RECOMMENDATION:	
Streaming of claims - https://irb-cisr.gc.ca/en/legal-policy/procedures/Pages/procedures-less-complex-claims-rpd.aspx	☐ File Review (In chambers decision)
	☒ Short Hearing (2 hours or less)
	☐ Regular Hearing: Half-Day (3 hours)
	☐ Complex Hearing (full-day)

Names and UCI of associated claimants, if applicable

	NAME	RELATIONSHIP TO PRINCIPAL CLAIMANT	DOB	UCI	RPD File N°
1.		spouse			
2.		child			
3.		child			
4.	Surname, First name		Click to enter date		
5.	Surname, First name		Click to enter date		

ADDITIONAL ADMINISTRATIVE DETAILS

REVIEWED

☒ Security Screening Completed	☒ IMM0008, Schedules A and 12
☒ Canadian Criminal Record Check completed at intake: 2019-10-01	☒ BOC ☐ Amended BOC (if applicable)
☒ Canadian Immigration History Check completed (if applicable)	Interview or Port-of-Entry notes ☐ Reviewed ☒ None available

CHARLES MWEWA

INTEGRATED CLAIM ANALYSIS CENTRE (ICAC)
CHECKLIST TO IRB

UCI: 1116915848
TBX-XXXXX

☒ Biometric checks completed for principal claimant

Country	Sent	Match	Non-resultant
USA	☐	☐	☒
United Kingdom	☐	☐	☐
Australia	☐	☐	☐
New Zealand	☐	☐	☐

☒ Biometric checks completed for all associated claimants 14 years of age or older. *Complete only if results are different than the principal applicant. Insert additional sheet as required.*

Associated claimant #1:

Country	Sent	Match	Non-resultant
USA	☐	☐	☒
United Kingdom	☐	☐	☐
Australia	☐	☐	☐
New Zealand	☐	☐	

Temporary Resident (TR) application(s) (only work permits, study permits and visitor visas issued outside of Canada)

☐ No application or no application within the last two years (from outside Canada only)

☒ TR application available in GCMS (if box is checked, include application with package)

☐ TR application requested from the appropriate mission
          Date requested   **Click here to enter date**
          Date received   **Click here to enter date**
          Not received ☐

REVIEWED FOR POSSIBLE 1E

☐   Possible 1E exclusion check completed for the following country(ies):

    1. _____
    2. _____

    ** *Note: The above review should not be interpreted as the Minister's position on possible 1E exclusion. Checking this box without intervening should not be interpreted as the Minister taking the position that exclusion is not an issue. It simply means the Minister does not have information to provide at this time, but reserves the right to intervene should additional information become available.*

INTERVENTION

☐   No intervention
       ☐   Additional relevant information for inclusion in scheduling ready package
            1. _____
            2. _____
            3. _____

    ***Note: The above should not be interpreted as the Minister's position on the merits of the claim.*

☐   Intervention
    (If box is checked, include notice of intervention and disclosure package)
       ☐   By documents
       ☐   In-person at the hearing

    Ground(s) for intervening:
       ☐   Credibility
       ☐   Identity
       ☐   Program Integrity
       ☐   Exclusion 1E
       ☐   Exclusion 1F(a)
       ☐   Exclusion 1F(b)
       ☐   Exclusion 1F(c)

Version 1.0 October 1, 2019

Page 3 of 3

INTEGRATED CLAIM ANALYSIS CENTRE (ICAC)
CHECKLIST TO IRB

UCI: 1116915848
TBX-XXXXX

SCHEDULING READY PACKAGE

Documents	In Package (check mark)
1. Standard disclosure letter	✓
2. ICAC checklist - **1 per family**	✓
3. Notice of Intent to Intervene and disclosure package, including statement of service *if applicable* (from CPA, SIO, Hearing Advisor, or Hearing Officer)	
4. Any other documents as provided by a CPA, SIO, Hearing Advisor or Hearing Officer (e.g. open source material or other relevant information *if applicable*)	
5. Interview or Arrest Notes *if applicable*	
6. Colour copies of all available identity documents (e.g. passport, national ID card etc.)	✓
7. Biometric information provided to the Minister by international partners within the context of the Migration 5 (M5) immigration information-sharing agreement (applies to claimants age 14 and older)	
8. Temporary resident (TR) applications (includes WP/SP) within the previous two years <u>or</u> TR ATIP reports if application not available from mission	✓

DATE SENT TO CLAIMANT/COUNSEL AND IRB: CLICK HERE TO ENTER DATE

NOTE: The content of this checklist should not be taken as conclusive and in no way restricts further action by the Board or the Minister in regard to this case.

APPENDIX VI:
Redacted Real Notices of Decision

(Selected few recent decisions the author has won)

- 1 -

IMMIGRATION AND REFUGEE BOARD

- REFUGEE PROTECTION DIVISION -

Reasons for the Decision in a Hearing under the

Immigration and Refugee Protection Act, concerning

HELD AT: Toronto, Ontario

DATE: December 16, 2019

BEFORE: K. Khamsi   - Member

APPEARANCES:

	▮▮▮ et al	- Claimants
	Charles Mwewa	- Counsel for Claimant
	A. Gholbeigi	- Interpreter

IRB/CISR

Unrevised Transcript
of decision delivered orally

Transcription non révisée d'une
décision rendue de vive voix

Certified True Copy
Copie Conforme

Case Officer
Agent proposé au cas

Hint: Member Khamsi is punctual and organized; make sure you know your story very well.

Immigration and
Refugee Board of Canada
Refugee Protection
Division

Commission de l'immigration
et du statut de réfugié du Canada
Section de la protection
des réfugiés

RPD File: TB██████96

NOTICE OF DECISION

[Immigration and Refugee Protection Act, subsection 107(1)]
[Refugee Protection Division Rules, rule 67]

K. Khamsi
Member

In the claims for refugee protection of:	Date of birth:	UCI:
██████████	██████	████46

The claims were heard on December 16, 2019.

The Refugee Protection Division determines that **the claimants are Convention refugees and therefore accepts the claims.**

The reasons for the decision are attached.

January 13, 2020

E. TRUONG,
For the Registrar
Tel: 1-866-790-0581

Certified True Copy
Copie Conforme

Case Officer
Agent préposé au cas

RPD.29.04 (July 31, 2019)
Disponible en français

Canada

Hint: Member Khamsi is punctual and organized; make sure you know your story very well.

- 1 -   TB9▓▓05

IMMIGRATION AND REFUGEE BOARD

- REFUGEE PROTECTION DIVISION -

Reasons for the decision in a Hearing under the

Immigration and Refugee Protection Act, concerning

▓▓▓▓▓▓▓▓▓▓▓▓▓▓▓

HELD AT:	Toronto, Ontario
DATE:	November 29, 2019
BEFORE:	C. Gibbs — Member
APPEARANCES:	
▓▓▓▓▓▓▓	- Claimant
Charles Mwewa	- Counsel
N/A	- Designated Representative
N/A	- Minister's Counsel
S. Hedayati	- Interpreter

IRB/CISR

Unrevised Transcript
of decision delivered orally

Transcription non révisée d'une
décision rendue de vive voix

Hint: Member Gibbs is very meticulous and pays attention even to overlooked details; make sure you understand your claim in and out.

CHARLES MWEWA

Immigration and
Refugee Board of Canada
Refugee Protection
Division

Commission de l'immigration
et du statut de réfugié du Canada
Section de la protection
des réfugiés

RPD File: TB█████05

NOTICE OF DECISION
[Immigration and Refugee Protection Act, subsection 107(1)]
[Refugee Protection Division Rules, rule 67]

C. Gibbs
Member

In the claim for refugee protection of: Date of birth: UCI:

████████████████   ██████   ███08

The claim was heard on November 29, 2019.

The Refugee Protection Division determines that **the claimant is a Convention refugee and therefore accepts the claim.**

The reasons for the decision are attached.

January 3, 2020   N. Deol, A/Case Management Officer
For the Registrar
Tel: 1-866-790-0581

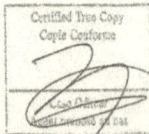

Certified True Copy
Copie Conforme

RPD.29.04 (July 31, 2018)
Disponible en français   Canada

Hint: Member Gibbs is very meticulous and pays attention even to overlooked details; make sure you understand your claim in and out.

REFUGEE PROTECTION IN CANADA

(

Immigration and Refugee
Board of Canada

Refugee Protection Division

Commission de l'immigration
et du statut de réfugié du Canada

Section de la protection des réfugiés

RPD File / Dossier de la SPR : T█████79
UCI / IUC : █████70

Private Proceeding / Huis clos

TRANSCRIPT OF THE REASONS AND DECISION

Claimant(s)	████████	Demandeur(e)(s) d'asile
Date(s) of hearing	December 12, 2019	Date(s) de l'audience
Place of hearing	Toronto, ON	Lieu de l'audience
Date of decision and reasons	January 2, 2020	Date de la décision et des motifs
Panel	Yonatan Rozenszajn	Tribunal
Counsel for the claimant(s)	Charles Mwewa	Conseil(s) du (de la/des) demandeur(e)(s) d'asile
Designated Representative	N/A	Représentant(e) désigné(e)
Counsel for the Minister	N/A	Conseil du (de la) ministre
Interpreter	Amir Ghofrani	Interprète

Certified True Copy
Copie Conforme

Case Officer
Agent préposé au cas

RPD.61.01 (October 4, 2019)
Disponible en français

Canada

CHARLES MWEWA

Hint: Member Yonatan thinks out of the box and goes even where you least expect. Remain steady, and have a global approach to your claim.

Immigration and
Refugee Board of Canada
Refugee Protection
Division

Commission de l'immigration
et du statut de réfugié du Canada
Section de la protection
des réfugiés

RPD File: TB█████79

NOTICE OF DECISION
[Immigration and Refugee Protection Act, subsection 107(1)]
[Refugee Protection Division Rules, rule 67]

Yonatan Rozenszajn
Member

In the claim for refugee protection of: Date of birth: UCI:

█████████   ████████   ██████70

The claim was heard on December 12, 2019.

The Refugee Protection Division determines that **the claimant is a Convention refugee** and **therefore accepts the claim.**

The reasons for the decision are attached.

January 3, 2020

N. Deol, A/Case Management Officer
For the Registrar
Tel: 1-866-790-0581

Certified True Copy
Copie Conforme

RPD.23.04 (July 31, 2018)
Disponible en français

Canada

Hint: Member Yonatan thinks out of the box and goes even where you least expect. Remain steady, and have a global approach to your claim.

490

TRANSCRIPT OF THE REASONS AND DECISION

Claimant(s)	████████	Demandeur(e)(s) d'asile
Date(s) of hearing	December 4, 2019	Date(s) de l'audience
Place of hearing	Toronto, ON	Lieu de l'audience
Date of decision and reasons	December 4, 2019	Date de la décision et des motifs
Panel	Robert Bafaro	Tribunal
Counsel for the claimant(s)	Charles Mwewa	Conseil(s) du (de la/des) demandeur(e)(s) d'asile
Designated Representative	N/A	Représentant(e) désigné(e)
Counsel for the Minister	N/A	Conseil du (de la) ministre
Interpreter	Gholamhossein Karami	Interprète

Hint: Member Robert is, probably, the fairest adjudicator out there – he knows exactly what a Claimant thinks, fears and responds. He exudes reasonableness without sacrificing law and process.

Immigration and
Refugee Board of Canada
Refugee Protection
Division

Commission de l'immigration
et du statut de réfugié du Canada
Section de la protection
des réfugiés

RPD File: TE██55

NOTICE OF DECISION
[Immigration and Refugee Protection Act, subsection 107(1)]
[Refugee Protection Division Rules, rule 67]

R. Bafaro
Member

In the claim for refugee protection of: Date of birth: UCI:

██████████████   ██████   ████53

The claim was heard on December 4, 2019.

The Refugee Protection Division determines that **the claimant is a Convention refugee** and **therefore accepts the claim.**

The reasons for the decision are attached.

December 30, 2019

N. Deol, A/Case Management Officer
For the Registrar
Tel: 1-866-790-0581

Certified True Copy
Copie Conforme

RPD.29.04 (July 31, 2018)
Disponible en français

Canada

Hint: Member Robert is, probably, the fairest adjudicator out there – he knows exactly what a Claimant thinks, fears and responds. He exudes reasonableness without sacrificing law and process.

Immigration and Refugee Board of Canada		Commission de l'immigration et du statut de réfugié du Canada
Refugee Protection Division		Section de la protection des réfugiés

RPD File / Dossier de la SPR : TB████49
UCI / IUC: ████████05

Huis clos / **Private Proceeding**

Reasons and Decision – Motifs et décision

Claimant(s)	████████████	Demandeur(e)(s) d'asile
Date(s) of hearing	IN CHAMBERS	Date(s) de l'audience
Place of hearing	Toronto, Ontario	Lieu de l'audience
Date of decision and reasons	December 11, 2019	Date de la décision et des motifs
Panel	Ana Rico	Tribunal
Counsel for the claimant(s)	Charles Mwewa	Conseil(s) du (de la/des) demandeur(e)(s) d'asile
Designated representative	N/A	Représentant(e) désigné(e)
Counsel for the Minister	N/A	Conseil du (de la) ministre

Certified True Copy
Copie Conforme

Case Officer
Agent préposé au cas

RPD.29.01 (October 4, 2019)
Disponible en français

Canada

Hint: Member Ana pays attention to even the tiniest textual nuances. Do not be general with her; be specific and rationally and logically connect your narrative with your evidence in order to have a chance of success.

RPD File: TB████9

NOTICE OF DECISION

[*Immigration and Refugee Protection Act*, subsection 107(1) and paragraph 170(f)]
[*Refugee Protection Division Rules*, subrule 67(1)]

Ana Rico
Member

In the claim for refugee protection of:	Date of birth:	UCI:
████████	████	███95

The claim was determined without a hearing on December 11, 2019.

The Refugee Protection Division determines that **the claimant is a Convention refugee and therefore accepts the claim**.

The reasons for the decision are attached.

December 16, 2019

E. TRUONG,
For the Registrar
Tel: 1-866-790-0581

Certified True Copy
Copie Conforme

Case Officer
Agent préposé au cas

Canada

Hint: Member Ana pays attention to even the tiniest textual nuances. Do not be general with her; be specific and rationally and logically connect your narrative with your evidence in order to have a chance of success.

- I -

TE██92

N⁺.

IMMIGRATION AND REFUGEE BOARD

- REFUGEE PROTECTION DIVISION -

Reasons for the decision in a Hearing under the

Immigration and Refugee Protection Act, concerning

HELD AT:	Toronto, Ontario
DATE:	July 15, 2019
BEFORE:	J. Campbell — Member
APPEARANCES:	
	██████████ — Claimant
	Charles Mwewa — Counsel
	N/A — Minister's Counsel
	G. Karani — Interpreter

> **IRB/CISR**
>
> Unrevised Transcript
> of decision delivered orally
>
> Transcription non révisée d'une
> décision rendue de vive voix

Hint: Member James could be very methodical and process-oriented. Make sure you are whole, from rule to narrative to process in order to succeed.

Immigration and
Refugee Board of Canada
Refugee Protection
Division

Commission de l'immigration
et du statut de réfugié du Canada
Section de la protection
des réfugiés

RPD File: TE▇▇92

NOTICE OF DECISION
[Immigration and Refugee Protection Act, subsection 107(1)]
[Refugee Protection Division Rules, rule 67]

James W. Campbell
Member

In the claim for refugee protection of: Date of birth: UCI:

▇▇▇▇▇   ▇▇▇▇   ▇▇99

The claim was heard on July 15, 2019.

The Refugee Protection Division determines that **the claimant is a Convention refugee** and therefore accepts the claim.

The reasons for the decision are attached.

August 8, 2019

N. Deol, A/Case Management Officer
For the Registrar
Tel: 1-866-790-0581

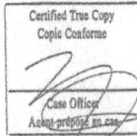

Certified True Copy
Copie Conforme

Case Officer
Agent préposé au cas

RPD.29.04 (July 31, 2018)
Disponible en français

Canada

Hint: Member James could be very methodical and process-oriented. Make sure you are whole, from rule to narrative to process in order to succeed.

ABOUT THE AUTHOR

Charles Mwewa (LLB, BA. Edu. + Engl., BA. Legal Studies, Cert. Law, DIBM., LLM.) is a Dad, author, and poet. Mwewa is the author of over 50 books and counting in all genres – fiction (novels), non-fiction and poetry. Mwewa, his wife, and their three girls, reside in the Capital City of Ottawa, Canada

Websites:
charlesmwewa.com
acpress.ca

Facebook:
https://www.facebook.com/authorcharlesmwewa

Email:
info@acpress.ca

Amazon
https://www.amazon.ca/dp/1988251206

INDEX

CBSA, 5, 11
checklist, 13, 126
child, 453
Chile, 82
Christian community,
146, 178, 179, 195,
266
Christian converts, 91,
144, 145, 146, 152,
157, 159, 164, 167,
171, 173, 175, 178,
184, 187, 192, 196,
197, 199, 224, 226,
236, 266, 274, 276,
282, 285
Christian faith, 450
Christian holidays, 212
Christian life, 189
Christian literature, 181
Christian ministries,
157, 269
Christian TV, 158, 271
Christianity, 32, 88, 90,
91, 145, 150, 152,
153, 154, 155, 156,
161, 164, 166, 174,
176, 177, 181, 182,
183, 184, 186, 190,
191, 198, 200, 203,
204, 205, 206, 207,
209, 211, 212, 215,
224, 225, 234, 235,
265, 267, 268, 274,

275, 278, 284, 285,
301, 302, 304, 305,
306, 307, 309, 313,
314, 315, 320, 328,
329, 330, 331, 332,
333, 337, 338, 341,
348, 351, 353, 354,
357, 360, 361, 463,
466, 471, 472
Christmas, 179, 212
Church, 457, 464, 465
church services, 162,
171, 178, 200, 201,
228
CIC, 5
circumstantial
evidence, 81
Citizenship Act, 3
Citizenship and
Immigration
Canada, 5
commitment (pledge),
25
condemns, 462
Constitution, 3, 172, 220,
221, 266, 275, 276
Contact Information, 6
contextual approach, 90
Convention Against
Torture, 10
Convention refugee, 9,
37, 50, 59, 65, 67,
70, 80, 87, 88, 94,

314, 336, 474, 478
Evin Prison, 177
examination, 12, 15,
    39, 67, 87, 110
execution, 32, 179, 197,
    223, 236, 337, 345,
    346, 361
express entry, 6
Extensive questioning, 125

F

Facebook, 186, 234,
    240, 244, 245, 246,
    248, 250, 252, 253,
    258
false documents, 43
Family in Canada, 45
Farsi, xxix, 161, 162,
    178, 273
FATA, 239, 240, 241,
    246, 248, 283
fatwas, 219, 220
Federal Court, 36, 40,
    52, 60, 63, 69, 77,
    85, 96, 97, 103, 106,
    108, 109, 110, 113,
    114, 115, 135
Federal Court of
    Appeal, 36, 52, 60,
    63, 69, 96, 97, 103,
    106, 108, 110, 114,
    115
fits of anger, 461
flee from persecution,

32
foreign national, 12, 13,
    14, 22
forgive sins, 449
Forgiveness, 462
former habitual
    residence, 1, 2, 3, 9,
    11, 18, 33, 34, 89,
    113, 114, 115, 116,
    144
founded fear of
    persecution, 2, 9, 11,
    52, 72, 82, 84, 89,
    116, 120, 144
freedom, 27, 165, 174,
    179, 197, 198, 209,
    230, 245, 337, 340,
    344
fruit, 472

G

gender-related
    persecutions, 1
Generic, 13, 15
Germany, 42, 155, 156,
    179, 285
Gethsemane, 459
glory, 451
God, 148, 203, 213,
    214, 216, 227, 228,
    236, 322, 331, 333,
    349, 351, 352, 354
good faith, 18, 24
good grounds, 35, 36,

J

450, 451, 452, 453,
454, 455, 457, 460,
462, 464, 465, 466,
467, 468, 470, 471
Jews, 146, 148, 149,
163, 194, 196, 213,
266, 274, 347, 455,
456, 468
John the Baptist, 454
John Zebedee. *See*
disciple
Joseph, 454
Judas Alpheus. *See*
disciple
Judas Iscariot. *See*
disciple
Jude. *See* Bartholomew
judicial review, 56, 127,
139
jurisdiction, 3

K

knowledge of
Christianity, 205
Kurdish, 152
Kurds, 152, 193, 196

L

Law of Moses, 458
Law Society, 6
lawyer, 6, 56, 128, 177,
336
Lazarus, 460

Legal Test, 36
Licensed Paralegals, 6
Life. *See* Jesus Christ
Light of the World,
448

M

Maji, 456
Martha, 460
Mary, 454, 460
Masoud Mohammad
Amin, 154
Matthew Levi. *See*
disciple
Members, 6, 22, 176,
182, 228, 231, 267,
270, 281
mercies, 450
Messiah. *See* Jesus
Christ
microphone, 28
Middle East, 149, 164,
170, 186, 219, 233,
234, 235, 236, 249
Minister of
Immigration, 14
Ministry of the Interior
and the Ministry of
Culture, 175
minor, 12, 59, 62, 69,
72, 79, 137, 139, 145
misrepresentation, 12,
14, 21
moharebeh, 148, 149,

rings, 22
orgies, 461

P

panel, 37, 40, 48, 59,
65, 119, 121, 124,
126, 127, 129, 139
Panel Physician, 15
particular social group,
2, 3, 9, 473
passports, 13
Pastors, 171
permanent residence,
5, 54
Persian, 171, 200, 201,
203, 210, 211, 214,
244, 316
Person in Need of
Protection, 9
Personal Information
Form or PIF, 13
Philip. *See* disciple
Point of Entry (POE),
11
police, 25, 96, 99, 101,
109, 112, 113, 129,
136, 169, 240, 248,
265, 277, 303, 304,
305, 314, 336, 349,
357
political opinion, 2, 3, 9
post-traumatic stress
syndrome, 74
pregnant. *See* Mary

presumption, 41, 52,
55, 72, 90, 91, 95,
97, 101, 102, 103,
104, 105, 112, 115,
116
prison, 164, 166, 167,
172, 176, 179, 184,
197, 232, 270, 274,
276, 308
prison sentences, 164,
167, 176, 276
prisoners, 168, 196,
197, 277
propaganda, 159, 171,
176, 178, 261, 271,
358
Prophet, 217, 220, 224
Protestant Christians,
146, 195, 266
Protestant churches,
161, 199, 273
Protestants, 150, 155,
199, 200, 210
PSEPC, 5
psychiatric assessment, 74
Psychological reports, 73
putative, 131, 132

R

race, 2, 9
Rapture, 466
reasonable chance, 36,
37, 39, 86
reasonable grounds, 70

98
tribulation, 450
Trinity, 467
trite law, 2, 10, 54
Trust, 23
Truth. *See* Jesus Christ
Turkey, 48, 85, 151,
152, 153, 154, 156,
180, 182, 186, 187,
208, 215, 224, 263,
264, 267, 268, 284,
285, 354, 358, 359,
360
Two-Prong Test, 119

U

U.K., 74
UN conventions, 3
UN General Assembly,
217, 286
UN Secretary-General,
217
United Kingdom, 156,
182, 186
United States, 42, 45,
46, 48, 49, 75, 76,
104, 116, 152, 162,
171, 195, 198
unusual treatment or
punishment, 10
unwilling to return, 2,
9, 115
Use of a
Representative, 6

V

victory, 452
Vine, 448
violence, 77, 136, 316,
318, 338, 352
Virgin. *See* Mary
visa, 53, 54, 55, 75, 80,
326, 343, 354

W

warrant, 5, 65, 304
water baptism, 456
Way. *See* Jesus Christ
well-founded fear, 2, 9,
35, 39, 40, 52, 62,
64, 72, 82, 84, 86,
116, 120
wine. *See* blood
witness, 23, 26, 27, 28,
109, 474, 478
Wonderful. *See* child
Work Permit, 15
World Wide Web, 260,
261

Y

Young children, 17

Z

Zachariah. *See* John the
Baptist

www.ingramcontent.com/pod-product-compliance
Lightning Source LLC
Chambersburg PA
CBHW021023210326
41598CB00016B/894